GRADING THE NATION'S REPORT CARD

Research from the Evaluation of NAEP

Committee on the Evaluation of National and State Assessments
of Educational Progress

Nambury S. Raju, James W. Pellegrino, Meryl W. Bertenthal,
Karen J. Mitchell, and Lee R. Jones, *editors*

Board on Testing and Assessment

Commission on Behavioral and Social Sciences and Education

National Research Council

NATIONAL ACADEMY PRESS
Washington, D.C.

NATIONAL ACADEMY PRESS • 2101 Constitution Avenue, NW • Washington, DC 20418

NOTICE: The project that is the subject of this report was approved by the Governing Board of the National Research Council, whose members are drawn from the councils of the National Academy of Sciences, the National Academy of Engineering, and the Institute of Medicine. The members of the committee responsible for the report were chosen for their special competences and with regard for appropriate balance.

This study was supported by Award No. EA95083001 between the National Academy of Sciences and the U.S. Department of Education. Any opinions, findings, conclusions, or recommendations expressed in this publication are those of the author(s) and do not necessarily reflect the views of the organizations or agencies that provided support for this project.

Suggested citation: National Research Council (2000) *Grading the Nation's Report Card: Research from the Evaluation of NAEP.* Committee on the Evaluation of National and State Assessments of Educational Progress. Nambury S. Raju, James W. Pellegrino, Meryl W. Bertenthal, Karen J. Mitchell, and Lee R. Jones, editors. Board on Testing and Assessment, Commission on Behavioral and Social Sciences and Education. Washington, DC: National Academy Press.

Additional copies of this report are available from:
National Academy Press
2101 Constitution Avenue, NW
Washington, DC 20418
Call 800-624-6242 or 202-334-3313 (in the Washington metropolitan area)

This report is also available online at **http://www.nap.edu**

Printed in the United States of America

THE NATIONAL ACADEMIES

National Academy of Sciences
National Academy of Engineering
Institute of Medicine
National Research Council

The **National Academy of Sciences** is a private, nonprofit, self-perpetuating society of distinguished scholars engaged in scientific and engineering research, dedicated to the furtherance of science and technology and to their use for the general welfare. Upon the authority of the charter granted to it by the Congress in 1863, the Academy has a mandate that requires it to advise the federal government on scientific and technical matters. Dr. Bruce M. Alberts is president of the National Academy of Sciences.

The **National Academy of Engineering** was established in 1964, under the charter of the National Academy of Sciences, as a parallel organization of outstanding engineers. It is autonomous in its administration and in the selection of its members, sharing with the National Academy of Sciences the responsibility for advising the federal government. The National Academy of Engineering also sponsors engineering programs aimed at meeting national needs, encourages education and research, and recognizes the superior achievements of engineers. Dr. William A. Wulf is president of the National Academy of Engineering.

The **Institute of Medicine** was established in 1970 by the National Academy of Sciences to secure the services of eminent members of appropriate professions in the examination of policy matters pertaining to the health of the public. The Institute acts under the responsibility given to the National Academy of Sciences by its congressional charter to be an adviser to the federal government and, upon its own initiative, to identify issues of medical care, research, and education. Dr. Kenneth I. Shine is president of the Institute of Medicine.

The **National Research Council** was organized by the National Academy of Sciences in 1916 to associate the broad community of science and technology with the Academy's purposes of furthering knowledge and advising the federal government. Functioning in accordance with general policies determined by the Academy, the Council has become the principal operating agency of both the National Academy of Sciences and the National Academy of Engineering in providing services to the government, the public, and the scientific and engineering communities. The Council is administered jointly by both Academies and the Institute of Medicine. Dr. Bruce M. Alberts and Dr. William A. Wulf are chairman and vice chairman, respectively, of the National Research Council.

CONTRIBUTORS

SHEILA BARRON, RAND Corporation, Washington, D.C.

ROBERT BORUCH, Graduate School of Education, University of Pennsylvania

PATRICIA ANN KENNEY, Learning Research and Development Center, University of Pittsburgh, Pennsylvania

MICHAEL J. KOLEN, Iowa Testing Programs, The University of Iowa, Iowa City

KEVIN MEARA, School of Education, University of Massachusetts, Amherst

JIM MINSTRELL, ACT Systems for Education, Bellevue, Washington

MICHELLE PERRY, School of Education, University of Illinois, Urbana-Champaign

FRÉDÉRIC ROBIN, School of Education, University of Massachusetts, Amherst

H. JANE ROGERS, Teachers College, Columbia University

STEPHEN G. SIRECI, School of Education, University of Massachusetts, Amherst

JAMES W. STIGLER, Psychology Department, University of California, Los Angeles

HARIHARAN SWAMINATHAN, School of Education, University of Massachusetts, Amherst

GEORGE TERHANIAN, Harris Black International Limited, Rochester, New York

JENNIFER R. ZIELESKIEWICZ, Institute of Psychology, Illinois Institute of Technology, Chicago

Contents

1   Introduction   1

ASSESSMENT DEVELOPMENT
2   Families of Items in the NAEP Mathematics Assessment   5
       Patricia Ann Kenney
3   Student Thinking and Related Assessment: Creating a Facet-Based
    Learning Environment   44
       Jim Minstrell

CONTENT VALIDITY
4   An External Evaluation of the 1996 Grade 8 NAEP Science
    Framework   74
       *Stephen G. Sireci, Frédéric Robin, Kevin Meara, H. Jane Rogers,
       and Hariharan Swaminathan*
5   Appraising the Dimensionality of the 1996 Grade 8 NAEP Science
    Assessment Data   101
       *Stephen G. Sireci, H. Jane Rogers, Hariharan Swaminathan,
       Kevin Meara, and Frédéric Robin*
6   Subject-Matter Experts' Perceptions of the Relevance of the NAEP
    Long-Term Trend Items in Science and Mathematics   123
       Jennifer R. Zieleskiewicz

NAEP DESIGN AND USE

7   Issues in Phasing Out Trend NAEP   132
        Michael J. Kolen
8   Issues in Combining State NAEP and Main NAEP   152
        Michael J. Kolen
9   Difficulties Associated with Secondary Analysis of NAEP Data   172
        Sheila Barron

EDUCATION INDICATOR SYSTEM DESIGN

10 Putting Surveys, Studies, and Datasets Together: Linking NCES
        Surveys to One Another and to Datasets from Other Sources   195
        George Terhanian and Robert Boruch
11 Developing Classroom Process Data for the Improvement of
        Teaching   229
        James W. Stigler and Michelle Perry

GRADING THE NATION'S
REPORT CARD

1

Introduction

The National Assessment of Educational Progress (NAEP), also known as the nation's report card, has chronicled American students' academic achievement for over a quarter of a century. It has been a valued source of information about the academic performance of students in the United States, providing among the best-available trend data on the achievement of elementary, middle, and secondary students in key subject areas. The NAEP program has set an innovative agenda for conventional and performance-based testing and in doing so has become a leader in American achievement testing.

NAEP's prominence and the important need for stable and accurate measures of academic achievement have prompted a legislative mandate for ongoing evaluation of the program. This mandate, levied by Congress, calls for evaluation of NAEP and an analysis of the extent to which its results are reasonable, valid, and informative to the public (P.L. 103-382). The legislative charge includes evaluation of the national assessment, the state program, and the student performance standards reported by NAEP.

A three-year evaluation of NAEP was recently conducted by the National Research Council. Its Committee on Evaluation of National and State Assessments of Educational Progress recently issued a report entitled *Grading the Nation's Report Card: Evaluating NAEP and Transforming the Assessment of Educational Progress* (National Academy Press, 1999). The present volume is a companion to the main report and consists of a collection of papers prepared to support the committee's evaluative analyses and deliberations. To assist in its work, the committee commissioned research and syntheses on four key topics: NAEP's assessment development, NAEP's content validity, NAEP's design and use, and the design of education indicator systems. This work helped to inform the committee's analysis, instigate debate, and push the committee's thinking on key topics and issues. Some of the papers in this volume are more directly relevant to and aligned with the committee's conclusions and recommendations than are others. In every case the papers represent the authors' views, not those of the committee.

The first topic addressed by this volume is the development of assessment materials by NAEP. In *Grading the Nation's Report Card*, the committee argued that NAEP's assessment development should be guided by a coherent vision of student learning and by the kinds of inferences and conclusions about student performance that are desired in reports of NAEP results. The committee concluded that multiple conditions should be met in assessment development for NAEP: (a) NAEP frameworks and assessments should reflect subject-matter knowledge; research, theory, and practice regarding what students should understand and how they learn; and more comprehensive goals for schooling; (b) assessment instruments and scoring criteria should be designed to capture important differences in the levels and types of student knowledge and understanding, through both large-scale surveys and multiple alternative assessment methods; and (c) NAEP reports should provide descriptions of student performance that enhance the interpretation and usefulness of summary scores. The first two authors, Patricia Ann Kenney and Jim Minstrell, discuss the development of frameworks, items, and reports for NAEP.

In Chapter 2, "Families of Items in the NAEP Mathematics Assessment," Kenney presents ideas for and gives examples of families of items in mathematics. She contends that families of items support fuller understanding and description of students' understanding in mathematics because students' responses can be examined across sets of related items rather than in isolation. In Chapter 3, "Student Thinking and Related Assessment: Creating a Facet-based Learning Environment," Minstrell suggests an approach to examining students' thinking in science and shows how the approach can be used to diagnose student difficulties and tailor instruction to address performance deficits. His paper discusses ways that research on learning and teaching can be used to inform instruction in science and speaks to the development of NAEP assessments.

The second topic area relates to the first and concerns the content validity of NAEP. In its final report the committee observed that many of the changes in NAEP instrumentation over the past 30 years reflect only minimally the changes that have occurred in certain critical areas of knowledge. The committee questioned whether NAEP's consensus-based frameworks and the assessments based on them lead to portrayals of student performance that deeply and accurately reflect student achievement.

Stephen G. Sireci and colleagues and Jennifer R. Zieleskiewicz examine the dimensionality and content validity of NAEP assessments. In Chapter 4, "An External Evaluation of the 1996 Grade 8 NAEP Science Framework," authored with Frederic Robin, Kevin Meara, H. Jane Rogers, and Hariharan Swaminathan, Sireci reports on the content validity of the NAEP science assessment to determine whether inferences derived from its scores can be linked to targeted content and skill domains. Sireci and his colleagues worked with science teachers to review items from the NAEP science assessment and solicit judgments about the knowledge and skills measured by sampled items. They compared teachers' judgments to developers' categorizations of the items. In Chapter 5, "Appraising the Dimensionality of the 1996 Grade 8 NAEP Science Assessment Data," Sireci, Rogers, Swaminathan, Meara, and Robin evaluate the structure of item response data gathered in the 1996 science assessment and compare this structure to that specified in the NAEP framework.

In Chapter 6, "Subject-Matter Experts' Perceptions of the Relevance of the NAEP Long-Term Trend Items in Science and Mathematics," Jennifer R. Zieleskiewicz asks whether NAEP's long-term trend items are up-to-date and relevant measures of student achievement in mathematics and science. She compares experts' ratings on the relevance of these items to relevance ratings for items created under the current frameworks. She presents data on the correspondence between long-term trend NAEP and main NAEP, national standards, and contemporary classroom practices in mathematics and science.

The third topic of this volume is NAEP's design and use. In its report the committee argues that the proliferation of NAEP's multiple independent data collections—national NAEP, state NAEP, and long-term trend NAEP—is confusing, burdensome, and inefficient and sometimes produces conflicting results. The committee recommended that NAEP reduce the number of independent large-scale data collections while maintaining trend lines, periodically updating frameworks, and providing accurate national and state-level estimates of academic achievement.

Michael J. Kolen and Sheila Barron make suggestions for streamlining NAEP's current designs and simplifying the secondary analysis of NAEP data. In Chapter 7, "Issues in Phasing Out Trend NAEP," Kolen considers ways that long-term trend NAEP can be phased out and replaced by the main NAEP assessments while still maintaining the long-term trend line. In Chapter 8, "Issues in Combining State NAEP and Main NAEP," Kolen examines options for combining the main and state NAEP designs. In both papers he focuses on sampling, operational and measurement concerns and lays out the strengths and weaknesses of varied designs. In Chapter 9, "Difficulties Associated with Secondary Analysis of NAEP Data," Barron outlines difficulties that secondary analysts face in using NAEP data. She discusses the means by which NAEP's sponsors have attempted to address these problems and gives recommendations for improving the usability of NAEP data.

The last two chapters of the volume provide suggestions for the design of education indicator systems. In *Grading the Nation's Report Card*, the committee argues that the nation's educational progress should be portrayed by a broad array of education indicators that include but go beyond NAEP's achievement results. The committee recommends that the U.S. Department of Education integrate and supplement the current collections of data on education inputs, practices, and outcomes to provide a more comprehensive picture of education in America. The committee commissioned the last two papers in this volume to help its members think about the development of an indicator system and about the collection of data on curriculum and instructional practice, academic standards, technology use, financial allocations, and other indicators of educational inputs, practices, and outcomes.

In Chapter 10, "Putting Surveys, Studies, and Datasets Together: Linking NCES Surveys to One Another and to Datasets from Other Sources," George Terhanian and Robert Boruch review research and experience on the integration of federal statistics to inform science and society. The authors take lessons from past data linkage efforts to make suggestions for the National Center for Education Statistics (NCES) and the U.S. Department of Education. They suggest policies for making statistical surveys and datasets linkable.

In Chapter 11, "Developing Classroom Process Data for the Improvement of Teaching," James W. Stigler and Michelle Perry argue for the collection of educational practice data. They contend that for achievement data to be informative such data must be accompanied by information about what is going on in classrooms and that it is important to relate changes in student learning outcomes to possible sources of achievement gains and decrements. The authors suggest the kinds of data to be collected as well as methods and costs for collecting them and ways to integrate the data into present NCES activities.

The committee deeply appreciates the time, energy, enthusiasm, and intellect dedicated to the evaluation by the authors. Their papers stand as important contributions to assessment research and the NAEP program.

2

Families of Items in the NAEP Mathematics Assessment

Patricia Ann Kenney

This paper discusses families of items in the National Assessment of Educational Progress (NAEP) mathematics assessment and presents a sample family of items for grade 4. Item families can serve as an illustration of how to more fully understand and describe levels of students' understanding by examining students' responses across a set of related items. The paper presents a brief overview of the NAEP mathematics framework developed for the 1996 assessment, the idea of families of items and how they have appeared in previous NAEP assessments, a rationale for the development of a sample family of items around the topic of number patterns at the fourth-grade level, and the family of items itself based on released NAEP pattern items and other items developed for this paper.

OVERVIEW OF THE 1996 NAEP MATHEMATICS FRAMEWORK

The 1996 NAEP mathematics assessment used a framework (National Assessment Governing Board, 1994) that was influenced by ideas presented in *Curriculum and Evaluation Standards for School Mathematics* of the National Council of Teachers of Mathematics (NCTM, 1989). The framework sampled the content domain of mathematics using five strands: Number Sense, Properties, and Operations; Measurement; Geometry and Spatial Sense; Data Analysis, Statistics, and Probability; and Algebra and Functions. Additional dimensions of the framework included mathematical abilities (Conceptual Understanding, Procedural Knowledge, Problem Solving) and mathematical power (Reasoning, Connections, Communication). In addition to defining the content, ability, and power dimensions along which to assess students' knowledge and understanding of mathematics, the NAEP framework document included recommendations concerning other aspects of the assessment, such as the distribution of items across the content strands for grades 4, 8, and 12; the use of calculators and manipulatives; and design considerations for special sets of items to appear on the test. One of these special sets of items, called "families of items," is described in more detail below.

Families of Items in NAEP

The 1996 NAEP mathematics framework document recommends that the assessment include sets of related tasks, called families of items, to "measure the breadth and depth of student knowledge in mathematics" (National Assessment Governing Board, 1994:5). The framework describes two types of item families: a vertical family and a horizontal family. A vertical family includes items or tasks that measure students' understanding of a single important mathematics concept in a content strand (e.g., numerical patterns in algebra) but at different levels, such as giving a definition, applying the concept in both familiar and novel settings, and generalizing knowledge about the concept to represent a new level of understanding. A horizontal family of items involves assessment of students' understanding of a concept or principle across the various content strands in NAEP within a grade level or across grade levels. For example, the concept of proportionality can be assessed in a variety of content strands, such as number properties and operations, measurement, geometry, probability, and algebra. The framework also suggests that a family of items could be related through a common mathematical or real-world context that serves as a rich problem setting for the items.

Although the notion of item families was first articulated in the 1996 mathematics framework document, sets of related items have appeared in prior NAEP assessments. However, these sets exhibited few characteristics of either horizontal or vertical item families. Instead, the relationships between items involved such features as a common stimulus (e.g., a table, chart, or graph), a rudimentary form of scaffolding in which one item draws on information from the preceding item(s), or a common context. Each of these relationships is discussed next.

The item set in Box 2-1 is an example of the first kind of relatedness in that the items share a common stimulus. These three items were administered to students in the grade 4 sample in 1992 and were classified by NAEP assessment developers in the content strand Numbers and Operations (as the strand was called then). While working on these items, students were permitted to use simple four-function calculators. A table that displayed the number of points earned from two school events for each of three classes served as the common stimulus for the items. The first item asked for a comparison based on adding the points earned by each class, comparing the total points per class, and selecting the class that earned the most points; the second item required students to obtain the

BOX 2-1 Set of Items that Share a Common Stimulus

Items 1, 2, and 3 refer to the following table:

Points Earned from School Events		
Class	Mathathon	Readathon
Mr. Lopez	425	411
Ms. Chen	328	456
Mrs. Green	447	342

1. Which class earned the most points from the two events?
   A. Mr. Lopez's class
   B. Ms. Chen's class
   C. Mrs. Green's class
   D. All classes earned the same amount

                                                    Correct answer: A

                                                    Percent correct: 66

2. What was the total number of points earned from the mathathon?

   Answer: _____

                                                    Correct answer: 1,200

                                                    Percent correct: 52

3. Ms. Chen's class earned how many more points from the readathon than from the mathathon?

   Answer: _____

                                                    Correct answer: 128

                                                    Percent correct: 49

Source: 1992 NAEP mathematics assessment

correct total number of points from the Mathathon column; and the third item involved a within-class comparison concerning the number of points earned for each event.

Because the items in Box 2-1 were related in only a cursory way (i.e., a table was used as a common stimulus), looking at performance across them reveals little about students' ability to select appropriate data from a chart and their use of arithmetic operations on those data. Performance results were not very different across items, and the results appeared to be related only to the item type; that is, students' performance was higher on the multiple-choice item (66 percent correct) than on either of the short constructed-response items (52 and 49 percent, respectively). It is well documented that, on the NAEP mathematics assessment, student performance is higher on multiple-choice items than on constructed-response items (Dossey et al.,1993; Silver et al., in press). With respect to the item set in Box 2-1, it is reasonable to suspect that guessing could be contributing to the higher performance on the first question (a multiple-choice item), but because the items are not related in other ways it is difficult to interpret performance among them on the basis of important mathematical concepts and principles.

Another way that sets of mathematics items in NAEP were related involved an attempt to scaffold items; that is, a particular item is based on important and purposeful ways on one or more items that precede it. For example, the answer from the first item is used again in later items, or the first item presents a simple concept that is elaborated on in the items that follow (e.g., the "superitems" as described in Collis et al., 1986, and Wilson and Chavarria, 1993). An example of a scaffolded item pair from the 1992 NAEP mathematics assessment appears in Box 2-2. This item pair, administered to students in the grade 4 sample and classified by NAEP assessment developers in the content strand Algebra and Functions, assessed students' understanding of a number relationship involving an arithmetic operation. In the first item, students were asked to identify the rule used to transform the numbers in column A to those in column B, and its companion item required them to use that *same* rule to generate another number in the pattern. Thus, the pair illustrates a simple form of scaffolding in which the first item provides important information to be used in the second item.

NAEP results show that 42 percent of the fourth-grade students chose the correct rule (divide the number in column A by 4) in the first item. However, as expected for constructed-response items, performance was lower on item 2: only 24 percent of the fourth-grade students found the correct value of 30. Given that the items were related, it is reasonable to think that students would use the rule they chose in the first item in order to answer the second item, but NAEP results show that this was not the case. For example, of the students who selected the correct rule in item 1, only about 50 percent also answered item 2 correctly, with about another 40 percent giving numerical values that were incorrect and the

BOX 2-2 Scaffolded Item Pair

Items 1 and 2 refer to the table below:

Column A		Column B
12	→	3
16	→	4
24	→	6
40	→	10

1. What is a rule used in the table to get the numbers in column B from the numbers in column A?

   A. Divide the number in column A by 4.
   B. Multiply the number in column A by 4.
   C. Subtract 9 from the number in column A.
   D. Add 9 to the number in column A.

   Answer: A

   Percent correct: 42

Column A		Column B
120	→	

2. Suppose 120 is a number in column A of the table. Use the same rule to fill in the number in column B.

   Answer: 30

   Percent correct: 24

Source: 1992 NAEP mathematics assessment

remaining 10 percent leaving the item blank. Unfortunately, NAEP does not provide additional information on the kinds of incorrect answers students produced for item 2. Thus, for example, there is no information on ways in which students could have implemented the correct rule from item 1 to get an incorrect answer in item 2. We can only speculate on some of these ways. For example, did students make an error in dividing 120 by 4 and give an answer of 3 instead of 30? Did students arbitrarily change the operation from division to multiplication, giving an answer of 480 (120 × 4)? Did students completely ignore their correct choice of the rule in item 1 and instead perform an arbitrary operation using an arbitrary divisor, such as dividing 120 by 10 for an answer of 12? Based on the way NAEP results were reported for the item pair, we have no answers to these and other questions about the kinds of errors students made.

The two kinds of related items just discussed, however, by no means match the definition of families of items in NAEP. And perhaps there is no reason to expect that they would, given that those related items appeared on the 1992 NAEP mathematics assessment and given that the directive about the assessment including item families was first prescribed in the 1996 version of the mathematics framework. Yet even in the 1996 NAEP there were few, if any, *true* families of items that match the horizontal or vertical description in the mathematics framework document. As was the case in 1992, the 1996 assessment included related sets of items, but the majority of these sets included only two or three items that were related by the common stimulus such as a graph or table or that were scaffolded in limited ways. The exception to this was the sets of items related by context and referred to as "theme blocks" (Hawkins et al., 1999).

In the 1996 mathematics assessment the theme blocks were the operationalization of the framework recommendation concerning *contextually related* sets of tasks. According to a recent NAEP report, the questions in each theme block "related to some aspect of a rich problem setting that served as a unifying theme for the entire block" (Reese et al., 1997:79). The theme blocks were designed as a special study at the national level in NAEP and as such the results were reported separately from the main NAEP assessment. For the 1996 assessment there were five different theme blocks, two at each grade level with one block common to grades 8 and 12. Each block, containing 6 to 10 items, was administered to a special sample of students at each grade level. The item formats included multiple-choice questions and short and extended constructed-response questions developed around important mathematical ideas set in a real-world context. Each student was allotted 30 minutes to complete the questions in the theme block. (To complete the 45-minute testing time allocated to the cognitive items, a student took another block of items consisting entirely of multiple-choice questions that had a 15-minute time limit.) While working on the items in the theme block, students were permitted to use calculators and were provided with other materials such as rulers, protractors, and models.

A released grade 4 theme block built around the context of a science fair project on butterflies appears in Appendix 2A.[1] While working on the six constructed-response items in this block, students had access to calculators and other materials (butterfly information sheet, butterfly cutouts, ruler). A close look at the six constructed-response items that make up the block reveals that, although all items involved the assessment of important mathematical concepts and all were set in the context of the butterfly display, the items themselves do not satisfy the definition of either a vertical or a horizontal family of items. Instead, the items individually assess mathematical topics that ranged from geometry to measurement to number concepts to proportions to patterns, with few if any connections between the items. The only obvious connection between items was that students had to use the wingspan measurements from the second item in order to answer the sixth item in the block.

The performance results for the six theme block items, shown in Table 2-1, cannot be interpreted in any connected way that has to do with the mathematics in the items. Moreover, the difficulty in making connections between performance on the items is exacerbated by differences in the number of score levels. With respect to the only two items that were connected, the results suggest that, although students could measure wingspan (40 percent correct on item 2), they had difficulty using these measurements as part of a complex problem (1 percent correct on item 6). However, these results were not presented so such direct comparisons can be made between students' performance on those two items. That is, we do not know the percentage of students who, having obtained the correct wingspan measurement in item 2, provided correct answers accompanied by reasonable work in item 6.

In recent NAEP mathematics assessments, then, there has been little implementation of the notion of families of items, although the 1996 framework document makes a case for their inclusion. What might a family of items look like? What kind of information would likely be generated about students' understanding of a particular concept presented at varying levels of complexity in a mathematical content area or their understanding of a concept presented across mathematical content areas? The next section of this paper investigates these questions in light of a suggested family of items structured around number patterns, an informal algebra topic for grade 4.

---

[1]A discussion of the grade 4 released theme block (as well as the released theme blocks from the grade 8 and grade 12 NAEP mathematics assessment in 1996) appears in Kenney and Lindquist (in press).

TABLE 2-1 Performance on Items in the Butterflies Theme Block: Grade 4

Item Description	% Scoring at Highest Level[a]
1. Draw four missing markings on pictures of two butterflies to make each butterfly symmetrical.	28
2. Obtain two correct measurements in centimeters for the wingspans of two butterfly models.	40
3. Determine the greatest number of butterflies that can be stored in a case and the number of cases needed to hold 28 butterflies; show how your answer was obtained.	5
4. Determine the maximum number of butterfly models that can be made from a given number of parts (wings, bodies, antennae); show or explain how your answer was obtained.	3
5. Given that two caterpillars eat five leaves per day, determine the number of leaves needed each day to feed 12 caterpillars; show how your answer was obtained.	6
6. Find the number of each type of butterfly needed to create a repeating pattern on a banner that is 130 centimeters long; show how your answer was obtained. (Note: measurements obtained in item 2 are needed in this problem.)	1

Note: All items in this block were either short or extended constructed-response items.
[a]Because of differences in the number of levels in scoring guides, the highest score level varied among the items from three to five levels. The highest score levels are as follows: "satisfactory" for items 1, 4, and 6 (based on four score levels); "extended" for items 2 and 3 (based on five score levels); and "complete" for item 5 (based on three score levels).

A Sample Family of Items Based on Number Patterns at Grade 4

This section of the paper is divided into three parts. The first part contains a discussion of the importance of number patterns in the elementary mathematics curriculum and of the appropriateness of this topic as the basis for an item family in NAEP. The purpose of the next part is to justify the use of released NAEP mathematics items as the basis for the family of items and the limitations inherent in this method. The concluding part contains the sample item family, an explanation of its structure, and the kinds of information that might be obtained from looking at students' performance across the items.

Number Patterns in Elementary Mathematics and in NAEP

The topic of patterns and relationships, particularly number patterns in elementary school mathematics, is an appropriate and important content topic around which to create a family of items. Exploring patterns helps students in the early grades develop the ability to think algebraically (Armstrong, 1995; National Council of Teachers of Mathematics [NCTM], 1989; Reys et al., 1995). In fact, the NCTM Algebra Working Group realized that "children can develop algebraic concepts at an early age" (NCTM, 1994:5) and suggested that working with patterns of shapes and numbers helps to build the foundation for algebraic thinking needed in later grades.

In addition to information about the importance of patterns and relationships in the elementary mathematics curriculum, there exists a body of research that examines elementary students' performance on various types of numerical series and pattern items (e.g., Holzman et al., 1982, 1983; Pellegrino and Glaser, 1982). Included in these studies is important information on the nature of pattern items and possible factors that affect their ease or difficulty. For example, Holzman et al. (1982) report that the degree of difficulty of a numerical pattern item depends on such factors as the *operations* used to generate the pattern (i.e., incrementing operations [addition, multiplication] are easier than decrementing operations [subtraction and division]); the *number of operations* used to generate subsequent numbers in the pattern (i.e., patterns based on one operation [e.g., add 4] are easier than those based on two operations [e.g., first multiply by 2 and then add 1]); and the *magnitude of the numbers* used (i.e., patterns based on increments or decrements of small numbers [5 or less] are easier than those based on larger numbers [11 or greater]).

The importance of patterns and relationships in the elementary mathematics curriculum is further supported by the fact that the NAEP mathematics framework included this topic at grade 4. There is evidence that patterns, particularly numerical patterns, were a topic assessed in NAEP. Within the Algebra and Functions content strand at grade 4, recent NAEP mathematics assessments have included items that assess informal algebraic thinking through patterns and relationships. In 1992 about 10 percent of the items on the grade 4 assessment dealt with informal algebra, and most of those items involved patterns of figures, symbols, or numbers (Kenney and Silver, 1997). The 1996 assessment had about the same percentage of items at grade 4, and most of them also involved a variety of patterns, including number patterns. Thus, given the importance of patterns in both the elementary mathematics curriculum and recent NAEP mathematics assessments as well as a research base that speaks to characteristics of pattern items that can affect performance, selecting this as the topic for a family of items was both reasonable and appropriate.

Released NAEP Pattern Items as the Basis for an Item Family

Not only did numerical pattern items appear on recent NAEP mathematics assessments, but also some of those items were released to the public. These released pattern items were not part of an item family in the assessment; instead, they appeared as single items in various parts of the assessment. However, because released pattern items and related performance data on those items were available from NAEP, it seemed reasonable to use these single items along with appropriate supplemental items to form a sample family of items. The advantage of this method of constructing a sample family of items is that the sample family uses items that have already appeared on a NAEP assessment, and we know how students performed on them. In addition, using existing items enabled the item family to be created with minimal time devoted to the development of original items. Finally, the existing items could be evaluated not only according to student performance but also using findings from published research studies (e.g., Holzman et al., 1982) and then organized into a family in a somewhat hierarchical fashion reflecting the level of cognitive demand.

However, this method of creating a sample item family using existing NAEP items carries with it potentially serious limitations. In particular, taking items developed individually and putting them together as a set post hoc has a degree of artificiality. The ideal method that should be used to create an item family is to begin with a particular topic and information based on research about students' understanding of that topic, build the family of items, and then validate the structure of the set by administering it to students and examining performance results. Obviously, this method was not used in this paper. As a consequence, the family of items presented herein should be considered as an illustrative but very modest example of what such a family might look like, with the understanding that better families of items will be created for future NAEP assessments. It is hoped that the simple example in this paper will be used as the basis for further thought about and discussion of important features of families of items in NAEP.

A Proposed Item Family Based on Numerical Patterns

The six items in Appendix 2B constitute a proposed family of items built around the topic of numerical patterns. The set was developed according to the following guidelines:

• Each item in the set involves an increasing pattern of numbers based on a particular rule that governs the growth. In the elementary mathematics curriculum, these kinds of patterns are often referred to as "growing patterns" (Reys et al., 1995; NCTM, 1992). In some items the pattern is based on constant increases between consecutive terms, and in others the pattern is based on nonconstant increases.

• The set represents an attempt to organize the items from the easiest to the most difficult. In the case of released NAEP items, performance data were used to determine the level of difficulty (e.g., an item for which performance was 75 percent correct was "easier" than an item for which performance was 53 percent correct). For items created especially for the set, the degree of difficulty was based either on a rational analysis of mathematical concepts or on factors found to influence the difficulty of number pattern item, such as kind of operation, number of operations, and magnitude of numbers, as presented in published research articles (e.g., Holzman et al., 1982).

• In some cases the items are presented in two formats: multiple choice and constructed response. Given that the NAEP has always advocated a judicious blend of multiple-choice and constructed-response items, presenting an alternative format for items (especially those developed specifically for the sample item family) seemed to be appropriate. However, because of the performance differences in NAEP concerning lower percent-correct results on constructed-response items, this could affect the hierarchy of items (easiest to more difficult) in the sample set.

The source is given for each item in Appendix 2B (e.g., a released NAEP item; an item created for the set). Following each item is a rationale for why the item was included in the item family and the kind of information that could be obtained from performance results. Figure 2-1 summarizes the concepts and progression of items in the sample family. Performance on these related items could provide insights into students' understanding of numerical patterns and where that understanding falters. For example, performance results could show that most fourth-grade students can work with patterns involving constant increases between the terms (items 1, 2, and 3), but performance levels could be lower for items involving patterns based on nonconstant increases (items 4 and 5), especially for complex problems (item 6). Performance results could also provide information on misunderstandings that students have about number patterns, with the same misunderstandings possibly occurring across items in the family. For example, some students may expect a number pattern always to have a constant increase between contiguous numbers. In this case, when faced with a pattern containing nonconstant increases such as the number pattern in item 4 (i.e., 8, 9, 12, 17, 24, 33, 44, . . . [increase based on the set of odd numbers]), those students could reason that, because the increase between the last two numbers shown in the pattern is 11, 55 (44 + 11) is the next number in the pattern. Because the next two items in the family (items 5 and 6) also involve nonconstant increases, results from those items can provide additional evidence about this misunderstanding.

Some might argue that such information about students' understanding and misunderstandings of numerical patterns is already available from the NAEP mathematics assessment results. All that would be needed would be to analyze

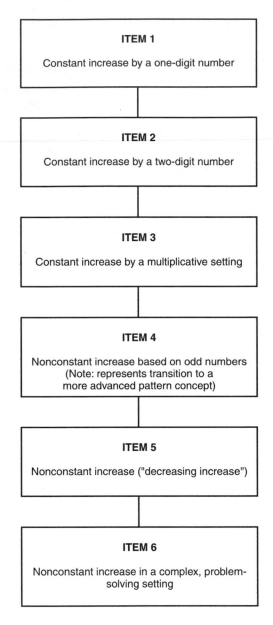

FIGURE 2-1 Progression of concepts in the number pattern family of items in Appendix 2B.

the performance results from the pattern items included on the assessment. While there is some truth to this argument, the fact remains that most NAEP items (other than the item pairs or triples or the theme block items) are discrete; that is, each item is essentially unrelated to any other item in the assessment. Therefore, identifying the numerical pattern items in NAEP and then analyzing the performance data as if those items had been developed as an intact set is likely to result in information about students' understanding that is fragmented and difficult to interpret. In fact, an attempt was made by Blume and Heckman (1997) to analyze student performance on the set of seven numerical pattern items that appeared on the grade 4 1992 NAEP mathematics assessment. Of those seven items, only two were related—the scaffolded item pair shown in Box 2-2. Because there were so few items and because most of them were discrete, Blume and Heckman were able to draw only limited conclusions about what students know about numerical patterns, such as: "[Number] patterns based on non-constant rates of change [e.g., the pattern shown above based on increasing by the set of odd numbers] are more difficult for fourth-grade students than patterns based on constant rates of change" (1997:232).

If those seven number pattern items had been developed as an item family, perhaps Blume and Heckman could have told a different story about student performance. As stated earlier, the advantage of an item family is that the items are purposely developed to be related in ways that could illuminate students' understandings and misunderstanding of important mathematical concepts. Analyzing the performance data from a related set of items, then, is more likely to provide results that are connected and interpretable. Also, expanding NAEP to include qualitative analyses of within-student performance across all items in a family (without identifying individual students) could provide information about patterns of performance concerning general knowledge about a particular topic and where such knowledge breaks down. This kind of information has the potential to make NAEP results more meaningful to teachers, parents, and others, thus satisfying an important recommendation of the National Research Council (1999).

CONCLUDING COMMENTS

The recommendation in the 1996 framework document about including families of items represents a positive direction for future NAEP mathematics assessments. The inclusion of item families can increase NAEP's potential to provide important information about the depth of students' knowledge in a particular content strand and across strands. The example given in this paper presents only one very limited way in which items can be related to make a family and how the results can be analyzed to provide a more complete picture of students' understanding. As stated previously, the best way to develop families of items is de novo, that is, after determining in advance the desired concepts to be assessed and examining existing research on mathematics learning in content areas. Current research does exist concerning a variety of mathematical topics such as fractions (e.g., Mack, 1990, 1995), decimals (e.g., Hiebert and Wearne, 1985), and probability (e.g., Jones et al., 1997) that could be used in the development of vertical item families, that is, those that assess students' understanding of important topics at a variety of levels.

It would also be wise to consider examples from the mathematics education literature that have some of the same features as described in the NAEP mathematics framework for horizontal item families that assess understanding of a mathematical concept (e.g., proportionality) across content strands. For example, in their framework for assessing conceptual understanding, Zawojewski and Silver (1998) propose that one way to ascertain the robustness of students' understanding of important mathematical concepts is to vary the context (e.g., content topics such as measurement, geometry, and number) in which the concept is presented. Their examples of "constellations" or collections of tasks that assess related aspects of a target concept might be useful to future development of related items in the NAEP.

By carefully choosing important mathematical topics and basing the development on prior research on the learning of mathematics, developers of the NAEP mathematics assessment can make better use of the idea of families of items. Reporting methods must also reflect the integrated nature of those item families. In particular, scoring schemes should be developed that link results on sets of items and perhaps even interpret those results in light of the concept assessed in the item familty. It is hoped that future NAEP assessments will include item families that reflect the intentions for the special sets of items in the 1996 NAEP mathematics framework document and that NAEP reports will take full advantage of the information provided by these related item sets.

REFERENCES

Armstrong, B.E.
    1995   Teaching patterns, relationships, and multiplication as worthwhile mathematical tasks. *Teaching Children Mathematics* 1:446-450.
Blume, G.W., and D.S. Heckman
    1997   What do students know about algebra and functions? Pp. 225-277 in *Results from the Sixth Mathematics Assessment of the National Assessment of Educational Progress*, P.A. Kenney and E.A Silver, eds. Reston, Va.: National Council of Teachers of Mathematics.
Collis, K.F., T.A. Romberg, and M.E. Jurdak
    1986   A technique for assessing mathematical problem-solving ability. *Journal for Research in Mathematics Education* 17:206-221.
Dossey, J.A., I.V.S. Mullis, and C.O. Jones
    1993   *Can Students Do Mathematical Problem Solving? Results from Constructed-Response Questions in NAEP's 1992 Mathematics Assessment.* Washington, D.C.: National Center for Education Statistics.

Hawkins, E.F., J.H. Mitchell, F.B. Stancavage, and J.A. Dossey
   1999   Estimation Skills, Mathematics-in-Context, and Advanced Skills in Mathematics: Results from Three Studies of the National Assessment of Educational Progress 1996 Mathematics Assessment. National Center for Education Statistics, Washington, D.C.
Hiebert, J., and D. Wearne
   1985   A model of students' decimal computation procedures. *Cognition and Instruction* 2:175-205.
Holzman, T.G., J.W. Pellegrino, and R. Glaser
   1982   Cognitive dimensions of numerical rule induction. *Journal of Educational Psychology* 74:360-373.
   1983   Cognitive variables in series completion. *Journal of Educational Psychology* 75:603-618.
Jones, G.A., C.A. Thornton, C.W. Langrall, T.M. Johnson, and J.E. Tarr
   1997   Assessing and Using Students' Probabilistic Thinking to Inform Instruction. Paper presented at the research presession to the annual meeting of the National Council of Teachers of Mathematics, April, Minneapolis, Minn.
Kenney, P.A., and M.M. Lindquist
   in   Performance of students on thematically related NAEP tasks. In *Results from the Seventh*
   press   *Mathematics Assessment of the National Assessment of Educational Progress*, E.A. Silver and P.A. Kenney, eds. Reston, Va.: National Council of Teachers of Mathematics.
Kenney, P.A., and E.A. Silver
   1997   Probing the foundations of algebra: Grade 4 pattern items in NAEP. *Teaching Children Mathematics* 3:268-274.
Mack, N.K.
   1990   Learning fractions with understanding: Building on informal knowledge. *Journal for Research in Mathematics Education* 21:16-32.
   1995   Confounding whole-number and fraction concepts when building on informal knowledge. *Journal for Research in Mathematics Education* 26:422-441.
National Assessment Governing Board
   1994   *Mathematics Framework for the 1996 and 2000 National Assessment of Educational Progress.* Washington, D.C.: National Assessment Governing Board.
National Council of Teachers of Mathematics (NCTM)
   1989   *Curriculum and Evaluation Standards for School Mathematics.* Reston, Va.: NCTM.
   1992   *Curriculum and Evaluation Standards for School Mathematics Addenda Series, Grades K-6: Fourth-Grade Book.* Reston, Va.: NCTM.
   1994   *A Framework for Constructing a Vision of Algebra.* Reston, Va.: NCTM.
National Research Council
   1999   *Grading the Nation's Report Card: Evaluating NAEP and Transforming the Assessment of Educational Progress*, J.W. Pellegrino, L.R. Jones, and K.J. Mitchell, eds. Committee on the Evaluation of National and State Assessments of Educational Progress, Board on Testing and Assessment. Washington, D.C.: National Academy Press.
Pellegrino, J.W., and R. Glaser
   1982   Analyzing aptitudes for learning: Inductive reasoning. Pp. 269-345 in *Advances in Instructional Psychology, Vol. 2*, R. Glaser, ed. Hillsdale, N.J.: Lawrence Erlbaum Associates.
Reese, C.M., K.E. Miller, J. Mazzeo, and J.A. Dossey
   1997   *NAEP 1996 Mathematics Report Card for the Nation and the States: Findings from the National Assessment of Educational Progress.* Washington, D.C.: National Center for Education Statistics.
Reys, R.E., M.N. Suydam, and M.M. Lindquist
   1995   *Helping Children Learn Mathematics,* Fourth Edition. Boston: Allyn and Bacon.

Silver, E.A., C. Alacaci, and D. Stylianou

in   Students' performance on extended constructed response tasks. In *Results from the*
press   *Seventh Mathematics Assessment of the National Assessment of Educational Progress,*
        E.A. Silver and P.A. Kenney, eds. Reston, Va.: National Council of Teachers of Mathematics.

Wilson, L.D., and S. Chavarria

1993   Superitem tests as a classroom assessment tool. Pp. 135-142 in *Assessment in the Mathematics Classroom: 1993 Yearbook of the National Council of Teachers of Mathematics,*
        N.L. Webb and A.F. Coxford, eds. Reston, Va.: National Council of Teachers of Mathematics.

Zawojewski, J.A., and E.A. Silver

1998   Assessing conceptual understanding. Pp. 287-295 in *Classroom Assessment in Mathematics: Views from a National Science Foundation Working Conference,* G.W. Bright and J.M. Joyner, eds. Lanham, Md.: University Press of America.

APPENDIX 2A: RELEASED GRADE 4 THEME BLOCK: 1996 NAEP MATHEMATICS ASSESSMENT

Materials Used in the Grade 4 Theme Block

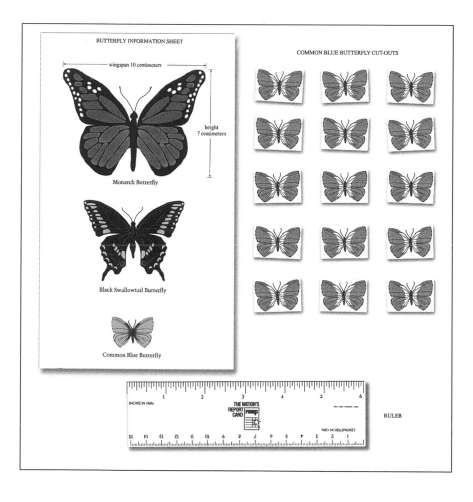

SOURCE: Hawkins et al. (1999).

This part has 6 questions. Mark your answers in your booklet. You will have to fill in an oval or write your answer as directed. In those questions where you must write an answer, it is important that your answer be clear and complete and that you show all of your work since partial credit may be awarded. Some questions may each require 5 minutes or more to think about and answer. After each question, fill in the oval to indicate whether you used the calculator.

Use the packet you have been given to help you answer the questions in this section.

Each class in Oakville School will have a booth at the Science Fair. Your class is planning to have a Butterfly Booth.

Your class has a lot to do to get ready for the Science Fair. You need to make decorations for the booth, plan activities, and order materials.

GO ON TO THE NEXT PAGE

1. The butterfly booth will be decorated with butterfly drawings. Draw only the missing markings on each picture to make each butterfly symmetrical.

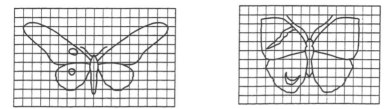

Did you use the calculator on this question?

   ○ Yes   ○ No

2. **Take the Butterfly Information Sheet from your packet.**

   On the Butterfly Information Sheet the wingspan of the Monarch butterfly is shown.

   Use your ruler to measure the <u>wingspans</u> of the other two butterflies on the sheet, the Black Swallowtail butterfly and the Common Blue butterfly, to the nearest centimeter.

   Black Swallowtail   Wingspan: _____   centimeters

   Common Blue   Wingspan: _____   centimeters

Did you use the calculator on this question?

   ○ Yes   ○ No

GO ON TO THE NEXT PAGE

3. Take the butterfly cutouts from your packet.

What is the greatest number of Common Blue butterflies that can be stored in the case below? (When you put butterflies in the case, you can't stack them. The butterflies can touch, but they can't overlap at all.)

Answer: _____

Show how the butterflies fit in the case.

Storage Case

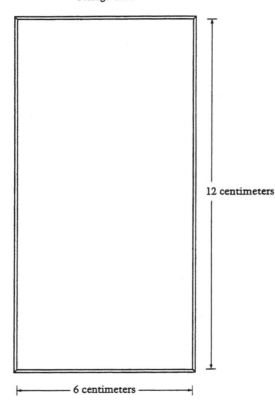

12 centimeters

|←——————— 6 centimeters ———————→|

GO ON TO THE NEXT PAGE

How many storage cases would you need to store 28 Common Blue butterflies?

Answer: _____

Use drawings, words, or numbers to explain how you got your answer.

Did you use the calculator on this question?

○ Yes ○ No

4. The children who visit your booth are going to build models of butterflies. For each model, they will need the following:

4 wing pieces   1 body   2 antennae

When the model is put together it looks like this:

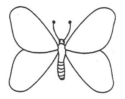

If the class has a supply of 29 wings, 8 bodies, and 13 antennae, how many complete butterfly models can be made?

Answer: _____

Use drawings, words, or numbers to explain how you got your answer.

Did you use the calculator on this question?

○ Yes   ○ No

GO ON TO THE NEXT PAGE

5. A fourth-grade class needs 5 leaves each day to feed its 2 caterpillars. How many leaves would they need each day for 12 caterpillars?

Answer: _____

Use drawings, words, or numbers to show how you got your answer.

Did you use the calculator on this question?

    O   Yes   O   No

GO ON TO THE NEXT PAGE

6. Use the Butterfly Information Sheet and your answer from question 2 to solve this question.

Your class has decided to have a banner that will be 130 centimeters long. This banner will have a repeating pattern of one Monarch butterfly followed by two Black Swallowtail butterflies, as shown here.

This part keeps repeating across the banner.

The butterflies will just touch but will not overlap.

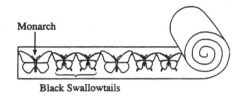

How many of each type of butterfly are needed for the banner?

Monarch _____

Black Swallowtail _____

Show how you got your answers.

GO ON TO THE NEXT PAGE

If you need more room for your work, use the space below.

Did you use the calculator on this question?

    O   Yes   O   No

APPENDIX 2B:
SAMPLE FAMILY OF ITEMS BASED ON NUMBER PATTERNS:
GRADE 4

ITEM 1

Version 1: Multiple choice

8, 14, 20, 26, 32, ...

If the pattern shown continues, which of the following numbers would be next in the pattern?

    A. 34
    B. 36
    C. 38
    D. 40

Version 2: Constructed response

Write the next two numbers in the number pattern.

    8   14   20   26   32   ____   ____

Version 3: Multiple-choice set within a context

Emily started her stamp collection with 8 stamps and added the same number of stamps to her collection each week. If she had 14 stamps after the first week, 20 stamps after the second week, and 26 stamps after the third week, how many stamps would she have after the fourth week?

    A. 28
    B. 32
    C. 38
    D. 40

Based on an example from Kenney and Silver (1997: 270).

Rationale for Item 1

This item would appear first in the family because nearly all the fourth-grade students should be able to produce a correct answer based on the constant increase of 6 between the numbers in the pattern. This conjecture concerning the ease of the item is supported by characteristics suggested in Holzman et al. (1982); that is, the pattern is based on a single incrementing operation (addition) and the use of a relative small number (6) as the increment between terms in the pattern.

The first version (multiple choice, no context) would best serve the purpose of determining the floor effect. The other versions are presented here as additional examples of simple pattern items based on a single-digit, constant increase between consecutive numbers. The last version set within a context could possibly be too difficult to appear as the first item in the set, but its multiple-choice format could make it more accessible to fourth-grade students.

ITEM 2

Original NAEP item [calculator use permitted]

In 1990 a school had 125 students. Each year the number of students in the school increases by 50. Fill in the table to show the number of students expected for each year.

Year	Number of Students
1990	125
1991	———
1992	———
1993	———

Source: 1992 NAEP mathematics assessment

Performance results:
All three answers correct:	51 percent
Any two answers correct:	3 percent
Any one answer correct:	9 percent
At least one answer correct:	63 percent

Version for the item family

In 1990 a school had 125 students. Each year the number of students in the school increases by 50. Answer the questions based on the table.

Year	Number of Students
1990	125
1991	———
1992	———
1993	———

1. How many students will the school have in 1991?
   Answer: _____

2. Complete the table to show the number of students expected for 1992 and 1993.

Rationale for Item 2

A version of the 1992 NAEP item would appear next in the item family. Although the pattern of numbers is still constantly increasing and although the operation is still addition, the increase itself is a double-digit number greater than 11, which adds to the difficulty of the item for elementary school students (Holzman et al., 1982). Despite the fact that the increase is a multiple of both 5 and 10 and that the increase is given in the problem, this item is considered as a "step up" from the first problem because of its constructed-response format and the need to work with a pattern involving a two-digit number increase.

The NAEP version, however, should be modified so that more information can be obtained from student responses. In particular, the original NAEP item asked for three numbers in the pattern based on a given constant increase of 50 students. The results showed that just over half the fourth-grade students gave completely correct responses. However, the results did not reveal which of the three numbers was the most difficult to obtain. The version proposed for the item family could remedy this situation by providing information on whether the students understood that the enrollment increases in the first year by 50 students, and then by that same number in each of the next two years.

ITEM 3

Original NAEP item pair [calculator use permitted]

Items 1 and 2 refer to the table below:

Column A		Column B
12	→	3
16	→	4
24	→	6
40	→	10

1. What is a rule used in the table to get the numbers in column B from the numbers in column A?

    A. Divide the number in column A by 4.
    B. Multiply the number in column A by 4.
    C. Subtract 9 from the number in column A.
    D. Add 9 to the number in column A.

Column A		Column B
120	→	

2. Suppose 120 is a number in column A of the table. Use the same rule to fill in the number in column B.

Source: 1992 NAEP mathematics assessment

Performance results:
    Item 1:   42 percent selected correct choice (A)
    Item 2:   24 percent obtained correct answer of 30

Version 1 for the item family: Division

The next questions use the following table:

Column A		Column B
12	→	3
16	→	4
24	→	6
40	→	10

Write the rule used to get the numbers in column B from the numbers in column A.

Rule:_____

Column A		Column B
120	→	

Suppose 120 is a number in column A of the table. Use the rule you wrote to fill in the number in column B.

Version 2 for the item family: Multiplication

The next questions use the following table:

Column A		Column B
3	→	12
4	→	16
6	→	24
10	→	40

Write the rule used to get the numbers in column B from the numbers in column A.

Rule: _____

Column A		Column B
30	→	

Suppose 30 is a number in column A of the table. Use the rule you wrote to fill in the number in column B.

Rationale for Item 3

The third item in the family represents a transition from patterns based on addition of a constant to patterns based on multiplicative models. This item would reveal whether students understand that patterns can be based on arithmetic operations other than addition, for example, multiplication or division.

The original NAEP item was discussed in an earlier section of this paper, and it was noted there that the results did not completely reveal the degree of consistency between the rule selected by students and whether they used that rule to answer the second question. Using one of the revised versions, both of which are constructed-response questions, perhaps we can better relate the students' description of the rule in part 1 and their use (or misuse) of that rule in part 2. For example, in version 1 for students who answered "Divide the number in Column A by 4," but who wrote "3" in Column B in the second part of the problem, we could more accurately attribute this incorrect answer to a place-value error or perhaps to carelessness. For other students who wrote the correct rule, but who answered "480" in the second part, it is likely that their error involved multiplying instead of dividing.

With respect to the two versions suggested for the family, one version might be preferable over the other depending on whether the multiplicative model (Version 2) or the division model (Version 1) is more easily recognized by students. Perhaps both versions could be pilot-tested to answer this question, with only one version included in the item family.

ITEM 4

Version 1: Multiple choice

8, 9, 12, 17, 24, 33, 44, ...

If the pattern shown continues, which of the following numbers would be next in the pattern?

A. 53
B. 55
C. 57
D. 59

Version 2: Constructed response

Write the next two numbers in the number pattern.

8   9   12   17   24   ____   ____

Source: Created as an example for this report.

Rationale for Item 4

The fourth item, presented in two versions (multiple choice and constructed response), serves as a transition between numerical patterns based on constant increases to those based on nonconstant increases. In an important way, nonconstant increases are in themselves a pattern within a pattern. For example, the pattern in the item (8, 9, 12, 17, 24, 33, 44, ...) also has a pattern of increases (1, 3, 5, 7, 9, ...)—the set of odd numbers. Because the notion of nonconstant increases is likely to be difficulty for some fourth-grade students, basing the nonconstant increases on the set of odd numbers could make the item more accessible. Also, the operation used to create the pattern is again simple addition.

As noted earlier in the paper, this item and the ones that follow could provide evidence about an important misunderstanding about patterns; that is, the notion that all patterns (even those that are based on nonconstant differences) contain pairs of numbers that have a constant difference. For item 4 in the family, it is likely that some students could choose B (55) for the multiple-choice version or write 31 and 38 as the next two numbers in the pattern for the constructed-response version. In both cases, such responses show evidence of changing the nonconstant increase to a constant increase based on the difference between the last two numbers shown in the pattern.

ITEM 5

Original NAEP item

Puppy's Age	Puppy's Weight
1 month	10 lbs.
2 months	15 lbs.
3 months	19 lbs.
4 months	22 lbs.
5 months	?

John records the weight of his puppy every month in a chart like the one shown above. If the pattern of the puppy's weight gain continues, how many pounds will the puppy weigh at 5 months?

A. 30
B. 27
C. 25
D. 24

Source: 1992 NAEP mathematics assessment

Performance results:
    Choice A   12 percent
    Choice B   24 percent
    Choice C   29 percent
    Choice D*   32 percent

*correct response

Note: Approximately 4 percent of the students did not answer this item, and it had a 20 percent "not reached" rate (i.e., 20 percent of the students in sample left this item and all items that followed it blank).

Version for the item family

Puppy's Age	Puppy's Weight
1 month	10 lbs.
2 months	15 lbs.
3 months	19 lbs.
4 months	22 lbs.
5 months	?

John records the weight of his puppy every month in a chart like the one shown above. Suppose the pattern of the puppy's weight gain continues.

1. How many pounds did the puppy gain from 1 month to 2 months?
   Answer: _____

2. How many pounds did the puppy gain from 2 months to 3 months?
   Answer: _____

3. If the pattern of the puppy's weight gain continues, how many pounds will the puppy weigh at 5 months?
   Answer: _____

Rationale for Item 5

This item within the family has the potential to be the most difficult question to this point. Results from the original NAEP version of the item showed that about the same percent of students selected choice C (25 pounds) as selected the correct choice D (24 pounds). This error pattern shows that some students may expect a number pattern to have a constant difference between some contiguous numbers: that is, in the puppy problem, students retained the 3-pound weight gain between the third and fourth months and used it as a constant to calculate the weight at 5 months (22 + 3 = 25). Also, the high omitted and not-reached rates suggest that some fourth-grade students thought that this problem was so difficult that they did not even try to answer it.

The version proposed for the item family attempts to make the question more accessible to students. It is scaffolded so that students must identify the first two nonconstant differences between the weights, in the hope that students will more easily recognize that the weight gains are decreasing between consecutive months. The final question involves a transition from the nonconstant differences to the actual weight of the puppy.

As for Item 4 in the family, this item has the potential to provide additional evidence of the misunderstanding about nonconstant increases. Despite the attempt at scaffolding, students could still change to a constant increase and answer 25 pounds or some other number based on a constant increase in weight.

ITEM 6

Original NAEP item [calculator use permitted]

A pattern of dots is shown below. At each step, more dots are added to the pattern. The number of dots added at each step is more than the number added in the previous step. The pattern continues infinitely.

(1st step)	(2nd step)	(3rd step)
		• • • •
	• • •	• • • •
• •	• • •	• • • •
2 dots	6 dots	12 dots

Marcy has to determine the number of dots in the 20th step, but she does not want to draw all 20 pictures and then count the dots.

Explain or show how she could do this and give the answer that Marcy should get for the number of dots.

Source: 1992 NAEP mathematics assessment—grade 8

Performance results:

Extended response	5 percent
Satisfactory response	1 percent
Partial response	6 percent
Minimal response	10 percent
Incorrect response	63 percent

Note: Approximately 16 percent of the eighth-grade students did not answer this question.

Version for the item family

A pattern of dots is shown below. At each step, more dots are added to the pattern. The number of dots added at each step is more than the number added in the previous step. The pattern continues and does not stop.

(1st step)   (2nd step)   (3rd step)

• •••• •

• • • • • • •

• • • • • • • •

2 dots   6 dots   12 dots

How many dots would be in the 4th step? Show how you got your answer.

Marcy has to determine the number of dots in the 10th step, but she does not want to draw all 10 pictures and then count the dots.

Explain or show how she could do this and give the answer that Marcy should get for the number of dots in the 10th step.

Rationale for Item 6

The original NAEP item, called Marcy's Dot Pattern in NAEP reports (e.g., Dossey et al., 1993), was administered to students in the 1992 eighth-grade sample as an extended constructed-response question in the Algebra and Functions content strand. As shown by the performance results, this question was difficult for the eighth-grade students: only 6 percent produced a response that was scored as satisfactory or extended. However, the fact that the item was last in an item block with previous items having little or no connection to number patterns could have affected performance levels. How would students have performed if this question, or an appropriate version thereof, appeared in a family of items devoted to number patterns?

Given the structure of the family of items describe thus far, it seemed reasonable to think about including an adaptation of the Marcy's Dot Pattern as the culminating item in the family. As the culminating item, it has characteristics based on work done on the previous items. For example, one way to view the pattern in this task is that the pattern involves nonconstant increases between the number of dots in each step. Solving the problem requires students to identify the rule that underlies the pattern of nonconstant increases. The version for the item family begins with an introductory question about the number of dots in the fourth step as a way to introduce students to the problem. Here, it would be reasonable for students to draw the fourth figure so that they can better understand the pattern. The next part of the problem is similar to that given to students in the eighth-grade sample, but the steps are reduced from the 20th step to the 10th step. This last decision needs careful thought, however, because drawing 7 more sets of dots is more accessible than drawing 17 more sets.

3

Student Thinking and Related Assessment: Creating a Facet-Based Learning Environment

Jim Minstrell

From the research literature we know that students come to our classes with preconceptions. Over the past 30 years there has been considerable research on students' conceptions. In a classic popularized article, McCloskey et al. (1980) identified several misconceptions in mechanics that they described as being consistent with the impetus theory, which predominated before Newton's synthesis. More recently, summaries of students' conceptual difficulties across the sciences have been published (Driver et al., 1994; Gabel et al., 1994; Project 2061, 1993). There is even at least one summary of international research on students' conceptions (Duit et al., 1991). How can these research results be incorporated into mainline assessment, curriculum, and instruction?

In topics new to their experience and thinking, learners construct understanding during class activities. The list of students' conceptions and reasoning has grown to be quite extensive and continues to grow. Consider the following student ideas:

- Are these ideas wrong?
- To find the average speed, divide the final position by the final time.
- Heavier things fall faster. Extremely light things don't even fall.
- A forward force is necessary to keep an object moving in the forward direction at a constant speed.
- Objects don't weigh anything in space.
- Balanced forces can't apply to both an at-rest object and an object moving at a constant velocity.
- In an interaction the bigger/heavier object exerts the greater force.

- The more pulleys the greater the mechanical advantage, or the less force one will need to exert.
- More batteries will make the bulb brighter.

Most of these statements seem valid on the surface. Several are true, depending on the context in which they are used. How can we honor the "sense making" learners have done and yet help them move toward a more scientific understanding?

What can research reveal about students' thinking, and what are the implications for instruction and assessment? This chapter illustrates some aspects of students' thinking, suggests a "facets of thinking" approach to organizing students' thinking, and shows that the facets approach can be useful to teachers in diagnosing student difficulties and designing or choosing instruction to address those difficulties. If it can be useful to teachers to effect better learning, it makes sense to incorporate the perspective into classroom assessment and even large-scale assessment in order to inform decisions at the program and policy levels. The purpose of the chapter is to demonstrate that research on learning and teaching can be used effectively to inform curriculum, instruction, and assessment at both the policy and especially the classroom levels.

THINKING ABOUT STUDENTS' THINKING

Background

Consider the following question:

A huge, strong magnet and a tiny, weak magnet are brought near each other. Which of the following statements makes the most sense to you?

A. The huge magnet exerts no force on the small one, which exerts no force on the large one.
B. The huge magnet exerts more force on the small magnet than the small one exerts on the large one.
C. The huge magnet exerts the same force on the small magnet as the small magnet exerts on the large one.
D. The huge magnet exerts less force on the small magnet than the small magnet does on the large one.
E. The huge magnet exerts no force on the small magnet, which does exert force on the large one.

Briefly explain how you decided.

Readers can most likely predict which is the most popular answer. In our classes, prior to instruction, nearly 85 percent of the students pick B and justify the choice by citing the fact that the one magnet is larger and stronger and therefore capable of exerting the larger force. It is also interesting that about 15 percent choose C. In this case their rationale comes from authority: "I remember that for every action there is an equal reaction." Asked to cite experience consistent with this idea, students report remembering "reading it in a book" or "hearing it from a former teacher." This does not represent an adequate understanding.

Consider a second question:

Sam is taller, stronger, and heavier than Shirley. They are both standing on level ground and lean on each other back to back without falling. Which seems to make the most sense with respect to the forces they exert on each other?

A. Sam exerts a greater force on Shirley.
B. Sam and Shirley exert equal forces on each other.
C. Shirley exerts a greater force on Sam.
D. Neither exerts a force on the other.

Briefly explain.

With the Sam and Shirley problem the reader may have more difficulty predicting the outcomes. In our classes about 50 percent of the students suggest that Sam will exert the larger force "because he is bigger and/or stronger." About 20 percent of the students suggest Shirley will exert the greater force, citing such evidence as, "she has the angle on Sam" or "he is just leaning [passive], but she will have to be pushing [active] to keep them from falling over." Nearly 30 percent suggest they will exert equal forces. While some students cite knowledge learned from authority, many cite as evidence the fact that "nobody is winning" and "they are not falling over" [no effect].

From these and similar questions it appeared that students were attending to surface features of problem situations rather than understanding and applying principles. From a formal physics perspective, it is clear the students are not being consistent. After all, these are both "third law" [Newton] questions and the students are not answering them the same. On the other hand, looking at the questions from the students' viewpoints, the questions are very different. The salient features in the two situations are different. In constructing their solutions the learners were considering such features as size, strength, "winning" or resulting movement effects, and level of activity or passivity of the interacting objects.

A tenet from cognitive psychology is that learners are naturally mentally active (Bruer, 1993). As humans, we try to make sense of the natural world and human-made artifacts in it. We organize it initially by surface features and then react on the basis of recognition of patterns. We see what we perceive to be a similar situation and make a similar prediction or action. If something does not work out as expected, we attempt to reorganize our understanding. It is around these impasses, where ideas do not work, that change in our thinking results. Making the leap to abstract scientific principles, like Newton's Third Law, to organize the world phenomena does not come naturally or quickly. It takes opportunities for development and time to develop our thinking to that level of principled performance.

To better understand my students' thinking so that I could create better instruction to address their cognition, I tried to think about the physical world like a student does. I assumed my students were trying to make sense of their world. I read their solutions and listened to their ideas with an eye and ear tuned to search for features that seemed to make sense to them in limited contexts.

From the field of research on students' conceptions and reasoning, I began identifying and organizing student thinking associated with various problematic situations. I identified the individual sorts of thinking (which I call facets) and clustered them around certain situations or ideas. I call these facet clusters (Minstrell, 1992). The term *facets* was used to avoid the "baggage" that goes with such terms as *misconceptions* or *alternative conceptions*. In fact, much of the thinking of students is useful and can be built upon, but it does not appear to be theoretically based, such as what would be part of an impetus theory or Newtonian theory. It seems rather to be based on salient features and a construction of explanations from "pieces" of understanding (diSessa, 1993).

Facets of Thinking

Facets are used to describe students' thinking as it is seen or heard in the classroom. Facets of students' thinking are individual pieces or constructions of a few pieces of knowledge and/or strategies of reasoning. While facets assumes a "knowledge in pieces" perspective like that of diSessa (1993), the pieces are generally not as small as the phenomenological primitives (p-prims) assumed by diSessa. Facets have been derived from research on students' thinking and from classroom observations by teachers. They are convenient units of thought for characterizing and analyzing students' thinking in the interest of making decisions to effect specific reform of curriculum, instruction, and assessment. Since facets are only slight generalizations from what students actually say or do in the classroom, they can be identified by teachers and used by them to discuss the phenomena of students' ideas. Some are content specific—for example, "horizontal movement makes a falling object fall more slowly." Others are strategic, like "average velocity is half the sum of the initial and final velocities" (in any situation). Still others are generic "more implies more," such as "the more batteries, the brighter the bulb." Typically they are (or seem to be) valid, depending on the context of usage.

Facet clusters are sets of related facets, grouped around a physical situation (e.g., forces on interacting objects) or around some conceptual idea (e.g., meaning of average velocity). Within the cluster, facets are sequenced in an approximate order of development and for recording purposes are coded numerically (see Figures 3-1 and 3-2). Those ending with 0 or 1 in the units digit tend to be appropriate, acceptable understandings for introductory physics. The facets ending in 9, 8, or so tend to be the more problematic facets in that, if this is not dealt with during instruction, the student will likely have a great deal of trouble with this cluster and with ideas in related clusters. For example, if students do not differentiate average speed from a change in position (facet 229-3), they will have great difficulty understanding many other ideas about motion. For some facets there are several "subspecies." For example, 229 has three ways that it represents what students do when they do not separate average rate (speed/velocity) from amount of distance or displacement. Those facets with middle digits frequently arise from formal instruction, but the student may have over-generalized or undergeneralized the application of an appropriate principle. The numerical code is intended as a descriptive aid. Thus, rather than simply a score, they suggest implications for what specifically needs to be addressed, where specific deficiencies exist. For additional information on facets and clusters see the following two Web sites: http://weber.u.washington.edu/~huntlab/diagnoser/facetcode.html and www.talariainc.com.

FIGURE 3-1 Cluster 470: forces on interacting objects.

*470   All interactions involve equal magnitude and oppositely directed action and reaction forces that are on the separate interacting bodies

474   Effects (such as damage or resulting motion) dictate relative magnitudes of forces during interaction.

474-1   At rest, therefore interaction forces balance.

474-2   "Moves," therefore interacting forces unbalanced.

475   Equal force pairs are identified as action and reaction but are on the same object

476   Stronger exerts more force

477   One with more motion exerts more force

478   More active/energetic exerts more force

479   Bigger/heavier exerts more force

FIGURE 3-2 Cluster 220: meaning of average speed or average velocity.

*220 avg. speed = (total distance covered)/(total amount of time)
*221 avg. velocity = $\Delta x/\Delta t$ (together with a direction)

225 Rate expression is over-generalized
225-1 avg. v = vf + vi/2 unless compensation between low and high values occurs
                        e.g., acceleration is constant
225-2 avg. v = xf / tf

226 Rate expression misstated
226-1 avg. v = $\Delta t/\Delta x$, i.e., change in time divided by change in position.
226-2 avg. v = $\Delta v/2$
226-3 avg. v = vf/2
226-4 avg. v = (vf+vi)/Δt

228 Average rate not differentiated from another rate
228-1 avg. v means constant velocity
228-2 Velocity = speed   Student doesn't differentiate between velocity and speed.
228-3 avg. v = vf, i.e., average v is the same as the final v.
228-31 greatest avg. vel = greatest Vf during any part of trip
228-4 avg. v = avg. a
228-5 avg. v = Δv or Δv divided by a quantity other than Δt

229 Average rate (speed/velocity) not differentiated from amount of distance or displacement.
229-2 avg.v = pf, i.e., the final position
229-21 avg.v = avg.p
229-3 avg.v = Δp

INSTRUCTIONAL DESIGN BASED ON STUDENTS' THINKING

Using Facets to Create a Facet-Based Learning Environment

This section demonstrates how having information from facet assessment can inform instructional decisions. Whether an assessment is done in the classroom or on a larger scale, such as state or national assessments, the results and implications must eventually be fed back to teachers to affect programs and instruction. Thus, the facet assessment examples presented here are at the classroom interface between teacher, student, and curriculum. Likewise, assessment implications can also affect curriculum development or adaptation to better address targeted learning difficulties with respect to particular learning goals (e.g., standards).

I will describe how the research on facets is used to create a facet assessment-based learning environment. The purpose of the environment will be to build

from assessments of students' initial and developing ideas toward a more principled understanding. Facets are used to diagnose students' ideas and to direct
the choice or design of instructional activities (Minstrell, 1989; Minstrell and
Stimpson, 1996). The main body of this paper discusses the value of teachers
having, and being able to use, facets and facet clusters. A particular facet cluster
is used to demonstrate the creation of such a facet assessment-based learning
environment.

Goals in our introductory physics course include understanding the nature of
gravity and its effects and understanding the effects of ambient fluid (e.g., air or
water) mediums on objects in them, whether the objects are at rest or moving
through the fluid. For many introductory physics students, an initial difficulty
involves a confusion between which effects are effects of gravity and which are
effects of the surrounding medium. When one attempts to weigh something, does
it weigh what it does because the air pushes down on it? Or is the scale reading
that would give the true weight of the object distorted somehow because of the
air? Or is there absolutely no effect by air? Because these have been issues for
beginning students, the students are usually highly motivated to engage in
thoughtful discussion of the issues.

Assessment for Eliciting Students' Ideas Prior to Instruction in Order to Build an Awareness of the Initial Understanding

At the beginning of several units or subunits, a preinstruction quiz is administered. One purpose is to provide the teacher with knowledge of the related
issues in the class in general and to provide specific knowledge of which students
exhibit what sorts of ideas. A second reason is to help students become more
aware of the content and issues involved in the upcoming unit.

To get students involved in separating effects of gravity from effects of the
ambient medium, we use the following question associated with Figure 3-3.
"First, suppose we weigh some object on a large spring scale, not unlike the ones
we have at the local market. The object apparently weighs ten pounds, according
to the scale. Now we put the same apparatus, scale, object and all, under a very
large glass dome, seal the system around the edges, and pump out all the air. That
is, we use a vacuum pump to allow all the air to escape out from under the glass
dome. What will the scale reading be now? Answer as precisely as you can at
this point in time. [pause] And, in the space provided, briefly explain how you
decided." Thus, students' ideas are elicited. (I encourage the reader to answer
this question now as best, and as precisely, as possible.)

Students write their answers and rationale. From their words a facet diagnosis
can be made relatively easily. The facets associated with this cluster, "Separating
medium effects from gravitational effects," can be seen in Figure 3-4. Students
who give an answer of zero pounds for the scale reading in a vacuum usually are
thinking that air only presses down and that "without air there would be no

FIGURE 3-3 Preinstruction question.

Name_____ School_____ Teacher_____
Period_____ Physics I.D. #_____

Nature and Effects of Gravity Diagnostic Quiz Problem 1.

Glass dome with air removed

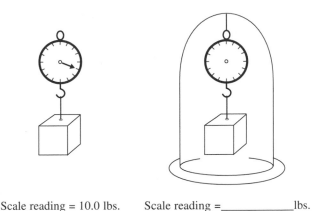

Scale reading = 10.0 lbs.   Scale reading =_____lbs.

Briefly explain how you decided.

weight, like in space" (facet 319). Other students suggest a number "a little less than 10" because "air is very light, so it doesn't press down very hard, but it does press down some"; thus, taking the air away will only decrease the scale reading slightly (facet 318). Other students suggest there will be no change at all. "Air has absolutely no effect on scale reading." This answer could result either from a belief that mediums do not exert any forces or pressures on objects in them (facet 314) or that fluid pressures on the top and bottom of an object are equal (facet 315). A few students suggest that while there are pressures from above and below there is a net upward pressure by the fluid. "There is a slight buoyant force" (facet 310, an acceptable workable idea at this point). Finally, a few students answer that there will be a large increase in the scale reading "because of the [buoyant] support by the air" (facet 317).

The numbering scheme for the facets allows for more than simply marking the answers "right" or "wrong." The codes ending with a high digit (9, 8, and sometimes 7) represent common facets used by our students at the beginning of instruction. Codes ending in 0 or 1 are used to represent goals of instruction. The

FIGURE 3-4 Separating medium effects from gravitational effects.

*310   Pushes from above and below by a surrounding fluid medium lend a slight support (net upward push due to differences in depth pressure gradient)

*310-1   The difference between the upward and downward pushes by the surrounding air results in a slight upward support or buoyancy.

*310-2   Pushes above and below an object in a liquid medium yield a buoyant upward force due to the larger pressure from below.

*311   A mathematical formulaic approach (e.g., rhoxgxh1 – rhoxgxh2 = net buoyant pressure)

314   Surrounding fluids don't exert any forces or pushes on objects

315   Surrounding fluids exert equal pushes all around an object

315-1   Air pressure has no up or down influence (neutral)

315-2   Liquid presses equally from all sides regardless of depth

316   Whichever surface has greater amount of fluid above or below the object has the greater push by the fluid on the surface.

317   Fluid mediums exert an upward push *only*

317-1   Air pressure is a big up influence (only direction)

317-2   Liquid presses up only

317-3   Fluids exert bigger up forces on lighter objects

318   Surrounding fluid mediums exert a net downward push

318-1   Air pressure is a down influence (only direction)

318-2   Liquid presses (net press) down

319   Weight of an object is directly proportional to medium pressure on it

319-1   Weight is proportional to air pressure.

319-2   Weight is proportional to liquid pressure

latter abstractions represent the sort of reasoning or understanding that would be productive at this level of learning and instruction. Middle number codes represent some learning. When data are coded, the teacher/researcher can visually scan the class results to identify dominant targets for the focus of instruction.

Benchmark Instruction to Initiate Change in Understanding and Reasoning

By committing their answers and rationale to paper, students express greater interest in coming to some resolution, in finding out what is "right." Students are now motivated to participate in activities that can lead to resolution. In the classroom this benchmark lesson usually begins with a discussion of students' ideas. We call this stage "benchmark instruction" since the lesson tends to be a reference point for subsequent lessons (diSessa and Minstrell, 1998). It unpacks the issues in the unit and provides clues to potential resolution of those issues. In this stage, students are encouraged to share their answers and associated rationales. Teachers attempt to maintain neutrality in leading the discussion, both to allow issues to be brought forth by students to maintain a focus on their thinking and to honor the potential validity of students' facets of knowledge and reasoning (van Zee and Minstrell, 1997).

Note that many of the ideas and their corresponding facets have validity. Facet 319: Some students have suggested a valid correlation between no air in space and no apparent weight in space. What they have not realized is that in an earth-orbiting shuttle one would likely get a zero spring scale reading, whether in the breathable air inside the shuttle or the airless environment outside. Facet 318: It is true that air is light, that is, its density is low relative to most objects we put in it. Air does push downward, but it also pushes in other directions. Facet 317: Air does help buoy things up, but the buoyant force involves a resolution of the upward and downward forces by the fluid, and that effect is relatively small on most objects in air (not so for a helium balloon). Facet 315: For many situations the difference between the up and down forces by air is so small that even the physicist chooses to ignore it. Thus, there is validity to most of the facets of understanding and reasoning used by students as they attempt to understand and reason about this problem situation.

By now many threads of students' present understanding of the situation are unraveled and lay on the table for consideration. The next phase of the discussion moves toward allowing fellow students to identify strengths and limitations of the various suggested individual threads. "Is this idea ever true? When and in what contexts? Is this idea valid in this context? Why or why not?" After seeing the various threads unraveled, students are motivated to know "what is the truth." The teacher asks: "How can we find out what happens?" Students readily suggest: "Try it. Do the experiment and see what happens." The experiment is run, air is evacuated, and the result is "no detectable difference" in the scale reading in the vacuum versus in air.

Facet-Informed Elaboration Instruction to Explore Contexts of Application of Other Threads Related to New Understanding and Reasoning

The initial activity was to address facet 319, considered the problematic understanding. But many of the students also thought that air only pushed down or only pushed up. Additional discussion and laboratory investigations allow students to test the contexts of validity for other threads of understanding and reasoning. Other activities involving ordinary daily experiences are brought out for investigation: an inverted glass of water with a plastic card over the opening (the water does not come out), a vertical straw dipped in water and a finger placed over the upper end (the water does not come out of the lower end until the finger is removed from the top), an inverted cylinder is lowered into a larger cylinder of water (it "floats" and as the inverted cylinder is pushed down, one can see the water rise relative to the inside of the inverted cylinder), and a 2-liter, water-filled, plastic soda bottle with three holes at different levels down the side (uncapped, water from the lowest hole comes out fastest; capped, air goes in the top hole and water comes out the bottom hole). These activities address students' hypotheses consistent with facets 318 and 317.

While each experiment is a new specific context, the teacher encourages the students to come to general conclusions about the effects of the surrounding fluid. "What can each experiment tell us that might relate to all of the other situations, including the original benchmark problem?" In addition to encouraging additional investigation of issues, the teacher can help students note the similarity between what happens to an object submerged in a container of water and what happens to an object submerged in the "ocean of air" around the earth.

A final experiment for this subunit affords students the opportunity to try their new understanding and reasoning in another more specific context. A solid metal slug is "weighed" successively in air, partially submerged in water (scale reading is slightly less), totally submerged just below the surface of the water (scale reading is even less), and totally submerged deep in a container of water (scale reading is the same as any other position, as long as it is totally submerged). From the scale reading in air, students are asked to predict (qualitatively compare) each of the other results, do the experiment, record their results, and, finally, interpret those results. This activity specifically addresses the students' hypotheses associated with facets 316, 315, and 314. This task asks the students to relate these results and the results of the previous experiments to the original benchmark experience.

By seeing that air and water have similar fluid properties, students are prepared to build an analogy between results. Weighing in water is to weighing out of water (in air) as weighing in the ocean of air is to weighing out of the ocean of air (in a vacuum). Thus, students are now better prepared to answer the original question about weighing in a surround of air, and they have developed a more principled view of the situation. Since students' cognition is associated with the specific features of each situation, a paramount task for instruction is to help students recognize the common features that cross the various situations. Part of coming to understand physics is coming to see the world differently, but the general principled view can be constructed inductively from experiences and from the ideas that apply across a variety of specific situations.

The facets are our representation of the students' ideas. They originate and are used by the students, although they may be elicited from the students by a skilled instructor or within the design of assessment items. Thus, the generalized understandings and explanations are constructed by students from their own earlier ideas. In this way I am attempting to bridge from students' ideas to the formal ideas of physics.

Assessment Embedded Within Instruction

The facet assessment can also be embedded within instruction and served technologically. This could be Web served giving policy and program people information, but the system I will describe here is one that our teachers are using to make instructional decisions.

Sometime after the benchmark instruction, after the class begins to come to tentative resolution on some issues, it is useful to give students the opportunity to individually check their understanding and reasoning. Although we sometimes administer these questions on paper in large-group format, we prefer to allow the students to quiz themselves when they are ready. To address this need for ongoing assessment, we have developed a computerized tool to assist the teacher in individualizing the assessment and keeping records on student progress. When students think they are ready, they are encouraged to work through computer-presented problems, appropriate to the unit being studied, using a program called DIAGNOSER (Levidow et al., 1991; Hunt and Minstrell, 1994).

The DIAGNOSER is organized into units that parallel units of instruction in our physics course. Within our example unit, there is a cluster of questions that focus on the effects of a surrounding medium on scale readings when attempting to weigh an object. Within each cluster the DIAGNOSER contains several question sets. Each set may address specific situations dealt with in the recent instruction to emphasize to students that we want them to understand and be able to explain these situations. Sets also may depict a new problem context related to this cluster. We want to continually encourage students to extend the contexts of their understanding and reasoning.

Each question set consists of four screens. The first screen contains a phenomenological question, typically asking the student "what would happen if . . . ?" The appropriate observations or predictions are presented in a multiple-choice format with each alternative representing an answer derivable from under-standing or reasoning associated with a facet in this cluster. From the student's choice, the system makes a preliminary facet diagnosis. For example, in Figure 3-5 the choices are facet coded as 315.1 (for A), 318.1 (B), 319.1 (C), 310.1 (D), 318.1 (E), and 317.1 (F), respectively.

The second screen asks the student: "What reasoning best justifies the answer you chose?" Again the format is multiple choice with each choice briefly paraphrasing a facet as applied to this problem context. For example, in Figure 3-6 the choices are facet coded as 319.1 (A), 318.1 (B), 315.1 (C), 317.1 (D), and 310.1 (E). From the student's choice of answer to the reasoning question, the system makes a second diagnosis.

Each screen also has an alternative "write a note to the instructor" button beneath the portion with the multiple choices. Clicking on this option will allow students to leave a note about their interpretation of the question, about their difficulties with the content, or if they have an answer other than the choices

Normal air pressure is about 15 lbs./sq. in. When a certain concrete block is weighed in normal air, the scale reading is 60 lbs. If the same block was weighed in a special room in which the air pressure has increased to 20 lbs./sq. in., what would the new scale reading be?

   A. Exactly the same; it still reads 60 lbs. even if we could measure very precisely
   B. Very slightly more than 60 lbs. (may not even show up on the scale).
   C. About 80 lbs .
   D. Very slightly less than 60 lbs (may not even show up on the scale).
   E. Much more than 60 but not 80 lbs.
   F. Substantially less than 60 lbs.

FIGURE 3-5 Phenomenological questions.

What reasoning would best justify the answer you chose?

   A. The weight of an object will change directly proportional to air pressure.
   B. Air is light, but greater air pressure will cause an additional downward push. Thus, a greater air pressure will result in a scale increased reading.
   C. Air has absolutely nothing to do with the scale reading.
   D. Air supports from below. More pressure implies much more support and so a substantially reduced scale reading.
   E. Air pressure is from all around an object, but it is slightly greater on the bottom of the object. That results in a very slight upward support.

FIGURE 3-6 Reasoning question.

offered. These notes can be scrutinized by the teacher/researcher to assist individual students, to improve DIAGNOSER questions and to modify activities to improve instruction. Students also are allowed to move back and forth between the question and the reasoning screens. This is done to encourage students to think about why they have answered the question the way they have, to encourage them to seek more general reasons for answering questions in specific contexts.

The "reasons" screen is followed by a diagnosis feedback screen. What this screen says depends on precisely what the student did on the question screen and the reasoning screen. The feedback basically says whether the student's answer and reasoning choices appear to be consistent. Consistency is important in all empirical and rationally based systems, especially in science. Then the card tells the student whether there seems to be a problem with his or her answer and/or reasoning. For example, if a student chose answers that were consistent but problematic, a screen like that in Figure 3-7 would appear.

The fourth screen in each sequence is the prescription screen. If a student's answers are diagnosed as being associated with productive understanding and reasoning, the student is mildly commended and is encouraged to try more questions to be more sure. The rationale here is that it should be recognized that while the student's ideas seem OK in this one context, overcongratulating the student may allow him or her to get by with a problematic idea that just did not happen to show up in this problem situation.

If the student's answers were diagnosed as potentially troublesome, they are issued a prescription associated with the problematic facet. Typically, the student is encouraged to think about how his or her ideas would apply to some common everyday experience or to do an experiment he or she may not yet have done. In either case the experience was chosen because the results will likely challenge the problematic facet apparently invoked by the student. For example, if the student had chosen answer E for the phenomenological question and B for the reasoning question, the system would serve the screen with a prescription consistent with facet 318.1, as in Figure 3-8.

> Both your answer to the question and your
> reasoning are consistent with each other, but
> it appears you are using a concept or strategy
> that will cause you some trouble. Move
> ahead for a prescription for help.

FIGURE 3-7 Feedback for consistent problematic answer.

If air pressure was down only, then the mountain climber would claim his pack was getting lighter (even without adding anything to or taking anything out). They don't tend to do that.

Suppose we do a thought experiment that goes beyond our lab experiences. Remember what happens when we "weighed" the cylinder in water versus "weighing" it out of the water. We can think of the air around the earth as an ocean of air. Consider the following analogy: Weighing in the ocean of air is to weighing it out of air as weighing in the ocean of water is to weighing it out of the water. What implication does that have for the direction of air pressure? Does air only push down?

FIGURE 3-8 Prescriptive lessons for facet 318.1.

The DIAGNOSER is run in parallel with other instructional activities going on in the classroom. Some students are working on DIAGNOSER, while others are working in groups on problem solving or additional laboratory investigations. In the case of our example subunit, the class may even be moving ahead into the next subunit. Students work on the program individually or in small groups of two (ideally). When they are finished with a session, they are presented with a summary of their performance but are not graded on it. It is a tool to help them assess their own thinking and a tool to help the teacher assess additional instructional needs for the class as a whole or for students individually. It is also a device to assist the students and teacher in keeping a focus on understanding and reasoning.

For additional information on DIAGNOSER, see the following two Web sites: http://weber.u.washington.edu/~huntlab/diagnoser/facetcode.html and www.talariainc.com. As of the writing of this paper, DIAGNOSER can be downloaded from the first site. Newer versions of DIAGNOSER-type assessment systems will be available on both sites as the assessments are ready.

Application of Ideas and Further Facet Assessment of Knowledge

A unit of instruction may consist of several benchmark experiences and many more elaboration experiences together with the associated DIAGNOSER sessions. Sometime after a unit is completed, students' understanding and reasoning are tested to assess the extent to which instruction has yielded more productive understanding and reasoning. When designing questions for paper-and-pencil assessment, we attempt to create at least some questions that will test for extension of application of understanding and reasoning beyond the specific contexts dealt with in class. Has learning been a genuine reweave into a new fabric of understanding that generalizes across specific contexts or has instruction resulted in brittle, situation-bound knowledge? In general, we find that students' answers and reasoning become progressively more consistent and they progress toward the goal facets, as will be seen under "Results."

In designing tests the cluster of facets becomes the focus for a particular test question. In the example cluster here, test questions probe students' thinking about situations in which the local air pressure is substantially changed. Have students moved from believing that air pressure is the cause of gravitational force? Other questions focus on interpreting the effects of a surrounding medium, as they help us infer the forces on an object in that fluid medium. Do students now believe that the fluid pushes in all directions? Do they believe greater pushes by the fluid are applied at greater depths? Can they integrate all of these ideas together to correctly predict, qualitatively, what effects the fluid medium will have on an object in the fluid? In future units—dynamics, for example—do students integrate this qualitative understanding of relative pushes to identify and diagram relative magnitudes of forces acting on submerged objects? DIAGNOSER-type questions, like those in Figure 3-9, can be used on end-of-unit or end-of-term tests as well as being used as assessment embedded in instruction.

Whether the question is in multiple-choice or open-response format, we attempt to develop a list of expected answers and associated rationale based on the individual facets in that cluster. After inventing a situation context relevant to the cluster, we read each facet in the cluster, predict the answer, and characterize the sort of rationale students would use if they were operating under this facet. Assuming we have designed clear question situations and our lists and characterizations of facets are sufficiently descriptive of students' understanding and reasoning, we can trace the development of their thinking by recording the trail of facets from preinstruction, through DIAGNOSER, to postunit quizzes and final tests in the course.

Results

For the sample of results described in this section, we continue to focus on separating gravitational effects from effects of the surrounding fluid. The answers for each question associated with diagnosis or assessment were coded using the facets from the cluster for "Separating medium effects from gravitational effects" (see Figure 3-4, 310 cluster of facets).

The preinstruction assessment called for free-response answers (Figure 3-3). On it 3 percent of our students wrote answers coded at the most productive level of understanding (see Table 3-1). On the embedded assessment (DIAGNOSER),

These pictures show three identical
blocks attached to the spring scale.
In one case the block is in water,
in another it is in air, and in a third
the block is in vacuum. In air the scale
reads 20 lbs. To the nearest 0.1 lbs.

The scale readings would be

A. About the same in all three environments.
B. Noticeably less in water but about the same
    in air and vacuum.
C. Noticeably less in air and in the water.
D. Noticeably more in water and noticeably
    less in the vacuum.

What reasoning would best justify the answer you
chose?

A. The weight of an object will change directly
    proportional to air pressure.
B. Air is light, but greater air pressure will cause an
    additional downward push. Thus, a greater air pressure
    will result in an increased scale reading.
C. Air has absolutely nothing to do with the scale reading.
D. Air supports from below. More pressure implies much
    more support and so a substantially reduced scale
    reading.

FIGURE 3-9 Examples of other relevant DIAGNOSER questions.

Identical blocks are supported by a spring scale
in water, in air, and in a vacuum. Suppose
the scale was INFINITELY PRECISE, that is,
the scale could be read precisely out to any
number of digits one wanted. In air suppose
the scale reads 20.0000000 etc. lbs. (exactly 20 lbs.).

How would the scale readings compare?

A. In water < in air < in vacuum
B. In water < in air = in vacuum
C. In water > in air > in vacuum
D. In water = in air = in vacuum
E. In air > in water, but in a vacuum it would be
     zero.

What reasoning would best justify the answer you chose?

A.   Mediums exert pressure downward on objects. The more
     dense the medium the more downward pressure.
B.   Mediums have no effect. They exert equal pressures from
     all sides
C.   Water creates a buoyant force, but objects don't weigh
     anything in a vacuum (like space).
D.   Mediums support objects. The more dense the medium, the
     more support from below.
E.   Water supports objects from below, but air has no effect at
     all.

FIGURE 3-9 Examples of other relevant DIAGNOSER questions.

A cubic object (10 cm on a side) is hung on a spring scale. The scale shows that the object weighs 30 lbs. in a normal air situation.

In a certain special room, if the air pressure is doubled,

A. The scale reading will be close to 60 lbs.

B. The scale reading will be pretty close to 30 lbs.

C. The scale reading will be very nearly zero pounds.

What reasoning would best justify the answer you chose?

A. Air pressure does not greatly affect scale readings.

B. Doubling the air pressure will double the downward pressure on the cube, which will double the scale reading.

C. Doubling the air pressure will cancel the downward influence of the weight and the object will almost seem to float.

FIGURE 3-9 Examples of other relevant DIAGNOSER questions.

In a severe storm, such as a hurricane, the local air pressure may drop by 10%. Under these conditions the scale reading when weighing an object will

A. Decrease by about 10%.

B. Decrease but not by as much as 10%.

C. Stay about the same.

D. Increase substantially.

What reasoning would best justify the answer you chose?

A. Air pressure tends to push downward on objects.

B. Weight scale reading is not greatly affected by air pressure.

C. The weight of an object is directly proportional to air pressure.

D. Air pressure helps greatly to support objects from below. It helps hold them up.

FIGURE 3-9 Examples of other relevant DIAGNOSER questions.

TABLE 3-1 Student Preinstruction Predictions for Scale Reading

Scale Reading[a]	Percent	Facet Code
s 20 lbs.	2	317
20 > s > 11	11	317
11 s > 10	3	310
s = 10	35	314/315
10 > s ≥ 9	12	318
9 > s > 1	17	318
1 ≥ s ≥ 0	20	319

Note: Table is ordered by predicted scale reading answer followed by the inferred facet associated with that answer.
[a]Represents the predicted scale reading.

after students completed the elaboration experiences for a similar multiple-choice question and reasoning combination, 81 percent of the answers to the phenomenological question and 59 percent of the answers to the reasoning were coded 310.

Apparently revisiting the "object in fluid" context in subsequent instruction helped maintain the most productive level of understanding and reasoning about buoyancy at nearly the 60 percent level. By the end of the first semester, the class had integrated force-related ideas (statics and dynamics) into the context of fluid effects on objects submerged in the fluid medium. On a question in this area 60 percent of the students chose, and then briefly defended in writing, an answer coded 310. On the end-of-year final, 55, 56, and 63 percent of students chose the answer coded 310 on three related questions.

At the other end of the understanding and reasoning spectrum of facets is a substantial development away from believing that "downward pressure causes gravitational effects" (facet 319) and "fluid mediums push mainly in the downward direction" (facet 318). On the free-response preinstruction assessment, these two facets accounted for 49 percent of the data (see Table 3-1). In the DIAGNOSER those facets accounted for about 5 to 20 percent of the data. Similar results were achieved on both the first- and second-semester finals. Much of this movement away from the problematic "pressure down" facets did not make it all the way to the most productive facet. Much student thinking moved to intermediate facets that involve thinking that there are no pushes by the surrounding fluid of air (facet 314) or that the pushes up and down by the surrounding air are equal (facet 315). Most of the students were not stuck on these intermediate facets in the water context. This makes sense since they have direct evidence that water pressure at different depths causes a difference in the scale reading. In the air case the preponderance of the evidence is that if there is any difference because of depth it does not matter (e.g., force diagrams on a metal slug hung in the classroom do not usually include forces by the surrounding air). Even low-achieving students made significant gains (see Tables 3-2 and 3-3). The semester test questions used were similar to the DIAGNOSER questions shown earlier.

Also from Tables 3-2 and 3-3 it can be seen that individual students do not always answer in consistent fashion. Across items and across time individual students exhibit various facets of thinking. Which pieces of their knowledge and understanding are brought to a particular problem depend on the features of the problem. Early in the instruction it is the salient physical or verbal features of the problem. At this time there is considerable inconsistency between their answers to problems that might be seen as similar when the questions are organized by formal topic (recall the questions about Newton's Third Law). Later in the

TABLE 3-2 Development of Understanding and Reasoning: Forces by Surrounding Air on Objects

Facet Code	Preair	Prewater	Sem1	Sem2
310	16, 55		64, 72, 74	5, 16, 19, 21, 25, 64, 72
315	66, 74		16, 31, 53, 66, 69	8, 27, 31, 53, 55, 66, 69, 74
317	21			
318	7, 19, 25, 27, 64, 69		5, 7, 8, 19, 21, 27, 55	7
319	5, 8, 31, 53, 72		25	

Note: Numbers at right are identification numbers for 16 low-achieving students.

TABLE 3-3 Development of Understanding and Reasoning: Forces by Surrounding Water on Objects (four days after preair)

Facet Code	Preair	Prewater	Sem1	Sem2
310		7, 8,16, 25 55, 64, 74	5, 7, 8, 16, 19, 21 ,27, 53, 55, 64, 66, 72, 74	5,7,16,19, 21 25, 27, 31, 53, 55, 64, 66, 72, 74
315		5, 19,27, 66	25, 31, 69	69
317				
318		21, 31, 53, 69		
319		72		

Note: Numbers at right are identification numbers for 16 low-achieving students.

instruction, as students become more expert like, their answers are based on threads of experience and understanding that are more principle based (Chi et al., 1981). Their answers become more consistent and converge on the target understandings.

Apparently about half of our students came to physics instruction believing that air and perhaps even water pressure effects are mainly in the downward direction. By the end of the year, through early specific instruction and later revisiting, this belief was greatly reduced, and over half of the students were able to demonstrate good productive understanding of buoyant effects. Given that this is a difficult topic conceptually even for many physics teachers, these results are encouraging.

Similar facet-based instruction is now being used by many physics teachers and some curriculum developers (Hunt and Minstrell, 1994). Facet-based instruction has also been effective in the learning of introductory statistics and in training health care providers in the management of pain.

IMPLICATIONS FOR LARGE-SCALE ASSESSMENT

The examples given above are primarily from the classroom. That is the source of most of our specific experience with facet-based assessment. But the classroom is also where the results of large-scale assessments must make sense and be useful if the large-scale assessments are to help effect reform and result in better learning. We are beginning to explore the application of facet-based assessment to large-scale assessment. Large-scale tests like the National Assessment of Educational Progress or the state assessments could include facet-indexed foils that could inform policy, program, and practice. While the preceding material is based on many years of research and practice, below are some speculations as we begin our exploration.

Implications for Policy, Program, and Practice

The National Science Education Standards advocate reform in assessment as well as curriculum and instruction (National Research Council, 1996). The test items and ranking purposes of the typical normative-based assessment system will not be sufficient. Universities and employers may still need to rank applicants against each other, and that has been accomplished reasonably well by normative testing, such as the SAT (Scholastic Assessment Test). But in a standards-based system, large-scale assessment needs to compare the performance of the unit (state, district, school, or individual) with the standard. There is a choice to be made for the criteria for making the comparison. One could set the large-scale standard to be a certain score that is deemed sufficient for certification. But such action would sidestep the intent of the standards effort. We would not know what the troubles are at a level of specificity that can help decide what to do about them. This would not be much different from what we presently have with respect to assessment.

Suppose instead that the learning target standards are integrated with the problematic understandings in facet clusters. Multiple-choice foils, or the rubrics for coding open-response items, could be tuned to the facets. Such a large-scale assessment system would be able to check on accountability for policy and program revision, but it would also allow sufficiently rich feedback to inform the system about what troubles exist. From identification of specific troubles, teachers and others creating or adapting a curriculum could design or choose lessons to address the problematic issues.

What might a test based on facets be like? To characterize thinking in any one cluster for a group of students would likely require incorporating two DIAGNOSER-type items, like those shown earlier, to each form of the test. If the two items incorporate the reasoning as well as the phenomenological question, that is like having four subitems per cluster. From our experience responding to these items takes about 1 minute per subitem for a total of about 4 minutes per cluster. At that rate we could test for 15 clusters per 60-minute test. For our physics program there are about 40 clusters, but several are not unique to physics. If a large-scale test is to cover the learning in science over a three-year period, I estimate that would represent about 100 clusters. (Note: that is not 100 topics. For example, the topics of force and motion would be represented by about eight clusters.)

For large-scale assessment in which not every student needs to take the same test, sampling procedures could be used to cover all clusters. Analysis from such an assessment could provide information about specifically where students were having trouble in each cluster. This is the sort of feedback that can inform curriculum and instruction decisions as well as teachers about what needs to be focused on in the classroom. It seems that something like this procedure could be used for NAEP and some state tests.

What about large-scale assessments where all students are to take equivalent forms of the same test? For example, in Washington state all students at grade 10 need to obtain a certificate of mastery in science. Would that imply that all students would have to be tested over the same clusters and that from one year to the next the clusters must be the same? Presently test developers include items in topical headings. If each topic contains several clusters, perhaps test developers could have the freedom to choose items from within clusters under the given topic heading. For example, the test contractor for the state of Washington was to choose or design two or three items associated with each topical strand. There are about 40 topical strands in the state science standards. Within each topical strand, I estimate there would be two or three clusters. Thus, I believe a facets and facet cluster base could be used as the basis for constructing and choosing items instead of using traditional methods or current ones. In this way the state would be able to certify students as meeting the general standard for science using a score from reduced test data. But the school could get facet cluster-based data from which to make program decisions, and teachers could get facet-based data from which they could make instructional decisions to improve practice and learning.

A facet-based system can also be used to tune expected learning targets. The setting of our present national and state standards is based to a considerable extent on what we "want our students to know and be able to do." To a much lesser extent, standards efforts have incorporated some implications from research on what students "do know and are able to do," especially when we set goals for "all" students. We could consider these goals as the top-level facets, but much more research is needed to determine the problematic constructions by students on their way to the goal (Minstrell, in preparation). This sets an item on the agenda for research. In the past, research on learning was set largely in clinical or classroom situations designed to teach particular topics, not particularly tuned to learning the standards. To the extent that we collectively believe the standards that have been set are the goals we want to achieve, we need to direct research on learning in the disciplines toward identifying the problematic issues and understanding on the way to the goals. Then in our teaching experiments the problematic ideas become the focus of our design of curriculum and instruction as we attempt to guide students toward the standards.

Facet-based assessment can provide information from which we can decide expected levels of understanding. If we had characterizations of various understanding and reasoning for students nationally, we might be better able to identify reasonable targets for learning. For example, using the previously stated results, is it reasonable to assume that all high school students can achieve the 310 level of understanding for the air contexts as well as the water contexts? For air contexts we might be willing to set the standard bar at 317 (air has some buoyant upward force somehow) or 315 (air pushes from above and below are equal). Yet requiring a 310 standard for all with respect to understanding water contexts seems reasonable, since we see (from Tables 3-2 and 3-3) that the water context is more achievable, even by lower achievers. Thus, a facet-like system can provide information for making cost-benefit decisions. For example, knowing that low-achieving students were diagnosed at 310 on the water cluster but at 315 in the air cluster would suggest that better activities are needed for demonstrating the similarity of fluid characteristics of air and water. Can we afford the extra instructional time to get from one level of understanding to the higher level? Should we invest the extra time?

For making practical classroom "next day" decisions, one or more facet-based questions can be used during one class period to inform the teacher about tomorrow's needs. More questions per cluster will be needed in the long run for periodic monitoring of learning by the teacher. Except on unit exams, the results of the monitoring can be low-stakes assessment, with grades assigned only on the basis of honest effort. Meanwhile, the results provide data from which teachers can make decisions on what might happen next.

Developing students' understanding in a cluster takes instructional time. Deep learning cannot be hurried. Judging from our experience in classes, it took four to five hours in class for students to develop their understanding in one cluster, like the clusters already demonstrated. Other clusters, such as the three for developing ideas of length, area, and volume, can be taken together as part of coming to understand spatial extent, about five hours at the high school level. Still other clusters involve the processes of scientific thinking and can be assessed across some of the other more subject-matter-oriented clusters. For example, the cluster for the meaning of explanation in science (Figure 3-10) can be applied across items that ask for explanation of specific events (e.g., explaining falling bodies or interpreting the resulting offspring from parent plants). As can be seen from Tables 3-2 and 3-3, not all of the understanding comes during the four days of instruction in that cluster. Some comes through revisiting the ideas and issues in subsequent subunits around related clusters. Thus, districts, departments, and individual teachers need to decide which clusters are more important or more difficult for their students and choose or design instruction to develop the more important ideas.

Need for Ongoing Research on Learning and Teaching

Although we have a good start for developing facets as they apply to high school physics, substantially more research needs to be done to characterize students' thinking across sciences and across grade levels. Consistent with this

FIGURE 3-10 Cluster: explanations or interpretations of phenomena.

*050—Explanations or interpretations involve conceptual modeling of multiple related science or math concepts, using experimental evidence and rational argument to address questions of "how do you know . . . ?" or "why do you believe the results, observation, or prediction?"

*051—Explanation involves a mathematical modeling approach, incorporating principles subsumed under that model.

053—Explanation involves identifying possible mechanisms involving a single concept causing the result.

055—Explanation involves identifying and stating a relevant concept.

057—Explanation constitutes a description of procedures that led to the result.

059—Explanations or interpretations are given by repeating the observation or result to be explained.

vision, we initiated an investigation into students' facets of thinking in probability and statistics at the introductory level at the university (Schaffner et al., 1997).

In collaboration with the University of Washington, the State Commission on Student Learning, selected school districts, and Talaria, Inc., Earl Hunt and I are directing the building of an assessment system to serve teachers as they focus on students' learning. This project involves identifying facets and developing a facet-based system for classroom assessment in the physical sciences and mathematics relevant to the quantitative sciences for grades 6 through 10 for Washington state. To follow this development, see the Web sites at http://weber.u.washington.edu/~huntlab/diagnoser/facetcode.html and www.talariainc.com.

Building a base of facets and facet clusters involves setting particular learning goals and doing the research to describe students' thinking in intermediate positions on the way to those goals. The top-level facets need to be described at a level of specificity that includes all of the "pieces" of knowledge and processing necessary to operationally define the goal. For our example 310 facet, the description fully written out is about a third of a page long. Defining these goals at this level requires deep knowledge of the content domain. For a large-scale facet assessment, the goals of learning will need to be carefully and specifically articulated.

To identify the other facets requires research. What do learners say and do when confronted with situations relevant to the learning goal? Some of the research on students' conceptions exists in the literature, but much more needs to be done in the context of the classroom. When we were building our present version of the facets, we identified situations or tasks we thought students should be able to explain if they had the goal understanding. Ideally, the tasks also involved many of the key issues related to the cluster. We collected 50 or so student responses to each task. As we read the responses, we sorted them according to similarities in answers and reasoning. Then we attempted to characterize the similarities among the several responses in one pile. Each characterization was the first try at identifying a facet. Next, using another task that was relevant to the same learning goal, the process was repeated for the responses to that second task. If the characterization of one of the piles for this set seemed similar to the characterization for a stack from the other set, we began to think we had validity and reliability for identifying that particular facet. But since particular tasks elicit particular ideas, not finding a similar pile for the second task analysis did not mean that the facet was not valid. The showing of a particular facet typically depends on context as well as content. To validate the facets associated with large-scale assessment would necessitate substantially more research on students' understanding of critical ideas in multiple contexts.

Once several facets in a particular cluster are identified, they can be used to predict typical responses on other tasks related to the cluster. It takes creativity to come up with novel problematic situations, but then the facets can be used to suggest responses to open-ended questions or to create foils for multiple-choice questions.

A facets perspective offers an opportunity to apply statistical analyses to determine prerequisite knowledge for the development of understanding of more complex ideas. Participation in large-scale assessment offers the opportunity to do research to determine what development is dependent on the development of what other ideas. Research on learning and teaching can benefit from development of understanding of students' facets of thinking resulting from large-scale assessment. Statistical analyses of large-scale test data could yield information on what facet in one cluster is related to what facets in other clusters. Thus, research on learning can identify what facets are in an ecological relationship (one of mutual existence and support) with other facets. Such research could serve curriculum program designers about what ideas to address as a set.

Computerized tools can assist teachers or large-scale assessment systems in diagnosing facets and handling electronically posted data from students. University of Washington colleagues Adam Carlson and Steve Tanimoto are building a computerized system for facet coding of electronically submitted open responses to questions and problems. Another colleague, Aurora Graf, has designed a DIAGNOSER-type module to address facets or thinking about ratio reasoning for middle-level students.

SUMMARY

Through a better understanding of students' thinking, we can characterize the sorts of problematic understandings that students exhibit on their way to learning goals. We can create facet clusters and individual facets. Using facet assessment can help teachers identify needs for particular learning activities. Curriculum developers or teachers adapting curriculum can better know and understand the targets for the lessons they engineer. Facet assessment can be used to monitor students' progress in the classroom. Large-scale facet-based assessments can identify particular curricular needs or suggest the need to revise standards or learning goals to make them more appropriate developmentally or with respect to time and other available resources. Finally, large-scale facet-based assessment will require support to clearly specify learning goals and research to identify more than just the "right" answers.

Through facets and tasks related to targeted facet clusters the thinking of large groups of students can be characterized and reported. From facet descriptions of groups of learners, policy and program decisions can be informed. Feedback and recommendations, specific to the facets, can be presented to teachers in the classroom and they can be better informed about what specifically to do to effect better learning.

ACKNOWLEDGMENTS

Several colleagues over the years have influenced this work or assisted in its progress. Arnold Arons, John Clement, Andrea diSessa, Virginia Stimpson, Dorothy Simpson, Emily van Zee, and Earl Hunt have contributed to the generation or revision of the ideas. They deserve much credit. Tens of other teachers and thousands of students have tested the ideas. I also want to thank the administrations of the school districts, especially Mercer Island School District, for their willingness to allow their teachers to think about facet assessment and the effects it can have on teaching and learning in the classroom.

The research and development described in this paper were supported by grants to Mercer Island School District and the University of Washington from the James S. McDonnell Foundation Program for Cognitive Studies for Educational Practice and the National Science Foundation: Program for Research in Teaching and Learning. Preparation of this paper was supported in part by a grant from the National Science Foundation to Talaria, Inc., a small research and development company that creates facet-based assessment and learning environments. The ideas expressed here are those of the author and do not necessarily reflect the beliefs of the sponsoring foundations.

REFERENCES

Bruer, J.
   1993   *Schools for Thought: A Science of Learning in the Classroom.* Cambridge, Mass.: MIT Press.
Chi, M., P. Feltovich, and R. Glaser
   1981   Categorization and representation of physics problems by experts and novices. *Cognitive Science* 5:121-152.
diSessa, A.
   1993   Toward an epistemology of physics. *Cognition and Instruction* 10(2-3):105-226.
diSessa, A., and J. Minstrell
   1998   Cultivating conceptual change with benchmark lessons. In *Thinking Practices in Learning and Teaching Science and Mathematics*, J.G. Greeno and S. Goldman, eds. Mahwah, N.J.: Lawrence Erlbaum Associates.
Driver, R., A. Squires, P. Rushworth, and V. Wood-Robinson
   1994   *Making Sense of Secondary Science: Research into Children's Ideas,* New York: Routledge.
Duit, R., F. Goldberg, and H. Niedder (eds.)
   1991   *Research in Physics Learning: Theoretical Issues and Empirical Studies: Proceedings of an International Workshop held in Kiel, Germany.* Institute for Science Education.
Gabel, D. (ed)
   1994   *Handbook of Research on Science Teaching and Learning.* New York: MacMillan.
Hunt, E., and J. Minstrell
   1994   A cognitive approach to the teaching of physics. In *Classroom Lessons*, K. McGilly, ed. Cambridge, Mass.: MIT Press.
Levidow, B., E. Hunt, and C. McKee
   1991   The Diagnoser: A HyperCard tool for building theoretically based tutorials. *Behavior Research Methods, Instruments, and Computers* 23(2):249-252.

McCloskey, M., A. Caramazza, and B. Green
   1980   Curvilinear motion in the absence of external forces: Naive beliefs about the motion of objects. *Science* 210:1139-1141.
Minstrell, J.
   1989   Teaching science for understanding. In *Toward the Thinking Curriculum: Current Cognitive Research*, L. Resnick and L. Klopfer, eds. 1989 Yearbook of the Association for Supervision and Curriculum Development, Alexandria, Virginia.
   1992   Facets of students' knowledge and relevant instruction. Pp. 110-128 in *Research in Physics Learning: Theoretical Issues and Empirical Studies: Proceedings of an International Workshop held in Kiel, Germany*. R. Duit, F. Goldberg, and H. Niedderer, eds. Kiel, Germany: Institute for Science Education.
Minstrell, J., and V. Stimpson
   1996   A classroom environment for learning: Guiding students' reconstruction of understanding and reasoning. In *Innovations in Learning: New Environments for Education*, L. Schauble and R. Glaser, eds. Mahwah, New Jersey: Lawrence Erlbaum Associates.
National Research Council
   1996   *National Science Education Standards*. Washington, D.C.: National Academy Press.
Project 2061
   1993   *Benchmarks for Science Literacy*. New York: Oxford University Press.
Schaffner, A., D. Madigan, A. Graf, E. Hunt, J. Minstrell, and M. Nason
   1997   Benchmark lessons and the World Wide Web: Tools for teaching statistics. In: *Proceedings of the Second International Conference on the Learning Sciences*, D.C. Edelson and E.A. Domeshek (eds.). Evanston, Ill: Northwestern University.
van Zee, E., and J. Minstrell
   1997   Reflective discourse: Developing shared understanding in a physics classroom. *International Journal of Science Education* 19(2):209-228.

4

An External Evaluation of the 1996 Grade 8 NAEP Science Framework

Stephen G. Sireci, Frédéric Robin, Kevin Meara,
H. Jane Rogers, and Hariharan Swaminathan

The National Assessment of Educational Progress (NAEP) is the most comprehensive evaluation of the educational achievement of U.S. students in history. Laudable features of the more recent NAEP tests are their breadth in terms of the content domains measured and the manner in which students are tested. For example, on the 1996 NAEP science assessment, the focus of this paper, three "fields" of science are measured—earth, life, and physical science—and students are required to perform "hands-on" science experiments, report the results of their experiments in written form, and respond to multiple-choice questions. Thus, the structure of the current NAEP science assessment is complex.

This study examined the content validity[1] of the 1996 grade 8 NAEP science assessment to determine how well items composing the assessment represent the framework that governed the test development process. This appraisal is important for determining whether the inferences derived from NAEP scores can be linked to the science content and skill domains the test is designed to measure. To accomplish the goals of this study, 10 carefully selected science teachers were recruited to review items from the 1996 grade 8 NAEP science assessment and provide judgments regarding the knowledge and skills measured by these items.

---

[1]Some measurement specialists (e.g., Messick, 1989) argue against use of the term *content validity* because it is does not directly describe score-based inferences. Although this position has theoretical appeal, in practice, content validity is a widely endorsed notion of test quality (Sireci, 1998b). Thus, the position taken here is similar to Ebel (1977:59), who claimed "content validity is the only basic foundation for any kind of validity. . . . One should never apologize for having to exercise judgment in validating a test. Data never substitute for good judgment."

These judgments were compared to the knowledge and skill domains the items were intended to measure.

OVERVIEW OF THE GRADE 8
SCIENCE ASSESSMENT FRAMEWORK

The 1996 grade 8 science assessment comprised 189 items. The intended structure of the assessment is characterized in the content frameworks, which specify four dimensions (National Assessment Governing Board, 1996). The first dimension is a content dimension comprising three separate "fields of science"— earth science, life science, and physical science. The committees involved in creating the test specifications concluded that these three fields of science are sufficiently unique as to warrant separate scales. Thus, for all 1996 NAEP science assessments, the results were to be reported along four separate scales: one for each of the three fields of science and a composite score scale summarizing science proficiency across the three fields.

The second dimension of the science framework is a cognitive dimension described as "ways of knowing and doing science." There are also three components to this dimension: conceptual understanding, practical reasoning, and scientific investigation. Separate score scales are not derived for these cognitive skills; however, these skill areas were critical in defining the domains measured on the assessment and in governing the item (task) development process. Every item on a NAEP science assessment is targeted to one of the three fields of science and one of the three ways of knowing and doing science.

Only some of the items were linked to the other two dimensions underlying the content frameworks. These two dimensions are described as a "themes of science" dimension and a "nature of science" dimension. The "themes" dimension comprised three areas: patterns of change, models, and systems. The nature of science dimension comprised two areas: nature of science and nature of technology. For the grade 8 assessment, 93 items (49 percent) corresponded to a "theme" dimension and 31 items (16 percent) to a "nature" dimension. The content, cognitive, theme, and nature test specifications are presented in Table 4-1.

Another conspicuous aspect pertinent to the content structure of the assessment is the diversity of item formats used. Students were required to both read assessment material and perform hands-on scientific experiments. The item formats tied to these tasks were multiple-choice items (with two to four response options per item); short constructed-response items (where students were required to write a short answer, usually a single word or a sentence or two); and extended constructed-response items (requiring students to supply a detailed response to the item). There were 73 multiple-choice and 116 constructed-response items on the grade 8 assessment.

TABLE 4-1 Cross-Tabulation of Item Specifications for 1996 Grade 8 NAEP Science Assessment

| Field of Science | Conceptual Understanding | Ways of Knowing and Doing Science | | Total |
		Practical Reasoning	Scientific Investigation	
Earth science	35	13	14	62 (33%)
(Theme)	(23)	(7)	(7)	(37)
[Nature]	[2]	[4]	[5]	[11]
Life science	42	14	9	65 (34%)
(Theme)	(29)	(5)	(4)	(38)
[Nature]	[2]	[3]	[0]	[5]
Physical science	32	16	14	62 (33%)
(Theme)	(9)	(6)	(3)	(18)
[Nature]	[1]	[9]	[5]	[15]
Totals	109 (57.7%)	43 (22.8%)	37 (19.6%)	189
	(61)	(18)	(14)	(93)
	[5]	[16]	[10]	[31]

Note: Entries in the table are the number of items in each cell of the framework.

METHOD

Ten science teachers were recruited to scrutinize a carefully selected sample of items from the 1996 grade 8 science assessment and provide judgments regarding the content characteristics of the items. As described below, these teachers provided both ratings of the content similarities among the items and ratings linking each item to the content, cognitive, nature, and theme dimensions defined in the frameworks.

Participants

The 10 science teachers who served as the subject-matter experts (SMEs) in this study were selected by contacting the state assessment directors in states that are currently active in developing state standards and assessments in science. The teachers were nominated by their state assessment director because of their involvement in science assessment movements in their state. Three of the teachers previously served on a national working group, convened by the National Assessment Governing Board, that helped clarify the achievement-level standards set on the 1996 science assessment. Seven of the 10 SMEs were women. All had extensive experience teaching science. These SMEs represented the following states: California, Delaware, Florida, Kentucky, Maryland, Ohio, South Carolina, Texas, Virginia, and Washington. The data from these SMEs were gathered during a two-day workshop in Washington, D.C. All SMEs received an honorarium for their participation.

Items Selected for Analysis

As noted above, 189 items comprised the grade 8 science assessment. Sixty items were selected for the purposes of this study to represent the test specifications in terms of the content and cognitive dimensions as well as item format (multiple choice, short constructed response, extended constructed response). In addition, items were selected that represented a theme or nature of science area. These items came from 9 of the 15 blocks comprising the grade 8 item pool. Item-objective congruence ratings (described below) were obtained for all 60 items. However, because of time and subject fatigue limitations, a subset of 45 of these items was chosen for the item similarity ratings (also described below). Table 4-2 presents the test specifications for the 60-item subset, and Table 4-3 presents the test specifications for the 45-item subset. A comparison of Tables 4-1 through 4-3 reveals that the percentages of items from each science field were relatively comparable across the item pool and the item subsets but that the two subsets had slightly more items measuring practical reasoning and scientific investigation.

Procedure

SME Training

Almost half (29) of the 60 NAEP items used in this study were associated with one of the four hands-on science tasks. Twelve of these 29 items were included in the similarity rating task involving the 45-item subset, and all 29 were included in the item-objective congruence rating task. Training of the SMEs began with a description of these hands-on tasks. The material kits for these tasks were presented to the SMEs, and an oral description of the experiments was provided. The descriptions focused on tasks the students were required to complete in conducting their experiments. Next, the judges were asked to complete a block of 14 test items as if they were students being tested. After completing the items, the judges were given the answer keys and asked to check their answers. Finally, the judges were given the operational test booklet sections for the nine-item blocks (i.e., all 60 items). The 45 items that were later used were highlighted. The SMEs were given time to familiarize themselves with the items and the scoring protocols.

TABLE 4-2 Cross-Tabulation of Specifications for 60-Item Subset Used in Item-Objective Congruence Study

| Field of Science | Conceptual Understanding | Ways of Knowing and Doing Science | | Total |
		Practical Reasoning	Scientific Investigation	
Earth science	10	6	6	22 (37%)
(Theme)	(8)	(1)	(1)	(10)
[Nature]	[0]	[1]	[1]	[2]
Life science	10	7	4	21 (35%)
(Theme)	(8)	(3)	(4)	(15)
[Nature]	[0]	[1]	[3]	[4]
Physical science	7	4	6	17 (28%)
(Theme)	(0)	(2)	(1)	(3)
[Nature]	[1]	[2]	[3]	[6]
Totals	27 (45.0%)	17 (28.3%)	16 (26.7%)	60
	(16)	(6)	(6)	(28)
	[1]	[4]	[7]	[12]

Note: Entries in the table are the number of items in each cell of the framework.

TABLE 4-3 Cross-Tabulation of Specifications for 45-Item Subset Used in Item Similarity Rating Study

| Field of Science | Conceptual Understanding | Ways of Knowing and Doing Science | | Total |
		Practical Reasoning	Scientific Investigation	
Earth science	9	3	3	15 (33%)
(Theme)	(8)	(1)	(0)	(9)
[Nature]	[0]	[1]	[0]	[1]
Life science	7	6	3	16 (36%)
(Theme)	(0)	(3)	(3)	(6)
[Nature]	[0]	[1]	[2]	[3]
Physical science	6	3	5	14 (31%)
(Theme)	(1)	(1)	(1)	(3)
[Nature]	[1]	[2]	[3]	[6]
Totals	22 (48.9%)	12 (26.7%)	11 (24.4%)	45
	(9)	(5)	(4)	(18)
	[1]	[4]	[5]	[10]

Note: Entries in the table are the number of items in each cell of the framework.

Item Similarity Ratings

Following these item familiarization steps, instructions for completing the item similarity ratings were provided. The SMEs were informed that they would be required to review pairs of NAEP items and provide a judgment regarding the similarity of the items in each pair to one another in terms of the science knowledge and skills tested. These instructions were intentionally general so that the SMEs' ratings were not influenced by anyone else's preconceived notions of what the items were measuring. Therefore, the content specifications for these items, and the content frameworks for the test, were *not* described to the SMEs.

To facilitate understanding of the item similarity rating task, three "practice" item pairs were distributed to the judges. The first pair involved two multiple-choice items; the second pair involved a short constructed-response item and an extended constructed-response item; and the third pair involved two extended constructed-response items. Each item pair was printed on a single page, and an eight-point similarity rating scale was printed at the bottom of each page. The numeral "1" on the scale was labeled "very similar," and the numeral "8" was labeled "very different." The SMEs rated the similarities among these three item pairs individually and then discussed the ratings as a group. The SMEs with the highest and lowest ratings for each item pair described the characteristics of the items that influenced their ratings. Common factors cited were cognitive complexity of the item and science content area the item was measuring. The SMEs were told that they were on task and were each given an item similarity rating booklet. The pages of these booklets each contained one item pair, with the same eight-point rating scale printed at the bottom of each page. A sample item similarity rating page is presented in Figure 4-1.

Consideration of all possible item pairings among the 45 items involved 990 item comparisons ([45 × 44]/2). Given the time constraints of the study, the judges were required to rate only 700 of these 990 possible item pairings. Ten separate booklets were created. Each booklet represented a different ordering of the item similarity pairs to control for a systematic item order effect. The 700 ratings required of each SME were selected such that for each item pair seven independent ratings would be provided. Five of the SMEs finished relatively early and completed some of the "missing" 290 ratings. In addition to the 700 required ratings, six specific item pairs were repeated in each booklet. These repetitions were included to provide an estimate of the reliability of the SMEs' ratings. The six replicated item pairs were placed near the end of each booklet, when the deleterious effects of fatigue and boredom were most likely to be present. Thus, the error associated with the similarity ratings as measured by these replicated item pairs most likely represents a worst-case scenario.

Upon completion of the item similarity ratings, the SMEs responded to a short questionnaire on which they listed the criteria they used in making the item similarity ratings. The questionnaire asked the SMEs how long they took to

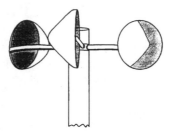

2. The instrument shown is used to measure

    ◎ wind direction

    ◎ wind speed

    ◎ air pressure

    ◎ relative humidity   JL001078

5. A space station is to be located between the Earth and the Moon at the place where the Earth's gravitational pull is equal to the Moon's gravitational pull. On the diagram below, circle the letter indicating the approximate location of the space station.

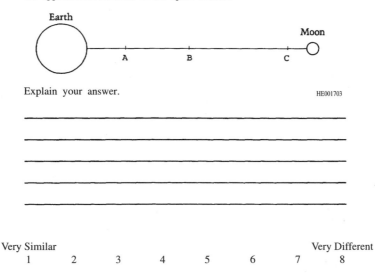

Explain your answer.   HE001703

_____

_____

_____

_____

_____

Very Similar   Very Different

   1   2   3   4   5   6   7   8

FIGURE 4-1 Sample item similarity rating sheet. Items are from National Center for Education Statistics, U. S. Department of Education, 1996 National Assessment of Educational Progress in Science released items; available at http://nces.ed.gov/naep.

complete the similarity ratings and listed seven item characteristics that were anticipated to influence their ratings: science discipline measured by each item, cognitive level measured by each item, item format, item difficulty, item length, item themes, and historical origin of each item. Space on the questionnaire was also provided for the SMEs to add any additional criteria they used that were not included on the list.

Item-Objective Congruence Ratings

The purpose of the item similarity rating task was to obtain the SMEs' "independent" appraisal of the knowledge and skills measured by the items (i.e., independent of knowledge of the content, cognitive, nature, and theme dimensions that governed item development). In this manner it was hoped that the content specifications for these 45 items would be "recovered" rather than confirmed. Thus, the similarity rating task tested the adequacy of the dimensions underlying the framework, given the items that were developed.

For the item-objective[2] congruence ratings, the SMEs were given an oral presentation describing the NAEP science frameworks as well as the public documentation of these frameworks (NAGB, 1996). The SMEs were then presented with a new booklet that listed the item numbers for each block (60 items total) and series of columns under which they were to provide ratings for each item. The task presented to the SMEs was to indicate their opinion regarding the "field of science," "way of knowing and doing science," "theme of science," and "nature of science" classification of each item. They were informed that each item was classified by the test developers into one of the three "fields" and into one of the three "ways" dimensions but that only some items were classified as a "nature" item or a "theme" item. These data provided a check on whether the SMEs would classify the items in a manner congruent with their test specifications. A sample item-objective congruence rating page is presented in Figure 4-2.

Exit Survey

Upon completion of the item-objective congruence ratings, the SMEs were given a brief survey. This survey asked them about their confidence in the similarity and congruence ratings they provided and asked them to provide suggestions for future research in this area. In addition, the survey asked the SMEs about their experience with science assessment standards at the local, state, and national levels and asked them to describe how well the NAEP science materials matched national, state, and local science standards.

---

[2]The term *objective* is used here in a general sense to describe the specific field of science, way of knowing and doing science, theme of science, and nature of science designations for each item.

Field of Science (choose one)			Knowing and Doing Science (choose one)			Themes of Science (choose one)				Nature of Science (choose one)	
Item #	Life Science	Physical Science	Earth Science	Conceptual Understanding	Scientific Investigation	Practical Reasoning	Patterns of Change	Models	Systems	None	Yes	No

FIGURE 4-2 Sample item-objective congruence rating form.

Data Analysis

The item similarity ratings were analyzed using multidimensional scaling (MDS). The purpose of MDS is to portray the similarities among objects visually, as in a map (Schiffman et al., 1981). This visual portrayal is accomplished by scaling the items along as many continuous dimensions as are necessary to adequately represent the similarity ratings. Each stimulus dimension in an MDS solution corresponds to an attribute or characteristic of the objects being scaled. The purpose of this analysis was to determine whether dimensions, such as those specified in the NAEP frameworks, would be perceived by the SMEs and whether the items would be configured in the MDS space in a manner congruent with the test specifications.

The model used was an "individual differences" or weighted MDS model. Weighted models allow for the scaling of SMEs in the same MDS space in which the items are configured. Thus, by using a weighted MDS model, similarities and differences among the SMEs, as well as among the items, could be observed. The weighted MDS model used was the INDSCAL model (Carroli and Chang, 1970) implemented in the ALSCAL procedure in SPSS, version 7.5 (Young and Harris, 1993). The distances among items and the dimensional weights for the SMEs are computed using the weighted distance formula developed by Carroll and Chang (1970). In the INDSCAL model the similarity data for each subject are transformed to derive coordinates on dimensions that are used to scale the items in Euclidean space. The perceptual space for each subject is related to a common "group space" by weighting the dimensions of the group space separately for each subject. That is, each subject's coordinate matrix is multiplied by a vector of weights (**w**) consisting of elements w_{ka} that represent the relative emphasis subject k places on dimension a. The distances between stimuli are computed by incorporating this weighting factor into the Euclidean distance formula used by classical MDS. The INDSCAL model defines the distance between two objects i and j as:

$$d_{ijk} = \sqrt{\sum_{a=1}^{r} w_{ka} \left(x_{ia} - x_{ja} \right)^2}$$

where: d_{ijk} is the Euclidean distance between points i and j for subject k, x_{ia} is the coordinate of point i on dimension a, and r is the number of specified dimensions. The INDSCAL analysis provides a multidimensional configuration of the attributes rated (the stimulus, or item space) and a multidimensional configuration of the subjects (the group, or SME space).

To facilitate interpretation of the MDS solutions, external information on the items was analyzed together with the MDS item coordinates. These external data included item difficulties, the item-objective congruence ratings, and dichotomous "dummy variables" reflecting the item content specifications (i.e., field, ways, theme, and nature designations for each item). These data were correlated with the coordinates from the MDS solution to determine whether the dimensions were related to these item attributes.

RESULTS

Although the SMEs completed the item similarity ratings before they completed the item-objective congruence ratings, the results of the item objective congruence ratings are presented first. These results involve all 60 items used in this study and are helpful for subsequent interpretation of the MDS results.

Item-Objective Congruence Ratings

Tables 4-4 through 4-7 summarize the results of the item-objective congruence ratings. An item was considered to be "correctly" matched to its framework designation if at least 7 of the 10 SMEs placed it in the same category that was specified in the test blueprint. In addition to providing the percentages of items correctly classified by the SMEs, these tables present the number of "unanimous" matches (i.e., all 10 SMEs correctly classified the item) and stem-and-leaf plots of the SMEs' ratings.

Those ratings pertaining to the field of science dimension of the NAEP framework are presented in Table 4-4. More than half of the items (31, or 52 percent) were unanimously matched to their fields of science specified in the test blueprint. Only nine items failed to be correctly matched to their corresponding fields by at least seven SMEs, yielding an item-objective congruence index of 85 percent for the 60 items. Three of the "misclassified" items were earth science items that were classified as physical science by at least eight SMEs. Four other items were physical science items, three of which were predominantly rated as earth science and one as life science. The two remaining misclassified items were life science items, one of which nine SMEs classified as earth science; the other item was classified as life science; by only six SMEs. The percentages of correct classifications for the earth, life, and physical science fields were 86, 90, and 76 percent, respectively. These results indicate that in general the SMEs supported the field of science designations of the items. However, they did not "agree" with the operational content classifications for 15 percent of the 60 items. The results for the cognitive dimension (ways of knowing and doing science) are presented in Table 4-5. The correct classifications were relatively lower for this dimension than for the field of science dimension. Using the same "7 of 10" SME criterion, only 60 percent of the items were matched to their cognitive area specified in the test blueprint. Unanimous ratings were observed for only eight items, all of which were conceptual understanding items. The percentages of correct classifications for the conceptual understanding, practical reasoning, and

TABLE 4-4 Summary of Item-Objective Congruence Ratings: Field of Science

Stem-and-Leaf Plots of SMEs' Congruence Ratings

Earth (22 items)		Life (21 Items)		Physical (17 Items)	
0		0		0	
1	111	1	1	1	11
2		2		2	22
3		3		3	
4		4		4	
5		5		5	
6		6	6	6	
7	7	7	7	7	
8	888	8	8	8	8
9	99999	9	999	9	99999
10	0000000000	10	00000000000000	10	0000000

Summary of Content-Area Classifications

Field of Science	Number of Items	Items Classified Correctly by All SMEs (%)	Items Classified Correctly by at Least Seven SMEs (%)
Earth	22	45	86
Life	21	71	90
Physical	17	41	76
Average		53	85

Note: "Leaves" represent the number of SMEs correctly classifying each item, with 0 indicating all 10 SMEs correctly classified the item.

scientific investigation cognitive areas were 70, 53, and 50 percent, respectively. These results suggest that the cognitive classifications of these items are more equivocal than their content classifications.

The results for the themes of science dimension are summarized in Table 4-6. The test development committee designated only 28 of the 60 items as corresponding to one of the three themes of science areas. However, the SMEs considered most of these items to be measuring this dimension. At least three SMEs linked each of these nontheme items to a theme of science area. Thus, the most common misclassification "error" made by the SMEs was classifying an item as a theme item when in fact it was not. For those items designated as theme items in the test blueprint, only 50 percent were correctly classified. The "patterns of change" theme exhibited the highest correct classification rate (six of eight items were classified correctly). The models and systems theme areas exhibited correct classification percentages of 22 and 55 percent, respectively.

TABLE 4-5 Summary of Item-Objective Congruence Ratings: Ways of Knowing and Doing Science

Stem-and-Leaf Plot of SMEs' Congruence Ratings

Conceptual Understanding		Practical Reasoning		Scientific Investigation	
0	*	0		0	*
1	111	1		1	1
2	2	2	2	2	22
3		3	3	3	3
4	4	4	4	4	4
5	5	5	5	5	5
6	6	6	6666	6	6
7	777	7	777	7	7
8	888	8	8	8	88
9	99999	9	99999	9	99999
10	00000000	10		10	

Summary of Cognitive-Area Classifications

Ways of Knowing	Number of Items	Items Classified Correctly by All SMEs (%)	Items Classified Correctly by at Least Seven SMEs (%)
Conceptual understanding	27	30	70
Practical reasoning	17	0	53
Scientific investigation	16	0	50
Average		13	60

Notes: "Leaves" represent number of SMEs correctly classifying each item, with 0 indicating all 10 SMEs correctly classified the item.

Only two items were classified correctly by all 10 SMEs, both of which were "systems" items.

The item-objective congruence ratings for the nature of science dimension of the framework are summarized in Table 4-7. The SMEs were not asked to indicate whether the items were "nature of science" or "nature of technology" but rather only to indicate whether the item corresponded to the nature of science dimension. Only 10 of the 60 items were designated as corresponding to this dimension by the test development committee. Of these 10 items, 9 were correctly identified as nature of science items by at least eight SMEs; the other item was correctly classified by five of nine SMEs (one SME omitted the rating for this item). Although these results appear to support the nature of science classification, the SMEs tended to rate almost *all* of the items as corresponding to this

TABLE 4-6 Summary of Item-Objective Congruence Ratings: Themes of Science

Stem-and-Leaf Plot of SMEs' Congruence Ratings

Patterns of Change		Models		Systems	
0	**********	0	*******************	0	***
1	1111111	1	**11111111111111111111**	1	1111111111
2	22222222	2	**2222222**	2	**2222222222222222222**
3	33333333	3	**3333**	3	**3333333333**
4	44444	4		4	**44444**
5	5555	5	**55**	5	**55**
6	666666	6	**66**	6	**66**
7	**7777777**	7	**7**	7	**7**
8	**88**	8	**8**	8	**888**
9	**99**	9		9	
10		10	0	10	**00**

Summary of Theme of Science Classifications

Themes	Number of Items	Items Classified Correctly by All SMEs (%)	Items Classified Correctly by at Least Seven SMEs (%)
No theme	32	0	3
Patterns of change	8	0	75
Models	9	0	22
Systems	11	18	55
Average		3	25

Notes: All 60 items are represented in each theme area. Entries indicate number of SMEs classifying each item into the theme area, with 0 indicating all 10 SMEs and * indicating one SME. Correct classifications are indicated in **boldface**.

dimension. For the 50 items *not* listed as nature of science in the test blueprint, the mean number of SMEs linking them to the nature dimension was 7.3. In fact, 20 of these items (40 percent) were *unanimously* judged to correspond to this dimension. Only two items were linked to this dimension by three or fewer SMEs.

Analysis of the exit survey data revealed that the SMEs were fairly confident in the validity of their item-objective congruence ratings. When asked how confident they were regarding how well their ratings reflected the way the items "should truly be classified," the median confidence rating on an eight-point scale (where 8 = very confident) was 7. The confidence ratings ranged from 5 to 8.

TABLE 4-7 Summary of Item-Objective Congruence Ratings: Nature of Science

Stem-and-Leaf Plot of SMEs' Congruence Ratings

Nature of Science

```
 0 |
 1 |
 2 | 2
 3 | 333
 4 | 444444
 5 | 555
 6 | 666666
 7 | 777
 8 | 8888888
 9 | 99999999999999999999999
10 | 0000000000
```

Summary of Nature of Science Classifications

Themes	Number of Items	Items Classified Correctly by All SMEs (%)	Items Classified Correctly by at Least Seven SMEs (%)
No theme	50	0	4
Nature Science	8	75	88
Nature of technology	2	50	100
Average		12	18

Notes: All 60 items are represented in each theme area. Entries indicate number of SMEs classifying each item into the theme area, with 0 indicating 10 SMEs. Correct classifications are indicated in **boldface**.

MDS Results

All SMEs completed the item similarity ratings within six hours. The shortest completion time was three hours, and the median completion time was 5.25 hours. Analysis of the follow-up surveys indicated that all 10 SMEs used the science discipline, cognitive level, and item format characteristics of the items in making their similarity judgments. Nine of the SMEs also reported using the difficulty level of the item, six SMEs reported using item themes, and four reported using the length of the item in making their judgments. Other similarity rating criteria reportedly used by one or more SMEs included consideration of the "learning styles of students," the number of steps required to complete a problem, item vocabulary considerations, perceived grade level of the items, and visual or reading cues. All SMEs seemed to stress particular attention paid to cognitive attributes of the items in responding to the open-ended question regarding criteria used to make their item similarity ratings. When asked how confident they were that their item similarity ratings accurately reflected the "content and cognitive similarities among the item pairs," the median confidence rating obtained (on the same eight-point scale, where 8 = very confident) was 6.5. The confidence ratings ranged from 4 (SME #10) to 8.

For each SME the six item pairings repeated in each booklet were evaluated to provide an index of the reliability of their ratings. Across these 60 ratings (10 SMEs × 6 item pairs) only one differed by as much as four points on the eight-point scale (a pair originally rated by SME #4 as 8 was later rated as 4), and two other pairs differed by three points (original ratings of 6 were later rated as 3 by SMEs #2 and #3). The vast majority of the replicated ratings (80 percent) were within one point of one another, and 38 percent were identical. In looking at the average discrepancy of ratings for each SME, 7 of the 10 SMEs had average discrepancies less than one point across the replicated pairs. The largest discrepancy was 1.5 points, for the SME who had the four-point discrepancy noted above. The median discrepancy across the 10 SMEs was 0.73. These results suggest that in general the similarity ratings can be considered reliable; however, it is likely that some specific item pairings for some SMEs are probably unreliable, which is not surprising given the large number of ratings completed. However, given that the replicated ratings were made toward the end of the rating task and that the average discrepancies for these pairs were small, it does not appear that the SMEs' similarity ratings are undermined by low reliability.

INDSCAL Model Fit to the Data

Two- through six-dimensional MDS solutions were applied to the data. Model-data fit and interpretability of the solution were used to select the appropriate dimensionality of the data. The fit values of STRESS (departure of data from the model) and R^2 (proportion of variance in the SMEs' similarity data accounted for by the model) are reported in Table 4-8. Using the rules of thumb and heuristics suggested by Kruskal and Wish (1978), MacCallum (1981), and Dong (1985), at least four dimensions appear to be required to adequately fit the data. Very little improvement in fit occurs in adding a sixth dimension. Further-

TABLE 4-8 Summary of Fit Indexes from MDS (INDSCAL) Solution

Number of Dimensions in Solution	STRESS	R^2
6	.12	.75
5	.14	.75
4	.16	.71
3	.20	.70
2	.25	.67

TABLE 4-9 Summary of SME Fit Statistics and Dimension Weights

SME	Stress	R^2	Subject Weights Dimension					Weirdness
			1	2	3	4	5	
1	.153	.655	.48	.28	.33	.33	.36	.15
2	.125	.803	.39	.39	.60	.28	.26	.31
3	.137	.749	.54	.54	.16	.29	.24	.28
4	.140	.717	.45	.53	.27	.29	.28	.14
5	.123	.797	.63	.46	.25	.27	.25	.21
6	.121	.812	.70	.34	.28	.22	.29	.27
7	.153	.658	.32	.53	.31	.30	.30	.17
8	.129	.818	.27	.29	.73	.26	.28	.47
9	.163	.615	.27	.31	.13	.49	.43	.40
10	.098	.853	.47	.48	.21	.47	.37	.22

more all dimensions from the five-dimensional solution were interpretable (see below), but the sixth dimension in the six-dimensional solution was not readily interpretable. Thus, the five-dimensional solution was selected as the appropriate model for these data. As indicated in Table 4-8, the five-dimensional solution accounted for 75 percent of the variance in the SMEs' (transformed) similarity rating data. The total variance in these data accounted for by each dimension was 22, 18, 14, 11, and 10 percent, respectively, for dimensions one through five.

SME Congruence

The model-data fit values for each SME are presented in Table 4-9. The model fit the data for SMEs 1, 7, and 9 least well (R^2 less than .7 and STRESS greater than .15); however, these levels of fit are on par with those found in previous research (e.g., Deville, 1996; Sireci and Geisinger, 1992, 1995). The congruence among the SMEs was evaluated by inspecting the individual subject weights and the subject weirdness indexes.[3] Although differences were observed in the weighting of the dimensions across SMEs, all SMEs appeared to be using all five dimensions in making their similarity ratings. Figure 4-3 presents separate two-dimensional subspaces from the five-dimensional SME weight space. These two subspaces highlight the differences among the SMEs. SME #8 exhibited the

---

[3]The weirdness index describes the relative weightings of the dimensions for each subject in proportion to the average dimension weights across all subjects. A subject with a large weight on one dimension and small weights on the other dimensions would have a weirdness index near one, which is the maximum value. Subjects with dimension weights proportional to the average weights have weirdness indexes near zero, which is the minimum value (see Young and Harris, 1993, for the full details).

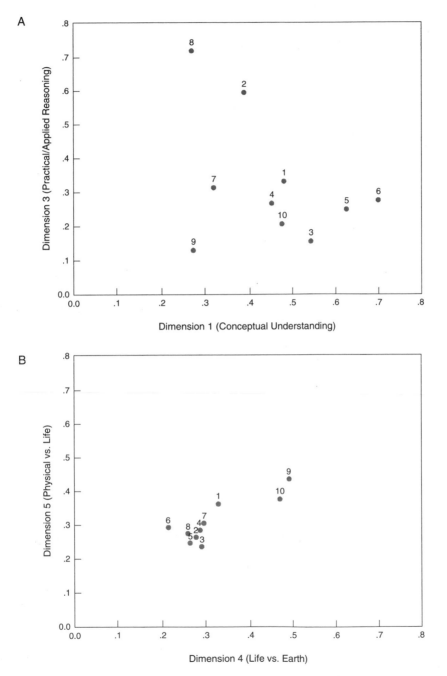

FIGURE 4-3 Two-dimensional subject weight subspaces. (a) dimensions 1 and 3; (b) dimensions 4 and 5.

largest weirdness index, due to his relatively large emphasis on dimension 3 (see Figure 4-3a). SME #9 and #10 had relatively larger weights on dimensions four and five (see Figure 4-3b). As described below, these two dimensions corresponded to the field of science characteristics of the items. Thus, these two SMEs emphasized content characteristics in their similarity ratings, whereas the other SMEs tended to emphasize cognitive characteristics of the items. Although these differences are interesting, the subject weights indicate that all five dimensions were used by all SMEs in making their ratings. Thus, we turn now to interpretation of these five dimensions.

Interpreting the Dimensions

The dimensions were interpreted visually and with the assistance of statistical analyses comparing known item characteristics with the item coordinates from the MDS solution. Visual interpretations were made separately by the first author and by a science content expert from the National Academy of Sciences. The statistical analyses involved computing correlations among the MDS item coordinates and content, cognitive, and format item attributes.

Because of the overlap of item characteristics (e.g., more of the practical reasoning items were also extended constructed-response items and most of the nature of science items were scientific investigation items), the visual interpretations were able to clarify some of the multiple interpretations that could be attributed to the dimensions using only the statistical results. Based on the (subjective) visual and (objective) statistical information, the following interpretations were given to the dimensions: dimension 1 is a "conceptual understanding" cognitive dimension that separates the "lower-order" cognitive skill items (e.g., factual recognition items) from those items requiring higher-order skills (e.g., design an experiment, interpret results); dimension 2 is an item format dimension that separates the multiple-choice items from the constructed-response items; dimension 3 is "practical/applied reasoning" cognitive dimension that separates the practical reasoning items from the scientific investigation items; dimension 4 is a content dimension that separates the life science items from the earth science items; and dimension 5 is a content dimension that separates the physical science items from the life science items. Thus, the first three dimensions are related to cognitive item attributes, and the fourth and fifth dimensions are related to content item attributes.

Figure 4-4 presents the two-dimensional item subspace for dimensions 1 and 2. A conspicuous "chasm" can be seen above the origin of dimension 1 (horizontal). This chasm roughly separates the lower cognitive level "conceptual understanding" (C) items (positive coordinates, or right side of the figure) from the higher-level "scientific investigation" (S) items (negative coordinates). Three conceptual understanding items have negative coordinates on this dimension; however, these same three items were rated as measuring higher-level cognitive

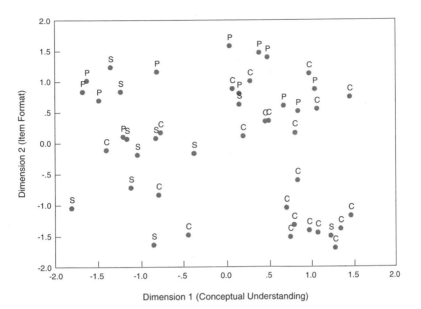

FIGURE 4-4 Two-dimensional MDS stimulus subspace: items plotted along dimensions 1 and 2 using cognitive classification symbols. C, conceptual understanding; P, practical understanding; S, scientific investigation.

areas by the SMEs in the item-objective ratings, as described earlier. Similarly, the two scientific investigation items with positive coordinates on this dimension tended to be "misclassified" with respect to cognitive area by the SMEs. Dimension 2 (vertical) separates the practical reasoning items from the others; however, all of the practical reasoning items, except one, were also constructed-response items. Figure 4-5 presents the same configuration but labels the items according to item format. As can be seen from this figure, all of the multiple-choice items have negative coordinates on dimension 2.

Figure 4-6 presents the item configuration for the two-dimensional subspace formed by dimensions 1 and 3. All but two of the scientific investigation items have negative or near-zero coordinates on dimension 3. Both of these items exhibited low item-objective congruence for scientific investigation. Similarly, all but two of the practical reasoning items had positive coordinates on dimension 3, both of which also had low item-objective congruence ratings for the practical reasoning cognitive area.

Figure 4-7 presents a three-dimensional subspace comprising the first three dimensions, which were related to cognitive area. Although some cognitive area

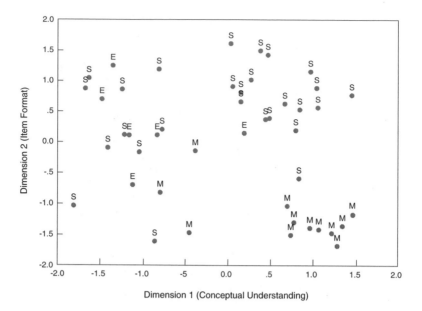

FIGURE 4-5 Two-dimensional MDS stimulus subspace: items plotted along dimensions 1 and 2 using item format symbols. E, extended constructed-response; M, multiple-choice; S, short constructed-response.

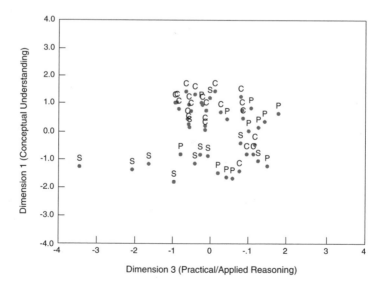

FIGURE 4-6 Two-dimensional MDS stimulus subspace: items plotted along dimensions 1 and 3 using cognitive classification symbols. C, conceptual understanding; P, practical reasoning; S, scientific investigation.

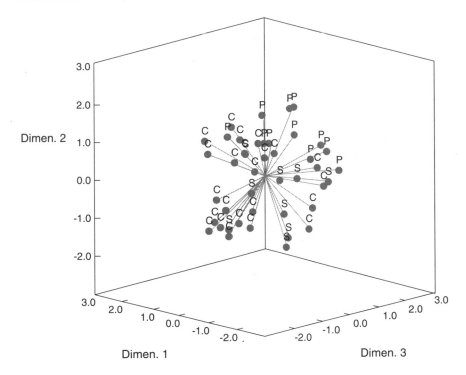

FIGURE 4-7 Two-dimensional MDS stimulus space illustrating cognitive groupings among grade 8 NAEP science items. C, conceptual understanding; P, practical reasoning; S, scientific investigation.

overlap is evident, clusters of items from the same content area occupy segregated regions of the subspace. In particular, the conceptual understanding items are primarily arranged in the left side of the figure (a tight cluster of these items appears in the lower left), and the practical reasoning items are configured near the top of the space.

Figure 4-8 illustrates the two-dimensional "content" subspace formed by dimensions 4 and 5. Dimension 4 (horizontal) tended to segregate the earth science (E) items (positive coordinates) and life science (L) items (negative coordinates). All but one of the life science items had negative coordinates on dimension 4. This item was classified as a life science item by seven of the 10 SMEs. Dimension 5 (vertical) appears to account for the degree to which the items measured physical science. Most physical science items had relatively large negative coordinates on this dimension; only one physical science item had a large positive coordinate. This item was classified as an earth science item by 8 of the 10 SMEs. Although some overlap among content areas is evident, in

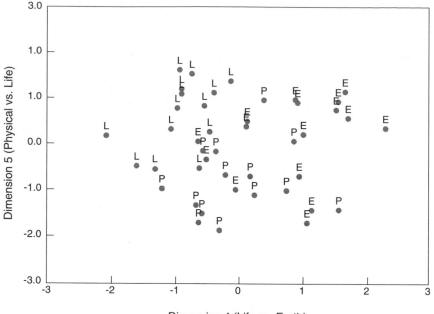

FIGURE 4-8 Two-dimensional MDS stimulus subspace: items plotted along dimensions 4 and 5 using content classification symbols. E, earth science; L, life science; P, physical science.

general the items comprising the three different fields of science tend to be segregated in the subspace. In particular, most of the life science items are configured more closely to one another than they are to items from other content areas.

To assist in verifying the visual interpretations given to the dimensions, correlations were computed between the MDS coordinates and external data on the items. These external data included the item-objective congruence ratings; item format information; and the content, cognitive, nature, and theme designations of the items. The content, cognitive, nature, and theme designations were "dummy" coded for this analysis. For example, an earth science dummy variable was created by coding all earth science items "1" and all other items "0." The cognitive, theme, and nature areas were also dummy coded, as well as an item format variable (multiple-choice/constructed-response). Two separate correlational analyses were conducted. The first analysis correlated the item-objective congruence ratings with the item coordinates. To conduct this analysis, the number of SMEs categorizing an item in each content, cognitive, nature, or theme area was calculated. These sums were then correlated with the MDS coordinates. The second analysis correlated the dummy variables with the item coordinates.

The results of the correlation analyses are presented in Table 4-10 (item-objective congruence correlations) and Table 4-11 (dummy variable correlations). Both sets of correlations lead to similar conclusions regarding the item characteristics defining each dimension. However, the correlations based on the item objective congruence data tended to be larger. The largest correlations for the coordinates on the first dimension were with the conceptual understanding and scientific investigation cognitive areas. The largest correlation for the second dimension was for the item format variable. For the third dimension, large correlations with the practical reasoning and scientific investigation cognitive areas were observed. The nature of the science dummy variable also exhibited a large correlation with this dimension, but the nature of science item-objective congruence ratings did not. This finding probably stems from the fact that 5 of the 10 nature of science items were also scientific investigation items. The coordinates from the fourth and fifth dimensions exhibited large correlations with the variables associated with the field of science designations of the items. Thus, in general, the correlation analyses supported the visual interpretations given

TABLE 4-10 Correlations Among MDS Item Coordinates and Item Objective Congruence Ratings

Item	Dimension				
Variable	1	2	3	4	5
Fields					
Earth science	−.04	−.15	−.01	.61*	.21
Life science	.06	.22	−.04	−.65*	.48*
Physical science	−.02	−.09	.07	−.07	−.75*
Ways of Knowing and Doing					
Conceptual understanding	.80*	−.51*	−.17	.01	.18
Practical reasoning	−.27	.56*	−.43*	−.12	.16
Scientific understanding	−.71*	.05	.66*	.11	−.38
Themes					
Models	.07	−.03	−.08	.68*	.20
Patterns	−.57*	.10	.10	−.14	−.02
Systems	.43*	−.02	−.08	−.49*	.22
Nature					
Yes	−.72*	.55*	.27	.14	−.11
No	.71*	−.52*	−.13	−.13	.17

*$P < .01$.

TABLE 4-11 Correlations Among INDSCAL Item Coordinates and Item Dummy Variables

Item	Dimension				
Variable	1	2	3	4	5
Fields					
Earth science	.02	−.04	.03	.61*	.02
Life science	−.02	.14	−.14	−.58*	.52*
Physical science	.00	−.10	.11	−.02	−.57*
Ways of Knowing and Doing					
Conceptual understanding	.57*	−.43*	−.03	.05	.08
Practical reasoning	−.16	.57*	.40*	−.18	.17
Scientific investigation	−.49*	−.12	−.40*	.14	−.28
Themes					
Models	−.11	.06	−.11	.61*	.17
Patterns	−.36	.02	.02	−.10	.40*
Systems	.28	.09	−.14	−.23	.25
Nature					
Science	−.44*	.29	−.46*	.08	−.04
Technology	.08	.24	.29	−.08	.01
Multiple Choice					
(Yes/No)	.40*	−.76*	.06	.12	.14
Difficulty	.09	−.52*	.28	.01	.02

$*P < .01.$

earlier. The first three dimensions correspond to cognitive and item format attributes, and the fourth and fifth dimensions correspond to fields of science attributes.

In summary, analysis of the item similarities data using MDS uncovered cognitive- and content-related dimensions that were congruent with those dimensions specified in the National Assessment Governing Board frameworks. Items that did not tend to group together with other items in their content or cognitive area tended to be the same items that were identified as problem items from analysis of the item-objective congruence ratings.

DISCUSSION

A fundamental requirement in educational assessment is operationally defining the construct(s) measured. Content validation involves determining whether a test actually represents the intended construct. Thus, it is an important step in evaluating the validity of inferences derived from test scores. As Sireci (1998b:106) has stated, "if the sample of tasks comprising a test is not representative of the content domain tested, the test scores and item response data used in studies of construct validity are meaningless."

Tests used in NAEP are operationally defined using test frameworks. This study sought to evaluate the content validity of a particular test in the NAEP battery—the 1996 grade 8 science assessment. An independent panel of science educators was convened, and these experts provided judgments of the content characteristics of items from this test over a two-day period. Two distinct methods for evaluating content validity were used, and both methods provided similar conclusions regarding how well a carefully selected subset of items represented the framework dimensions.

Does the grade 8 1996 NAEP science assessment measure what it purports to measure? The results from this study suggest that, in general, the two major dimensions composing the framework were supported by the SMEs' judgments. The majority of the items studied (85 percent) were judged to be measuring the content areas they were designed to measure. Although less congruence was observed for the cognitive classifications of the items, it was clear the SMEs thought that both higher- and lower-order thinking skills were measured across all three fields of science. These two major dimensions ("fields of science" and "ways of knowing and doing science") were also uncovered from the SMEs' item similarity ratings taken *before* the SMEs were aware of these dimensions. Sireci (1998a, 1998b) argues that this type of rating task provides a more rigorous appraisal of content validity. Thus, the results of the item-objective congruence and MDS analyses provide strong evidence that the content and cognitive dimensions of the framework were represented well by the actual items composing the assessment. However, given the fact that 15 percent of the studied items were classified differently by the SMEs with respect to field of science, a concern remains regarding which items to include in which field of science scale when the data are scored, calibrated, and reported. It is also interesting that the SMEs saw cognitive distinctions among the items first and foremost, before distinguishing among the items in terms of the fields of science content areas.

The item-objective congruence ratings, and the dimensions observed in the SME-derived MDS solution, did not strongly support the themes of science or nature of science dimensions of the framework. However, like the ways of knowing and doing science dimension, separate scores are not reported for these dimensions, and including them in the frameworks probably enhanced item development and contributed to the overall quality of the item pool. The lack of congruence between the SMEs and test developers regarding these two dimensions may be due to problems in the item classifications or to a lack of clarity regarding the descriptions of these dimensions. Thus, the utility of these two dimensions deserves further study.

Although the results of this study are encouraging, they are limited only to the 1996 grade 8 science assessment. Similar studies are recommended for other tests in the NAEP battery.

ACKNOWLEDGMENTS

The authors thank Karen Mitchell, Lee Jones, and Holly Wells for their invaluable assistance with this research and an anonymous reviewer for helpful comments on draft of this paper.

REFERENCES

Carroll, J.D., and J.J. Chang
  1970   An analysis of individual differences in multidimensional scaling via an *n*-way generalization of "Eckart-Young" decomposition. *Psychometrika* 35:238-319.
Deville, C.W.
  1996   An empirical link of content and construct validity evidence. *Applied Psychological Measurement* 20:127-139.
Dong, H.
  1985   Chance baselines for INDSCAL's goodness of fit index. *Applied Psychological Measurement* 9:27-30.
Ebel, R.L.
  1977   Comments on some problems of employment testing. *Personnel Psychology* 30:55-63.
Kruskal, J.B., and M. Wish
  1978   *Multidimensional Scaling.* Newbury Park, Calif.: Sage.
MacCallum, R.
  1981   Evaluating goodness of fit in nonmetric multidimensional scaling by ALSCAL. *Applied Psychological Measurement* 5:377-382.
Messick, S.
  1989   Validity. Pp. 13-103 in *Educational Measurement*, 3rd ed., R. Linn, ed. Washington, D.C.: American Council on Education.
National Assessment Governing Board (NAGB)
  1996   *Science Framework for the 1996 National Assessment of Educational Progress.* Washington, D.C.: NAGB.
Schiffman, S.S., M.L. Reynolds, and F.W. Young
  1981   *Introduction to Multidimensional Scaling.* New York: Academic Press.
Sireci, S.G.
  1998a   Gathering and analyzing content validity data. *Educational Assessment* 5:299-321.
  1998b   The construct of content validity. *Social Indicators Research* 45:83-117.
Sireci, S.G., and K.F. Geisinger
  1992   Analyzing test content using cluster analysis and multidimensional scaling. *Applied Psychological Measurement* 16:17-31.
  1995   Using subject matter experts to assess content representation: A MDS analysis. *Applied Psychological Measurement* 19:241-255.
Young, F.W., and D.F. Harris
  1993   Multidimensional scaling. Pp. 155-222 in *SPSS for Windows: Professional Statistics*, computer manual, version 6.0, M.J. Noursis, ed. Chicago: SPSS.

5

Appraising the Dimensionality of the 1996 Grade 8 NAEP Science Assessment Data

Stephen G. Sireci, H. Jane Rogers,
Hariharan Swaminathan, Kevin Meara, and
Frédéric Robin

The science assessment of the 1996 National Assessment of Educational Progress (NAEP) represents significant advances in large-scale assessment. In particular, this assessment featured carefully constructed "hands-on" performance tasks considered to better measure real-world science knowledge and skills. Furthermore, like the other subject tests in the NAEP battery, these assessments used comprehensive and innovative sampling, scoring, and scaling procedures. To document the science knowledge and skills of our nation's students, great care was taken in operationally defining the science domains to be measured on the assessment. For the 1996 grade 8 science assessment, which is the focus of this paper, three separate score scales were derived for three separate fields of science—earth science, life science, and physical science.

The purposes of the research presented here were to evaluate the structure of the item response data gathered in the 1996 NAEP science assessment and compare this structure to the one specified in the framework that governed the test development process. The dimensions composing this framework are described in detail by the National Assessment Governing Board (1996) as well as by Sireci et al. (Chapter 4, this volume). In brief, the framework specified four dimensions: "fields of science" (a content dimension), "ways of knowing and doing science" (a cognitive skill dimension), "themes of science," and "nature of science." The first dimension is particularly important for evaluating the structure of the assessment data because each item in the assessment was linked to one of the three fields of science, and separate score scales were derived for each field. Thus, this first dimension was influential in determining how the test booklets were constructed, how the booklets were spiraled during test administration, and how the scores were derived to report the results.

The word *dimension* as used in the NAEP frameworks refers to theoretical components that provide a structure for describing what NAEP tests and items measure. However, *dimension* has several different meanings in the psychometric literature (Brennan, 1998). For example, a dimension could be defined statistically as a latent variable that best accounts for covariation among test items. Sireci (1997) points out that these two different conceptualizations of test dimensionality should be related to one another. In summarizing dimensionality issues related to NAEP, he concludes that "there is an absence of research relating the theoretical dimensions specified in the content frameworks to the empirical dimensions arising from analysis of item response data" (p. i).

The present study represents an assessment of the dimensionality of the 1996 grade 8 NAEP science assessment data. The purposes motivating this research are straightforward and specific. In scaling the data for this assessment, the contractor (Educational Testing Service, ETS) used unidimensional item response theory (IRT) models fit separately to each of the three fields of science. Thus, the intended structure of this assessment comprised three unidimensional scales, one each for the earth, life, and physical sciences. The analyses carried out were aimed at evaluating whether the observed item responses conformed to this intended structure. A further purpose of the analyses was to determine if systematic sources of multidimensionality (that would threaten the validity of the IRT scaling procedure) were present in these data. These analyses were aimed at gathering critical evidence for evaluating the validity of inferences derived from the NAEP scores.

METHOD

Data

A comprehensive set of analyses was performed on the data obtained from the 1996 grade 8 NAEP science assessment. Item response data (test data) were available for 11,273 students. The item pool comprised 189 items partitioned into 15 blocks. Each student responded to three blocks of test items, one of which comprised items associated with one of the four hands-on tasks. These data were provided by the ETS and were the same data used for scoring, scaling, and reporting the results. A description of these blocks in terms of the item types, item content and cognitive specifications, and sample sizes is presented in Table 5-1.

The results for the 1996 grade 8 NAEP science assessment were reported on a composite score scale, which was a weighted composite of the three fields of science scales. Thus, there are four score scales of interest in evaluating the assessment: the composite score scale and the earth, physical, and life sciences scales.

TABLE 5-1   Composition of Item Blocks on Grade 8 NAEP Science Assessment

	Number of Items Categorized as									
	Field of Science			Ways of Knowing			Item Format			
Block	Earth	Life	Physical	CU	PR	SI	MC	CR	Hands on?	N
S3			6	1		5		6	Yes	2,961
S4	5	1	3	3	1	5	3	6	Yes	2,739
S5	7				4	3		7	Yes	2,711
S6		2	4	4		2		6	Yes	2,861
S7	12			7	2	3	2	10	No	2,401
S8		10		9	1		5	5	No	2,424
S9		13		10	3		3	10	No	2,401
S10	6	6	4	10	3	3	8	8	No	1,784
S11	7	2	7	8	6	2	8	8	No	1,797
S12	3	7	6	11	2	3	8	8	No	1,806
S13	6	4	5	7	4	4	8	7	No	1,947
S14	3	5	8	13	3		7	9	No	2,412
S15	4	5	6	8	3	4	6	9	No	1,836
S20	6	4	6	8	7	1	8	8	No	1,939
S21	3	6	7	10	5	1	7	9	No	1,797
Total:	62	65	62	108	43	36	73	116		

Correlational Analyses

Raw Score Correlations

For each test booklet, correlations were computed among the raw scores for the field of science content areas. These raw scores were computed by summing the item scores for those items in a booklet that corresponded to the same content area. These correlations based on the raw score metric are not representative of the scaled scores for each field of science derived using IRT. However, the correlations do provide a preliminary and straightforward indication of the similarities among the three fields of science. High correlations among these subscores (e.g., .9 or higher) would provide evidence that the same proficiencies are being measured by the respective fields of science. On the other hand, moderate correlations would suggest that more unique proficiencies were being measured. Both raw correlations and correlations corrected for unreliability were examined. To obtain disattenuated correlations among the subscores, coefficient alpha reliabilities were used.

IRT-Derived Theta Correlations

While correlations among the raw subscores present useful information regarding the structure of the data, correlations among the IRT-derived ability, or theta, scores may be more appropriate for examining the dimensionality of the scaled scores since NAEP analyses are based on these derived scores. To determine these ability scores, the items comprising each block were calibrated separately using IRT (see description below). Subsequently, these item parameters were used to compute a "block proficiency estimate" (block theta estimate) for each student. Because each student responded to three item blocks, three separate theta estimates were computed. The correlations among these theta estimates were compared with the content composition of each block. The logic motivating this analysis was that if high (disattenuated) correlations were observed among blocks that measured more than one field of science, evidence was obtained that the three fields were measuring one general dimension of science proficiency. On the other hand, if the correlations based on blocks measuring different fields of science were substantially lower than those measuring the same field of science, evidence of relatively unique dimensions measured by each field would be obtained. Thus, we were interested in both the magnitude and the pattern of these correlations. The theta correlations were disattenuated (corrected for unreliability) using the marginal reliabilities estimated in the calibration in each block. As described below, the sample sizes per block were sufficient for estimating individual student thetas. However, our block-level scaling treated each block as if it measured a single latent trait, thus ignoring the explicit scaling structure used in the operational NAEP scaling. Another potential limitation of this analysis is that there may be too few items per field within a block to provide unique variance associated with that field. Nevertheless, inspecting these correlations with the expectations described above provided a different lens through which to view the idea of composite and separate science proficiency scales.

Principal Components Analysis

As a preliminary check on dimensionality, data from four test booklets were analyzed using principal components analysis (PCA). PCA could not be used to simultaneously evaluate the dimensionality of the whole set of 189 items because of the balanced incomplete block (BIB) spiral design. The four booklets chosen (numbers 209, 210, 231, and 232) involved 12 of the 15 blocks (152 of the 189 items) and included all four hands-on tasks. Separate PCAs were conducted on each booklet. The eigenvalues associated with the extracted components and the percentages of variance in the item data accounted for by these components were used to evaluate the dimensionality of each booklet.

IRT Residual Analyses

The fit of IRT models to the data was evaluated directly by calibrating each block using a unidimensional IRT model. The decision to calibrate each block separately was motivated by sample size considerations (i.e., the booklet-level sample sizes were too small for IRT scaling) and the presence of large blocks of incomplete data in the student-by-item matrix (11,273 students by 189 items). Because each student responded to only about 36 items on average, the entire pool could not be calibrated concurrently due to the inability to properly estimate the interitem covariance matrix. In the operational scaling of NAEP, this problem is overcome by using the plausible values methodology (i.e., by conditioning calibration on a comprehensive vector of covariates derived from student background variables; see Mislevy et al., 1992, for more complete details of the NAEP scaling methodology). This conditioning was not possible given the time and software limitations of this study. Thus, these block-specific calibrations evaluated model-data fit in a manner independent of the plausible values methodology. If the data comprising a block are essentially unidimensional, these IRT calibrations should exhibit good fit to the data. As can be seen from Table 5-1, the sample sizes were appropriate for calibrating each block using an IRT model. The smallest sample size was 1,784, and the largest number of parameters estimated in any of the calibrations was 49.

All IRT calibrations were conducted using the computer program MULTILOG, version 6.1 (Thissen, 1991). The multiple-choice items were calibrated using a three-parameter IRT model (3P),[1] and short constructed-response items that were scored dichotomously were calibrated using a two-parameter IRT model (2P). These models were identical to those used by the ETS in calibrating these same items. For the constructed-response items that were scored polytomously (i.e., a student could earn a score greater than one), Samejima's (1969) graded response (GR) model was used. The GR model is similar but not equivalent to the Generalized Partial Credit (GPC) model (Muraki, 1992) used by ETS to calibrate these items. In both the GPC and the GR models, a common slope (discrimination) parameter is assumed for the response functions of each item score category while separate threshold (location) parameters are assumed for each score category. However, because of the dependency that exists among the threshold parameters (i.e., the choice of the first $k-1$ categories determines whether an examinee chooses the last category), the number of location parameters for an item is one less than the number of response categories. For example, a constructed-response item scored from zero to three (i.e., four response catego-

---

[1] For the 3P models, priors were used on the c parameters, where the prior was equivalent to the reciprocal of the number of response options for each item. The effect of these priors was evaluated by also calibrating the items without the priors. The results were very similar, which was not surprising given the relatively large sample sizes.

ries) is modeled using four parameters: one common slope parameter for each score category and three location parameters.

Although calibrating the polytomously scored items with the GR model using MULTILOG differs from the GPC model fitted using PARSCALE (which was used by ETS), the effects of this difference are considered to be minimal given the purpose of the analyses (i.e., to determine departure of the response data from unidimensionality). MULTILOG was used in this study because the modified version of PARSCALE used by ETS to calibrate the NAEP items was not publicly available.

To evaluate IRT model-data fit, a residual analysis was performed using the program POLYFIT (Rogers, 1996). The POLYFIT program uses the item and person parameter estimates obtained from MULTILOG to compute the expected score for examinees at a given proficiency (theta) level. These expected scores are compared with the corresponding average observed scores and residuals are computed. Specifically, the group of examinees is divided into 12 equal theta intervals constructed in the range (mean theta ± 3 standard deviations), with interval width equal to .5 standard deviations. The midpoint of each interval is used to calculate the expected score in that interval, where k is the category score and $P(k)$ is the probability that an individual with given theta will score in category k. The difference between the average observed score and the expected score in each interval is computed. This residual is then standardized by dividing by the standard error, which is obtained from the standard deviation of the discrete random variable

$$\sum_k k^2 P(k) - \left(\sum_k kP(k)\right)^2,$$

where k and $P(k)$ are defined above. The standardized residuals computed at the score level are analogous to those routinely computed for dichotomous IRT models by comparing observed and expected proportions correct. Standardized residuals are reported only for cells with a frequency of 10 or more. The standardized residuals may be examined for each item to assess the fit of individual items. In addition, a frequency distribution of the standardized residuals over items is provided as a summary of the overall fit of the model.

When the model fits the data, the distribution of standardized residuals should be symmetric with a mean close to zero. While there is no theory to show that the residuals are normally distributed when the model fits the data, it is reasonable to expect a roughly normal distribution, with few standardized residuals with an absolute value greater than three.

A chi-square statistic is also calculated using observed and expected frequencies of examinees in each score category. Expected frequencies are obtained by calculating the probability that an examinee at the midpoint of each theta interval would score in each response category. Results of the chi-square analysis should be interpreted with caution. The chi-square statistic is at best only approximately distributed as a chi-square; it has the usual failings of IRT chi-square fit statistics in that it is sensitive to sample size, the arbitrary nature of the theta intervals, and heterogeneity in the theta levels of examinees grouped in the same interval. Hence, it should be used only descriptively and the significance level ignored.

It was *not* hypothesized that all of the 15 blocks could be fit adequately using a single unidimensional scale. In fact, such a hypothesis is contrary to the scaling models used to score the assessment. As seen in Table 5-1, all blocks do *not* comprise items from a single field of science. Those blocks that *do* comprise items from a single field of science (blocks 3, 5, 7, 8, and 9) should conform to a unidimensional scale (i.e., exhibit relatively small, normally distributed standardized residuals). Conversely, those blocks containing items from more than one field may, unsurprisingly, depart from unidimensionality (i.e., exhibit relatively larger, nonnormally distributed standardized residuals). Thus, the hypotheses motivating our block calibration/residual analysis evaluations involved comparing the results of the residual analyses with the a priori expectations of dimensionality given the content-area designations of the items composing a given block. More specifically, if blocks containing items from only one field of science exhibited small residuals and the blocks containing items from two or three fields exhibited larger residuals, evidence of three separate scales corresponding to the three fields of science specified in the framework would be obtained.

Factor Analyses

Factor analyses (FAs) were also conducted to evaluate the dimensionality of each block. Evaluation of the dimensionality of each block using FA provides an independent assessment of dimensionality from that obtained by assessing the fit of an unidimensional IRT model to the data. It should be pointed out that FA is appropriate only when the relationship between item responses and the underlying trait is linear. When the relationships between the item responses and the underlying traits are nonlinear, procedures based on nonlinear factor models are necessary. Item response theory is an example of a nonlinear factor analysis procedure and is the procedure of choice for evaluating the dimensionality of nonlinear data. The problem is that currently only unidimensional IRT models (for dichotomous and polytomous responses) have been developed with commercially available software. Multidimensional IRT models have been proposed, but these do not have the necessary software for data analysis. One exception is the nonlinear factor analysis procedure developed by McDonald (1967) in which nonlinear trace lines are approximated by polynomials. The computer program NOHARM implements this procedure; however, the program is not designed to handle polytomous data. Given these considerations, the linear factor model was used as an approximation to nonlinear models to evaluate the dimensionality of the data especially when the hypothesis that several dimensions underlie the responses is examined.

A one-factor model was fit to the data for each block of items. If the blocks contained items from two fields, a two-factor model was fit to the data with items from each field constrained to load on two separate factors. If the blocks contained items from all three fields, a constrained three-factor model was fitted to the data. Because of constraints, the two- and three-factor models are analyzed using the confirmatory, rather than exploratory, factor analysis procedure; there is no distinction between confirmatory and exploratory procedures with the one-factor model.

The analyses were carried out using the LISREL 8 computer program (Jöreskog and Sörbom, 1993). The correlation matrix analyzed was based on product moment as well as tetrachoric and polyserial correlations. When the correlation matrix was based on the tetrachoric or the polyserial correlations, the generalized least squares procedure rather than the maximum likelihood procedure was used when the correlation matrix was not positive definite.

The fit of the model was evaluated by examining the goodness of fit index (GFI), adjusted goodness of fit index (AGFI), and residuals rather than the likelihood ratio statistic. When the data are nonlinear, particularly when they are nonnormal, and when tetrachoric/polyserial correlations are used, the likelihood ratio statistic is unreliable. The GFI and the AGFI provide adequate assessments of dimensionality (Tanaka and Huba, 1985). For this study, values of GFI and AGFI greater than .90 were taken as indications of adequate fit of the model.

Multidimensional Scaling Analyses

Multidimensional scaling (MDS) was used to evaluate the dimensionality of all the dichotomously scored items. These analyses followed the unidimensionality testing procedure developed by Chen and Davison (1996). This procedure involves computing pseudo-paired comparison (PC) statistics that represent the similarity between two dichotomously scored items, as determined from examinees' performance on the items. Given this restriction, the MDS analyses were conducted using only the multiple-choice items and those short constructed-response items that were also scored dichotomously. Chen and Davison recommend fitting one- and two-dimensional MDS models to the matrix of item PC statistics and comparing the results. If the one-dimensional model fits the data well, the coordinates correlate highly with the item difficulties (p values), and an n-shape or u-shape pattern is observed in two dimensions (suggesting overfitting the data), the data can be considered unidimensional. This comparison is qualitative, rather than relying on a statistical index. Two descriptive fit indices were used to evaluate fit of the MDS models to the data: STRESS and R^2. The STRESS index represents the square root of the normalized residual variance of the monotonic regression of the MDS distances on the transformed PC statistics. Thus, lower values of STRESS indicate better fit. The R^2 index reflects proportion of variance of the transformed data accounted for by the MDS distances. Thus, higher values of R^2 indicate better fit. In general, STRESS values near or below .10 and R^2 values of .90 or greater are indicative of reasonable data-model fit. There were 91 dichotomously scored items (73 multiple-choice and 18 short constructed-response items) analyzed using MDS.

RESULTS

Principal Components Analysis

As mentioned above, data from four test booklets were analyzed using principal components analysis (PCA). These four booklets (booklets 209, 210, 231, and 232) involved 12 of the 15 blocks (152 of the 189 items) and included all four hands-on tasks. Separate PCAs were conducted on each booklet. The number of items composing each booklet ranged from 33 to 40. The sample sizes for each booklet were approximately the same, ranging from 274 to 284.

Booklet 209 comprised 38 items from blocks S3, S11, and S12: 10 earth, 9 life, and 19 physical science items (16 multiple-choice and 22 constructed-response items). The first principal component (eigenvalue = 12.4) accounted for 33 percent of the variance. However, the second factor was also relatively large (eigenvalue = 5.8) and accounted for 15 percent of the variance. Inspection of the unrotated component (factor) loading matrix revealed 10 items with loadings below .3 on the first factor. These items came from different blocks and content areas, but all were constructed-response items. (Five of these items had loadings larger than .30 on the second factor.) The scree plot for booklet 209 is presented in Figure 5-1.

Booklet 210 comprised 40 items from blocks S4, S13, and S14: 14 earth, 10 life, and 16 physical science items (18 multiple-choice and 22 constructed-response items). The first principal component (eigenvalue = 11.0) accounted for 28 percent of the variance, and the second principal component (eigenvalue = 3.3) accounted for 9 percent of the variance. Inspection of the unrotated factor loadings revealed three items with loadings less than .3 on the first factor. Two items came from block S4; the other was from block S13. All three items were earth science items. One item was a constructed-response item from block S13; the other two were from block S4, one of which was a multiple-choice item. The scree plot for this booklet is presented in Figure 5-2.

Booklet 231 comprised 40 items from blocks S5, S10, and S21: 17 earth, 12 life, and 11 physical science items (15 multiple-choice and 25 constructed-response items). The first principal component (eigenvalue = 17.0) accounted for 45 percent of the variance and the second principal component (eigenvalue = 4.0) for 11 percent. Inspection of the unrotated factor loadings revealed five items

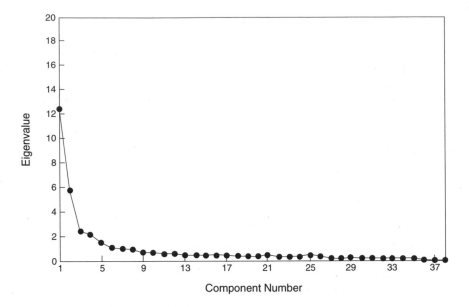

FIGURE 5-1   Scree plot from PCA for booklet 209.

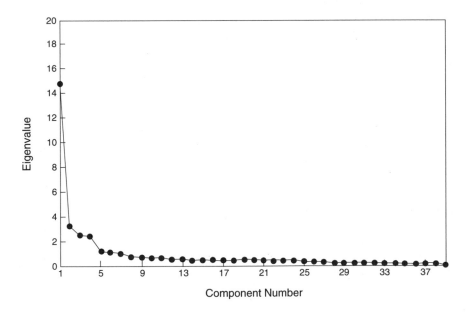

FIGURE 5-2   Scree plot from PCA for booklet 210.

with loadings less than .3 on the first factor: four constructed-response earth science items from block S5 and a constructed-response life science item from block S10. Only one of the five constructed-response items had a relatively large loading on the second factor. The scree plot for this booklet is presented in Figure 5-3.

Booklet 232 comprised 33 items from blocks S6, S7, and S15: 16 earth, 7 life, and 10 physical science items (8 multiple-choice and 25 constructed-response items). The first principal component (eigenvalue = 9.3) accounted for 28 percent of the variance and the second principal component (eigenvalue = 4.9) for 15 percent. Inspection of the unrotated factor loadings revealed five items with loadings of less than .3 on the first factor: three constructed-response life science items (one from block S6 and two from block S15) and two physical science items from block S15 (one of which was a multiple-choice item). The scree plot for this booklet is presented in Figure 5-4.

Using the ratio of the percentage of variance accounted for by the first two components, booklets 210 and 231 appear to be unidimensional. The first component accounts for three times as much variance as the second component in each of these two booklets. A case for unidimensionality may also be made for all four booklets because of the relatively large percentage of variance accounted for by the first component (minimum 28 percent). However, a substantial proportion of variance is accounted for by the second factor underlying all four booklets (especially for booklets 209 and 232), and each booklet exhibited some items with higher loadings on a factor other than the first. Thus, the PCAs indicate a small degree of multidimensionality in these data. This multidimensionality was not linked to content area or cognitive level, but it was noted that some of the constructed-response items had small loadings on the first factor. It should also be noted that PCA has been widely criticized for producing spurious factors when applied to test score data.

Raw Score Correlational Analysis

The relationship among the three fields of science was also evaluated at the booklet level by deriving three "content-area raw scores" for each student. The correlations among these earth, life, and physical science raw scores were then calculated. Raw scores derived from booklets containing only a few items corresponding to a field of science (specifically, those raw scores that produced a scale less than 10 points in length) were eliminated from this correlational analysis. In addition, raw scores with internal consistency (coefficient alpha) reliabilities of less than .50 were eliminated. This process resulted in 21 correlations among earth and physical science raw scores, 17 correlations among life and physical science raw scores, and 15 correlations among earth and life science raw scores. The 21 earth-physical correlations ranged from .61 to .79, and the median corre-

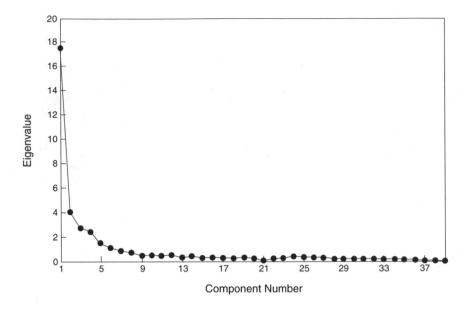

FIGURE 5-3 Scree plot from PCA for booklet 231.

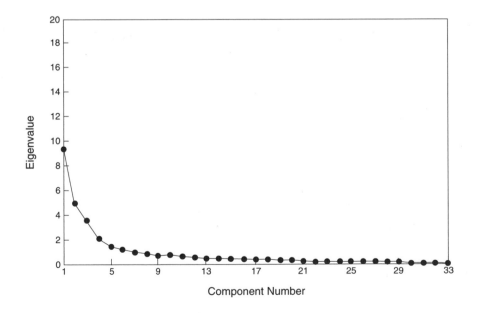

FIGURE 5-4 Scree plot from PCA for booklet 232.

lation was .69. After disattenuation (correction for measurement error[2]), these correlations ranged from .83 to 1.0, and the median correlation was .99. The 17 physical-life correlations ranged from .54 to .73; the median correlation was .64. After disattenuation, these correlations ranged from .83 to 1.0, with a median correlation of .97. The 15 earth-life correlations ranged from .53 to .71, with a median correlation of .62. After disattenuation these correlations ranged from .83 to 1.0, with a median correlation of .91. The magnitudes of the median disattenuated correlations (.99, .97, and .91) suggest that the three fields of science were essentially measuring the same construct. The results of these correlations are summarized in Table 5-2.

Results Stemming from IRT Analyses

As described earlier, MULTILOG was used to calibrate each of the 15 science item blocks. Unfortunately, an unidentifiable problem, internal to MULTILOG, prevented calibration of block S7 (a block comprising 12 earth science items). Successful item calibrations were obtained for the other 14 blocks; however, we were unable to estimate thetas based on students' responses to block S14 (a block comprising eight physical, five life, and three earth science items).

The marginal reliabilities for the 14 blocks that were calibrated ranged from .39 (block S6, which was a hands-on block containing four physical and two life science constructed-response items) to .80 (block S4, which was a mixed hands-on block comprising six constructed-response items and three multiple-choice items). The median marginal reliability across the 14 blocks was .75.

Correlations Among Separate (Block) Theta Estimates

As the description "balanced incomplete block spiraling design" indicates, not all of the 15 item blocks were paired with each other. Thus, our analyses of the block-specific thetas estimated for each student included all available correlations among the blocks that were successfully calibrated and scored using MULTILOG (except block S6, which exhibited inadequate marginal reliability) and that were paired together in at least one test booklet. Each student responded to three blocks of items; thus, three separate "block" thetas were computed for each student. A total of 56 block theta correlations were computed. There were no data available for computing correlations among an earth science block and a

---

[2]The disattenuated correlations were computed by dividing the raw score correlation by the square root of the product of the reliability estimates for each content-area raw score. Because the alpha coefficient is known to be an underestimate of reliability (Novick, 1966), the disattenuated correlations are overestimates and may at times be greater than one. Nine of the 53 disattenuated correlations were greater than one: six earth-physical correlations, two earth-life correlations, and one physical-life correlation. These correlations were truncated to 1.0.

TABLE 5-2 Summary of Field of Science Raw Score Correlations

Scores Correlated	Number of Correlations	Unadjusted Correlations		Disattenuated Correlations	
		Range	Median	Range	Median
Earth and physical	21	.61 to .79	.69	.83 to 1.0	.99
Life and physical	17	.54 to .73	.64	.83 to 1.0	.97
Earth and life	15	.53 to .71	.62	.83 to 1.0	.91

physical science block; however, there were two correlations available for both earth-life science comparisons and life-physical science comparisons. The remaining 52 correlations involved seven correlations among an earth science block (block S5) and "mixed"-item blocks (i.e., blocks containing items from all three fields of science), 23 correlations among life science (blocks S8 or S9) and mixed-item blocks; seven correlations among a physical science block (block S3) and mixed-item blocks, and 15 correlations among mixed-item blocks. All correlations were disattenuated using the MULTILOG marginal reliability estimates.

A summary of the theta-based correlational analyses is presented in Table 5-3. The unadjusted correlations among thetas derived from mixed-item blocks (15 correlations) ranged from .50 to .79. After correcting for measurement error, these correlations ranged from .76 (S21, S10) to 1.00,[3] with a median correlation of .87. The range and relatively large disattenuated correlations suggest that these mixed blocks, containing items from all three fields of science, were probably measuring the same general science proficiency construct. The magnitude of these correlations among the mixed-item blocks was similar to or higher than the observed marginal reliabilities for these blocks.

The unadjusted correlations for the earth-mixed comparisons ranged from .40 to .59 and after disattenuation from .58 (S5, S21) to .77 (S5, S12); the median disattenuated correlation was .68. The two disattenuated earth-life correlations were .63 and .72. These correlations are lower than those observed for the mixed-block correlations, leaving the door open for the conclusion that the earth science items, at least those included in block S5, do measure a slightly different construct than general science proficiency.

The unadjusted correlations for the physical-mixed comparisons ranged from .44 to .60 and after disattenuation from .63 (S3, S21) to .82 (S3, S11), with a median disattenuated correlation of .76. The two life-physical disattenuated correlations were .72 and .85. These correlations are also relatively low, suggesting that the physical science items may also be measuring a somewhat unique domain of science proficiency.

---

[3]Actually, three of the 56 disattenuated correlations were slightly greater than one; all were from correlations of thetas derived from two mixed blocks.

TABLE 5-3 Summary of Block-Derived Theta Correlations

Types of Blocks Correlated	Number of Correlations	Unadjusted Correlations Range	Median	Disattenuated Correlations Range	Median
Mixed and mixed	15	.50 to 79	.66	.76 to 1.0	.87
Life and mixed	14	.50 to .70	.64	.73 to .94	.88
Physical and mixed	7	.44 to .60	.56	.63 to .82	.76
Earth and mixed	7	.40 to .59	.51	.58 to .77	.68

Notes: The earth and mixed correlations are between block S5 and mixed blocks; the physical and mixed are between block S3 and mixed blocks; and the life and mixed are between blocks S8 or S9 and mixed blocks. Mixed blocks contain items from all three fields of science.

The unadjusted correlations for the life-mixed comparisons ranged from .50 to .70. The disattenuated correlations ranged from .73 (S5, S8) to .94 (S9, S20), and the median correlation was .88. The magnitudes of the disattenuated correlations suggest that the life science items (blocks S8 and S9) may be more closely related to general science proficiency than the earth and physical science items.

POLYFIT Analyses

The fit of the IRT models for each block was evaluated using POLYFIT (Rogers, 1996). Distributions of the standardized residuals generated from the POLYFIT program are presented in Table 5-4. Estimates could not be obtained for four of the 15 blocks (S4, S7, S9, and S14). For blocks S10 through S21 the unidimensional IRT models appear to fit the data adequately. The residual analy-

TABLE 5-4   Distribution of Standardized Residuals for Each Block

Block	Theta Interval < −3	−3 to −2	−2 to −1	−1 to 0	0 to 1	1 to 2	2 to 3	> 3	Mean
S3	4.55	0	4.55	42.42	42.42	1.52	1.52	3.03	−0.05
S5	3.90	1.30	2.60	40.26	40.26	1.30	2.60	7.79	0.13
S6	1.67	1.67	5.00	33.33	48.33	3.33	1.67	5.00	0.11
S8	11.00	3.00	7.00	28.00	30.00	13.00	6.00	2.00	−0.15
S10	2.50	3.13	5.63	36.25	36.25	9.38	5.63	1.25	0.04
S11	3.13	3.75	6.88	35.00	37.50	8.75	3.75	1.25	−0.04
S12	2.78	3.47	5.56	32.64	40.97	9.72	2.78	2.08	−0.01
S13	2.96	3.70	8.89	23.70	39.26	8.89	8.89	3.70	0.11
S15	2.67	2.67	5.33	39.33	36.00	12.00	2.00	0	−0.04
S20	3.13	3.13	10.00	31.88	31.88	16.25	3.13	0.63	−0.04
S21	1.88	0.63	7.50	41.88	38.13	6.88	2.50	0.63	−0.02

Notes: Table entries are percentages of residuals falling within each interval. Estimates could not be obtained for blocks 4, 7, 9, and 14.

ses show that most residuals are close to zero, with only a small proportion (no more than about 5 percent) falling outside the range (-3,3).

For blocks S3, S5, S6, and S8, the model did not fit as well. Blocks S3, S5, and S6 consist of performance tasks. These blocks have six, eight, and six items, respectively. Blocks S3 and S5 contain items from only one scale, while block S6 has four physical items and two life items. Block S8 consists of 10 items, all measuring life science.

For block S3, examination of the residuals reveals that most of the large ones were obtained from item 1. This was the only dichotomously scored item in the block, fitted using the two-parameter model. For this item the residuals tended to be negative at the low end of the proficiency continuum and positive at the high end, suggesting that the a-parameter may have been underestimated. In block S5, items 5 and 7 appeared to fit poorly. Both of these items were dichotomously scored and fitted using the two-parameter model. Item 5 showed no clear pattern in the residuals, while item 7 produced large positive residuals at the upper theta levels. In block S6, item 4 yielded poor fit. This item, again, was a dichotomously scored item, fitted using the two-parameter model. It was a very difficult item. The residuals showed the same pattern as was observed for the other poorly fitting items. For block S8 all of the dichotomously scored items (5 MC, 1 2P) showed some degree of misfit, with the largest (negative) residuals occurring at the low end of the proficiency continuum. A summary of the POLYFIT analyses is presented in Table 5-5.

The summary of the POLYFIT analyses presented in Table 5-5 illustrates that the results were contrary to our expectations. We expected blocks comprising items from only one field of science to be fit well by the unidimensional IRT models, and blocks comprising items from more than one field of science not to be fit well by these models. However, the opposite pattern emerged. Blocks

TABLE 5-5 Summary of POLYFIT Results

Block	Content	Item Types	Expectation	Result	Problem Items
S3	P	6 CR	Good fit	Poor fit	1 2P item
S5	E	8 CR	Good fit	Poor fit	2 2P items
S6	L, P	6 CR	Poor fit	Poor fit	1 2P item
S8	L	5 MC, 5 CR	Good fit	Poor fit	5 MC, 1 2P item
S10	E, L, P	8 MC, 8 CR	Poor fit	Adequate fit	
S11	E, L, P	8 MC, 8 CR	Poor fit	Adequate fit	
S12	E, L, P	8 MC, 8 CR	Poor fit	Adequate fit	
S13	E, L, P	8 MC, 8 CR	Poor fit	Adequate fit	
S15	E, L, P	6 MC, 9 CR	Poor fit	Adequate fit	
S20	E, L, P	8 MC, 8 CR	Poor fit	Adequate fit	
S21	E, L, P	7 MC, 9 CR	Poor fit	Adequate fit	

Notes: E = earth science, L = life science, P = physical science; CR = constructed-response item, MC = multiple-choice item; 2P = dichotomously scored constructed-response item.

comprising items from all three fields of science were fit adequately using IRT, and those blocks comprising items from a single field of science exhibited relatively poor fit.

Factor Analyses

A summary of the results of the factor analyses is presented in Table 5-6. A one-dimensional factor model was fit to each block. Fortunately, the results obtained with the Pearson product-moment correlations and the tetrachoric/polyserial correlations did not differ substantially; hence, only the results based on the product-moment correlations are provided. The goodness-of-fit indices (GFI and AGFI) were used to evaluate the model-data fit. The model-data fit was considered to be reasonable when GFI and AGFI were equal to or greater than .90. As shown in Table 5-6, 12 of the 15 blocks were adequately fit using the one-factor model, indicating that the data can be considered unidimensional. Blocks S3 and S14 came close to meeting the fit criterion—the GFI for both blocks exceeded .90, but the AGFI was .89 for both blocks. The only block that did not meet the fit criterion was block S5, which was a block of hands-on earth science items—the GFI was .84, while the AGFI was .72. The other hands-on tasks (blocks S3, S4, and S6) fitted the one-factor model adequately. Since S5 was made up of items from one content area, a multifactor model was not fit to the item responses. Given the high fit index values obtained with the one-factor model for all of the blocks, the acceptable fit values obtained with S3 and S14,

TABLE 5-6   Summary of Confirmatory Factor Analysis Results

Block	Content	Item Types	GFI/AGFI Areas
S3	P	CR	.95/.89
S4	E, L, P	CR, MC	.95/.92
S5	E	CR	.84/.72
S6	L, P	CR	.99/.99
S7	E	CR, MC	.99/.98
S8	L	CR, MC	.99/.99
S9	L	CR, MC	.99/.99
S10	E, L, P	CR, MC	.99/.98
S11	E, L, P	CR, MC	.98/.98
S12	E, L, P	CR, MC	.98/.98
S13	E, L, P	CR, MC	.99/.96
S14	E ,L, P	CR, MC	.91/.89
S15	E, L, P	CR, MC	.99/.98
S20	E, L, P	CR, MC	.99/.98
S21	E, L, P	CR, MC	.99/.98

Notes: E = earth science, L = life science, P = physical science, CR = constructed-response, MC = multiple-choice.

and the fact that S5 was comprised of items from a single content area, only the results obtained from fitting a one-factor model are presented in Table 5-6. Nevertheless, two- and three-factor confirmatory factor analyses were carried out for block S14. Unfortunately, the two- and three-factor solutions did not converge for S14, and hence the improvement in fit that may have resulted from fitting multifactor models could not be examined.

MDS Analysis of All Dichotomous Items

As described earlier, the PC statistic suggested by Chen and Davison (1996) provides a formal analysis of unidimensionality of dichotomous test data using MDS. Because of its limitation to analysis of only dichotomously scored items, we applied the procedure to only the multiple-choice and dichotomously scored short constructed-response items. Almost half (91 of 189) of the items were scored dichotomously: 73 multiple-choice items and 18 short constructed-response items. Although the results of this analysis cannot be generalized to the dimensionality of the complete dataset, which includes the polytomously scored items, it does evaluate whether the 91 dichotomous items can be considered unidimensional.

The one-dimensional MDS solution did not display adequate fit to the data (STRESS = .20, R^2 = .88). The item p values correlated .88 with the one-dimensional coordinates; however, they correlated .93 with the coordinates of the first dimension from the two-dimensional MDS solution. The two-dimensional solution fit the data well (STRESS = .10, R^2 = .97). Inspection of the item coordinates on the second dimension indicated that the four easiest items (with p values equal to or greater than .87) and the eight most difficult items (with p values equal to or less than .18) had large negative coordinates on this dimension. The item standard deviations correlated .98 with the item coordinates on dimension 2. These coordinates were unrelated to item type (multiple-choice or short constructed-response), field of science, cognitive area, or other item framework characteristics. Therefore, although the one-dimensional MDS solution did not fit these data, the second dimension appears to be a statistical artifact and not a substantive unique dimension.

The Chen-Davison procedure was also used to appraise the dimensionality of the 73 multiple-choice items. The one-dimensional model displayed adequate fit to the data (STRESS = .13, R^2 = .95). However, improved fit was obtained using two dimensions (STRESS = .10, R^2 = .96), and 10 items exhibited large negative coordinates on the second dimension. As expected, the coordinates from the one-dimensional solution and those from the first dimension of the two-dimensional solution were highly correlated with the item p values (both r's were around .99). Similar to analysis of the 91 dichotomous items reported above, dimension 2 corresponded to the extremely easy or extremely difficult items.

Thus, the MDS analysis of the PC statistics for the multiple-choice items suggests that these items are essentially unidimensional.

DISCUSSION

This study involved several different data analytic strategies for evaluating the dimensionality of the grade 8 NAEP science item response data. Some consistencies were observed across these analyses. For the most part, unidimensional models displayed adequate fit to the data. When multidimensionality was observed, it was generally linked to a few items in a block. The analyses most supporting unidimensionality of the data were the FA, the MDS analyses of the dichotomous items using the PC statistic, and the disattenuated field of science raw score correlations. The PCA and the POLYFIT analyses identified some booklets or blocks that were not fit well using a unidimensional model. The observed multidimensionality was not linked to differences among the fields of sciences or other content characteristics of the items. However, the POLYFIT results indicated poorest fit for the dichotomously scored constructed-response items from the three hands-on task blocks, as well as for all of the dichotomously scored items from block S8.

The results of the theta-based correlations are difficult to interpret. The correlations observed among the "mixed" blocks (blocks comprising items from all three fields of science) were larger than those observed among blocks comprising items from a single field of science. This finding could be taken as evidence of multidimensionality in the data resulting from the field of science designations of the items. However, there were only four blocks of items comprising items from a single field of science, and the residuals from IRT models fit to these blocks were larger than residuals from IRT models fit to mixed blocks (see Table 5-5). Therefore, it is difficult to conclude that these lower correlations are due to field of science content distinctions. It is noteworthy to reiterate that the block-level IRT calibrations we conducted differ from the field-of-science-specific IRT-derived scale scores used in the operational scoring of NAEP. Thus, the nature of the different "proficiencies" (i.e., thetas) resulting from our block-level calibrations is unknown. In general, however, the relatively high correlations observed among the mixed blocks suggests that the fields of science are highly related.

Although not explicitly explored in this study, a potential cause for the small degree of multidimensionality observed is "local item dependence" (Sireci et al., 1991; Chen and Thissen, 1997; Yen, 1993). If students' responses to one item are determined in part from their responses to another item (e.g., as in a multistep problem), this interitem dependence could show up as multidimensionality. Because local item dependence violates the conditional independence assumption of IRT, it could affect the plausible theta values computed for students and the NAEP scale values computed for groups. Thus, evaluating the fit of items likely to be locally dependent is an important area for future research. Unfortunately, we did not have access to the text for the actual items and so were unable to determine if some of the larger IRT model residuals or aberrant factor loadings were due to local item dependence.

Does the scale structure specifying three separate fields of science appear reasonable? Can the entire NAEP grade 8 science assessment be considered unidimensional? Even after the comprehensive series of analyses performed here, unequivocal answers to these questions cannot be provided. It appears that many of the blocks can be considered unidimensional even though they contain a mix of items from the three separate fields of science and a mix of multiple-choice and constructed-response items. For if the three fields of science represented very different proficiencies, we would expect relatively poor fit for the mixed-item blocks in the POLYFIT and unidimensional FA analyses. However, for the most part, the blocks were fit well using a unidimensional IRT or an FA model. The large disattenuated correlations observed among the field of science raw scores also argues against three separate scales. It is possible that there were too few items in each content area at the block or booklet level to uncover their uniqueness, but it is clear that these three fields of science are highly related. Therefore, reporting the assessment results on a composite score scale certainly seems appropriate. A more equivocal issue is the necessity of three separate score scales.

The results of this study suggest that it may be possible to represent the three fields of science using a unidimensional model. If these three fields do not represent distinct dimensions and can be calibrated onto a common scale, it is possible that the number of items required to represent all three fields of science could be reduced (since separate scales would not need to be calibrated). This possibility has implications for reducing the size of the item pool and consequently increasing the proportion of items taken by each student. This possibility should be explored further because with fewer items needed to represent general science proficiency a simpler, more "complete" spiraling design is possible, thus reducing the necessity for the complex plausible values scaling methodology. For example, Mislevy et al. (1992) compared plausible values estimation methodology with (unconditional) maximum likelihood estimation. Their results suggest that, with a sufficient number of items (e.g., 20 or 30), the two procedures provide comparable results (Sireci, 1997). On average, each student who took the 1996 NAEP grade 8 science assessment responded to about 36 items. Thus, an area of future research is evaluation of the utility of the separate field of science subscores with respect to information gained beyond the composite score. Given the strong relationships among the fields exhibited in this study, if the grade 8 NAEP science results continue to be aggregated and reported only at the group level, it is unlikely that subscores will provide unique diagnostic information.

The results from this study are consistent with those of Zhang (1997), who analyzed two of the grade 8 science blocks (S14 and S21) using "theoretical DETECT" and concluded that these mixed blocks were essentially unidimensional. In the current study, block 21 displayed adequate fit to a unidimensional IRT model and displayed adequate fit to the one-factor FA model. Block S14 could not be evaluated using POLYFIT but displayed close fit to the one-factor FA model. These two blocks contained a mix of multiple-choice items and constructed-response items and items from all three fields of science, making them good candidates for discovering multidimensionality. The fact that both the Zhang study and the present study were consistent in supporting the unidimensionality of these blocks suggests that a unidimensional scale could be used to represent all three fields and that the different item types are measuring the same proficiency. However, the present study looked at all 15 blocks, and two areas of concern were noted: (1) relatively poor fit to an IRT model for three of the four hands-on tasks analyzed using POLYFIT and (2) relatively poorer fit for those constructed-response items that were scored dichotomously. Whether these observations reflect real-item type differences or are specific to a small number of items from the much larger pool should be determined from future research.

It is important to bear in mind that this study only analyzed data from the 1996 grade 8 NAEP science assessment. Thus, the results may not generalize to the science assessments administered at other grade levels, to other subject tests in the NAEP battery, or to other NAEP tests administered in different years.

ACKNOWLEDGMENTS

The authors thank Karen Mitchell and Lee Jones for their invaluable assistance with this research; James Carlson, Al Rogers, and Steve Szyszkiewicz for providing the data; and Nambury Raju and an anonymous reviewer for their helpful comments on an early version of this paper.

REFERENCES

Brennan, R.L.
    1998   Misconceptions at the intersection of measurement theory and practice. *Educational Measurement: Issues and Practice* 17(1):5-9, 30.
Chen, T., and M.L. Davison
    1996   A multidimensional scaling, paired comparisons approach to assessing unidimensionality in the Rasch model. In *Objective Measurement: Theory into Practice*, vol. 3, G. Engelhard and M. Wilson, eds. Norwood, N.J.: Ablex.
Chen, W-H, and D. Thissen
    1997   Local dependence indices for item pairs using item response theory. *Journal of Educational and Behavioral Statistics* 22:265-289.
Jöreskog, K.G., and D. Sörbom
    1993   *LISREL-8 User's Reference Guide*. Mooresville, Ind.: Scientific Software.
McDonald, R.P.
    1967   Non-linear factor analysis. *Psychometrika Monograph Supplement*. No. 15.

Mislevy, R.J., A.E. Beaton, B. Kaplan, and K.M. Sheehan
   1992   Estimating population characteristics from sparse matrix samples of item responses. *Journal of Educational Measurement* 29:133-161.
Muraki, E.
   1992   A generalized partial credit model: Application of an EM algorithm. *Applied Psychological Measurement* 16:159-176.
National Assessment Governing Board (NAGB).
   1996   *Science Framework for the 1996 National Assessment of Educational Progress.* Washington, D.C.: NAGB.
Novick, M.R.
   1966   The axioms and principal results of classical test theory. *Journal of Mathematical Psychology* 3:1-18.
Rogers, H.J.
   1996   POLYFIT. Unpublished computer program, Teachers College, Columbia University, New York, N.Y.
Samejima, F.
   1969   Estimation of latent ability using a response pattern of graded scores. *Psychometrika Monograph Supplement* 4(Part 2):Whole #17.
Sireci, S.G.
   1997   Dimensionality Issues Related to the National Assessment of Educational Progress. Commissioned paper by the National Academy of Sciences/National Research Council's Committee on the Evaluation of National and State Assessments of Educational Progress. Washington, DC: National Research Council.
Sireci, S.G., D. Thissen, and H. Wainer
   1991   On the reliability of testlet-based tests. *Journal of Educational Measurement* 28:237-247.
Tanaka, J.S., and G.J. Huba
   1985   A fit index for covariance structure models under arbitrary GLS estimation. *British Journal of Mathematical and Statistical Psychology* 38:197-201.
Thissen, D.
   1991   MULTILOG: Multiple Categorical Item Analysis and Test Scoring Using Item Response Theory, Version 6. Computer program. Mooresville, Ind.: Scientific Software.
Yen, W.M.
   1993   Scaling performance assessments: Strategies for managing local item dependence. *Journal of Educational Measurement* 30:187-214.
Zhang, J.
   1997   A New Approach for Assessing the Dimensionality of NAEP Data. Paper presented at the annual meeting of the American Educational Research Association, Chicago, March.

6

Subject-Matter Experts' Perceptions of the Relevance of the NAEP Long-Term Trend Items in Science and Mathematics

Jennifer R. Zieleskiewicz

The National Assessment of Educational Progress (NAEP), a congressionally mandated project of the National Center for Education Statistics (NCES), evaluates American students' educational accomplishments in a variety of disciplines. Since 1969, assessments have been conducted periodically in reading, mathematics, science, writing, and other subjects. There are two types of trend assessments at the national level: the main NAEP or short-term trend NAEP assessments and the long-term trend NAEP assessments. The main NAEP assessments are given every few years and were designed to adapt to changes in assessment approaches. The long-term trend NAEP assessments were designed to be stable and measure specific trends in educational performance over time.

Because the long-term trend items were developed well before the current main NAEP frameworks and assessments, some have questioned whether the long-term trend items are up-to-date and relevant measures of student achievement. Thus, the purpose of this study was to evaluate long-term trend NAEP for its relevance compared with the classroom, national standards, and main NAEP assessments using item-level data. This study is only a first step toward evaluating the relevance of long-term trend NAEP.

BACKGROUND

The NAEP assessments used in this study were the main NAEP and the long-term trend NAEP assessments for mathematics and science. The main NAEP mathematics assessment was first administered in 1990 and then again in 1992 and 1996. The main NAEP science assessment was first administered in 1996.

The long-term trend NAEP assessments are based on a collection of items originally administered in NAEP assessments during the 1970s and 1980s. The current form of long-term trend NAEP was first administered in 1988 and has been administered every two years through 1999. Both the mathematics and science NAEPs are scheduled to be administered in 2000.

The development processes were different for each of the NAEP trend assessments. The main NAEP trend assessments framework was developed through a consensus-building process that resulted in a very specific definition of what is important to assess in education. Prior NAEP evaluators provided evidence of relevance by evaluating the framework; relying on groups of subject-matter experts to provide evidence that the consensus process resulted in a "good" and current framework; and conducting item classification/content congruence studies, such as the Sireci et al. analysis of the 1996 NAEP science assessment (Chapter 4, this volume), to show whether the items reflect the goals in the framework. However, long-term trend NAEP was not based on a consensus-building process or development of frameworks but was based on educational standards from the 1950s. Thus, for the purposes of this study it was suggested that some of the long-term trend NAEP items be evaluated to provide evidence that the long-term trend assessment was a "good" and current method of evaluating education, like that of main NAEP. Researchers were interested in answering the following questions:

1. Do the long-term trend items in mathematics and science adequately assess knowledge and skills taught in grade 8 classrooms today?

2. Do the long-term trend items in mathematics and science adequately assess what national standards should be taught in grade 8 classrooms today?

3. How do long-term and main NAEP items compare with one another? A survey was developed to assess these research questions.

METHOD

Sample

The survey sample consisted of two groups of 30 raters selected to evaluate the mathematics and science items. Each discipline had three groups of raters, containing 10 participants each. The three groups were eighth-grade district faculty, eighth-grade reform faculty, and disciplinary specialists. The groups were defined as follows:

Eighth-Grade District Faculty

Eighth-grade schoolteachers who were representative of typical schools and classrooms were used as raters. The participating states were chosen based on the random selection of one state from each of the Census Bureau divisions. These states were Kansas, Arkansas, Indiana, Georgia, New York, Oregon, Idaho, South Dakota, Vermont, and Alabama. One school district was randomly selected from each of these states, regardless of population size. All participating school districts are identical for the mathematics and science surveys, but for one instance in the science survey, where the Platt school district in South Dakota was used. The mathematics and/or science coordinator for each school district was contacted and asked to nominate an eighth-grade school teacher for each discipline. The coordinator was asked to nominate someone believed to be a good representative of the science or mathematics taught in the school district and who would also be interested in participating in a study on education.

Eighth-Grade Reform Faculty

Eighth-grade schoolteachers currently in the classroom or on leave, who had some knowledge of local and state reform issues, were selected to participate as raters. The National Research Council (NRC) provided the names and contact information for the science participants in this group because they participated in a prior study in the summer of 1997. The states included were Maryland, Florida, Virginia, Ohio, Kentucky, Texas, Delaware, California, Washington, and South Carolina. From these same states the NRC provided the names of state assessment directors who were asked to nominate a mathematics teacher with some knowledge of local and state reform issues.

Disciplinary Specialists

Disciplinary specialists consisted of professionals, such as university professors and leaders in professional organizations, who are considered experts in national mathematics or science standards assessments, were nominated by the NRC. Disciplinary specialists for science were from the University of Minnesota; Assessment Curriculum & Teaching Systems; Science Examination for New Standards Project in California; Bedford, New York Public Schools; University of Oklahoma; Alaska Department of Education; West ED; University of California; Vanderbilt University; and Colorado Department of Education. Disciplinary specialists for mathematics were from the University of Wisconsin, University of Iowa, University of Georgia, University of Delaware, Michigan State University, Colgate University, University of California at Los Angeles, Connecticut Department of Education, and San Diego State University.

Instruments

Two surveys were developed: one for mathematics and one for science. Each included a subset of items from the long-term trend NAEP assessments as well as the released items from the main NAEP assessments.

The Math Survey

There were 22 main NAEP and 37 trend mathematics items, making a total of 59 items for the mathematics survey. The main NAEP items were released items from the 1990, 1992, and 1996 assessments. The trend items were from the current long-term trend assessments. All selected items from the main and long-term trend assessments were randomly ordered in the survey.

The Science Survey

There were 16 main NAEP and 25 trend science items, making a total of 41 items for the science survey. The main NAEP science items were released from the 1996 assessment. The trend items were from the current trend assessment. All selected items from the main and long-term trend assessments were randomly ordered in the survey.

Survey Questions

For each item a set of two or four questions was asked of each rater.

Questions A and B

Questions A and B provided information to answer the question, "Do the long-term trend items in mathematics and science adequately assess knowledge and skills taught in today's grade 8 classrooms?" If the rater answered "no" to question A, the rater did not proceed to question B. But if the rater answered "yes," they did proceed to B (see Appendix).

Questions C and D

Questions C and D provided information to answer the question, "Do the long-term trend items in mathematics and science adequately assess what national standards state should be taught in today's grade 8 classrooms?" If the answer was "no" to question C, the rater did not proceed to question D. But if the answer was "yes," they did proceed to D (see Appendix).

The eighth-grade district faculty and the eighth-grade reform faculty were given questions A through D, whereas the disciplinary specialists were given only questions C and D. The two groups of faculty were given the four questions because this information requires eighth-grade teaching experience. The disciplinary specialists were given only questions C and D because it was thought they would have a good understanding of their field and educational national standards but did not currently teach eighth grade. Surveys were sent out and participants were asked to return the materials within two weeks of receipt. Sixty surveys were mailed, and there was a 100 percent response rate.

Statistical Analysis and Results

Means and standard deviations were computed for each group in mathematics and science for the main and long-term NAEPs. It should be noted that, while the sample size for questions A and C is either 8, 9, or 10 for each of the subgroups, the sample sizes are smaller for questions B and D and vary from item to item. The reason for the reduced and variable sample sizes is that only those who answered "yes" to question A(C) answered question B(D). Since there is no direct item-level correspondence between the main and long-term NAEP items, the mean and standard deviations of item means were computed for items in the main and long-term NAEP, separately, for comparison across the two NAEPs. Table 6-1 displays means for mathematics for questions A through D, separately for the three groups. Similar information is shown for science in Table 6-2.

TABLE 6-1 Means and Standard Deviations of Responses to Questions A, B, C, and D Across Groups and Combined for Mathematics

Question	District Teachers		Reform Teachers		Disciplinary Specialists		Combined	
	Short-Term (22)[c]	Long-Term (37)	Short-Term (22)	Long-Term (37)	Short-Term (22)	Long-Term (37)	Short-Term	Long-Term
A Mean[a]	0.832	0.946	0.954	0.940	X	X	0.893	0.943
SD	0.164	0.128	0.061	0.050	X	X	0.085	0.058
N (Range)[b]	10	9–10	9	9–10				
B								
Mean	3.916	4.252	4.174	3.876	X	X	4.045	4.064
SD	0.438	0.430	0.390	0.298	X	X	0.324	0.305
N	6-10	4–10	8–10	9–10				
C								
Mean	0.941	0.911	0.968	0.943	0.950	0.915	0.953	0.923
SD	0.067	0.062	0.048	0.051	0.074	0.084	0.039	0.035
N	10	9–10	9–10	9–10	9–10	9–10		
D								
Mean	4.043	4.375	4.155	3.820	3.937	4.045	4.045	4.080
SD	0.356	0.386	0.347	0.277	0.485	0.314	0.272	0.225
N	8–10	8–10	9–10	9–10	8–10	6–10		

NOTE: Means and standard deviations by item are also available by short-term and long-term, respectively.

[a]Mean of item means and standard deviation of item means.

[b]Number of respondents for questions B and D are conditional on responses to questions A and C. See Appendix for exact wording of these questions.

[c]Number of items.

TABLE 6-2 Means and Standard Deviations of Responses to Questions A, B, C, and D Across Groups and Combined for Science

Question	District Teachers		Reform Teachers		Disciplinary Specialists		Combined	
	Short-Term (16)[c]	Long-Term (25)	Short-Term (16)	Long-Term (25)	Short-Term (16)	Long-Term (25)	Short-Term	Long-Term
A Mean[a]	0.724	0.824	0.869	0.917	X	X	0.797	0.870
SD	0.173	0.188	0.087	0.161	X	X	0.121	0.156
N (Range)[b]	9–10	10	10	9–10				
B								
Mean	4.067	3.943	3.994	3.959	X	X	4.030	3.951
SD	0.447	0.364	0.400	0.342	X	X	0.400	0.221
N	4–9	4–10	7–10	2–10				
C								
Mean	0.831	0.868	0.900	0.873	0.863	0.868	0.865	0.870
SD	0.154	0.144	0.097	0.149	0.154	0.111	0.101	0.101
N	9–10	10	10	9–10	10	9–10		
D								
Mean	3.991	3.986	4.070	4.044	4.027	3.617	4.029	3.882
SD	0.449	0.325	0.388	0.313	0.459	0.477	0.314	0.217
N	5–10	5–10	7–10	5–10	5–10	7–10		

NOTE: Means and standard deviations by item are also available by short-term and long-term, respectively.

[a]Mean of item means and standard deviation of item means.

[b]Number of respondents for questions B and D are conditional on responses to questions A and C. See Appendix for exact wording of these questions.

[c]Number of items.

Means in Tables 6-1 and 6-2 are quite similar for main and long-term NAEP. The means for questions A and C vary between .724 and .968, with most of the means in the .80s and .90s. Standard deviations for questions A and C range from .048 to .188. The differences between means for A and C range from zero to 10 percentage points for science, with most at five percentage points or less. The differences between means for A and C range from zero to 10 percentage points for mathematics, with most at three percentage points or less. These high and comparable mean results indicate that study participants strongly feel that both frameworks, as reflected in the selected items, adequately assess mathematics and science concepts taught in today's classrooms as well as what national standards say should be taught in today's classrooms. The results also indicate a high degree of comparability across the two NAEPs.

Means for questions B and D are around 4.0, again indicating that study participants strongly feel that both frameworks, as reflected in the selected items, adequately assess the importance of mathematics and science concepts taught in today's classrooms as well as what national standards say should be taught. Standard deviations for questions B and D range from .277 to .485. The results also indicate a high degree of comparability across the two NAEPs. The differences between the main and the long-term NAEP items are in the second decimal place on a scale ranging from 1 to 5. Because of the small sample sizes involved, no significance tests were performed.

DISCUSSION

The research conducted on the subject-matter experts' perceptions of the relevance of the NAEP long-term trend items in mathematics and science for eighth graders has provided relevant information on the importance of the long-term trend assessment. These findings can be summarized as follows:

- The long-term trend and main NAEP mathematics and science items evaluated in this study appear to reflect important content and skills that grade 8 teachers cover in their classes.
- This subset of items also appears to reflect what grade 8 teachers and disciplinary specialists believe are important parts of national standards in mathematics and science.
- For both mathematics and science there do not appear to be any meaningful differences in grade 8 teachers' or disciplinary specialists' perceptions of the relevance of long-term trend items and main NAEP items, as measured by coverage in current classrooms or reflection in national standards.

The results taken as a whole suggest that these long-term trend items are up to date in measuring student achievement. Findings suggest that these long-term trend and main NAEP items reflect what is important for eighth-grade students to know and be able to do as well as what national standards say should be taught in today's eighth-grade classrooms. It also appears that teachers and disciplinary specialists agree on the relevance of the selected long-term trend and main NAEP items as measured by coverage in current classrooms or reflection in national standards. Although this study is only a first step toward evaluating the relevance of the long-term trend NAEP, one could suggest that the long-term trend NAEP, as a whole, may be relevant in today's classroom, reflects current national standards, and is as equally valuable as the main NAEP assessments. However, more research is needed to clarify this conclusion.

No meaningful differences were found between rating groups on questions A through D, suggesting that the selected long-term trend and main NAEP items are reflective of what is being taught in the classroom as well as what national standards say should be taught. This implies that these long-term NAEP trend items are not out of date for use in the 1990s and provide the same information as the main NAEP items. These findings also suggest that national standards are visible to individuals in the teaching professions, although to what degree is uncertain. It is likely that some teachers will recognize the national standards, but it is unclear whether all of those in the teaching profession have knowledge of them.

These results have important implications for the future of the long-term trend assessment. For several decades the NAEP trends have provided information about the educational achievements of students in American schools. The goal has been to assess information on what American students know and can do in the classroom and to compare their current performance with that of similar students assessed in the past. The main and long-term NAEP trends were designed to assess this achievement but using different frameworks. The results of this study give some suggestion that both this subset of main and long-term NAEPs items are equally valuable in their assessment and provide similar information. Perhaps one day the two trends may be combined into one assessment, eliminating the use of multiple measures over time and simplifying the testing process in general. More research is needed to investigate this possibility.

Because the results are preliminary, any interpretation or speculation on their use should be weighed against a small sample size and the use of a subset of trend items. As a result, caution should be taken in generalizing these results to populations outside the parameters of this study. A small sample may not adequately assess the differences in educational content from one state to the next, particularly in those states where there is no mandated curriculum or textbook adoption. Also, a subset of trend items was used, thus providing information about those national standards and content reflected only in those items. The results have shown that those items are reflective of what is important for eighth-grade students to know and be able to do as well as what national standards say should be taught in today's eighth-grade classrooms. It would be premature to assume, since only a portion of the national standards and content were represented in this study, that all national standards and content are reflected in classroom curriculum.

To learn more about the long-term trend NAEP assessment, research should be performed to focus on several aspects of it. Future research should consider the use of a larger sample of raters and the inclusion of a larger, more representative sample of items from the mathematics and science assessments. It may also be appropriate to include other disciplines in the research.

SUMMARY

Researchers were interested in knowing if the long-term NAEP is an up-to-date and relevant measure of student achievement in mathematics and science compared with the main NAEP frameworks and assessments developed more recently. Subsets of items from the long-term and main NAEP assessments were combined into two surveys, one for mathematics and one for science, and were sent to 60 subject-matter experts.

The long-term trend and main NAEP science and mathematics items evaluated in this study appear to reflect important content and skills that grade 8 teachers cover in their classes. These select items also appear to reflect what grade 8 teachers and disciplinary specialists believe to be important parts of national standards in science and mathematics. Lastly, in both science and mathematics there do not appear to be any meaningful differences in grade 8 teachers' or disciplinary specialists' perceptions of the relevance of long-term trend items and main NAEP items as measured by coverage in current classrooms or reflection in national standards.

APPENDIX

Question A: Does this item assess knowledge and/or skills that students in your school will have covered in science (mathematics) by the end of the eighth grade? (Please check one)

No __ Yes __

Question B: If *yes*, relative to all of what students cover in science (mathematics) in your school, how important is it for students to know/be able to do what is covered in the item by the end of the eighth grade? (Please circle one)

1	2	3	4	5
Not important		Somewhat important		Very important

Question C: Does this item assess knowledge and/or skills that students should have covered in science (mathematics) by the end of the eighth grade according to your best understanding of national standards? (Please check one)

No __ Yes __

Question D: If *yes*, relative to all of what national standards say students should cover, how important is it for students to know and be able to do what is covered by this item by the end of the eighth grade? (Please circle one)

1	2	3	4	5
Not important		Somewhat important		Very important

7

Issues in Phasing Out Trend NAEP

Michael J. Kolen

This paper considers ways in which the long-term trend National Assessment of Educational Progress (NAEP) can be phased out and replaced by the main NAEP while still maintaining a long-term trend line. Relevant history of NAEP is presented with a focus on those aspects that led to separating long-term trend NAEP and main NAEP. Differences between the two assessments are discussed, including differences in content, operational procedures, examinee subgroup definitions, analysis procedures, and results. Four designs for assessing long-term trends with NAEP are considered. Evaluation of these designs addresses how their implementation would affect main NAEP and the assessment of long-term trends. The paper concludes with recommendations for research and recommendations for the designs that should receive further consideration.

The recommendations focus on two designs. In one promising design, long-term trends are monitored with main NAEP, and overlapping main NAEP assessments are used whenever an assessment is modified. Implementation of this design requires extensive research. Because long-term trends are assessed with main NAEP in this design, modifications of main NAEP to reflect curricular changes must be tightly constrained. In another promising design, a separate long-term trend assessment is used that is periodically updated. This design can continue to provide long-term trends without an extensive research program. It also allows for main NAEP to change, as necessary, to reflect curricular changes. Drawbacks of this second design are that it requires continuing both the main NAEP and the long-term trend NAEP programs and it allows for only small changes in long-term trend NAEP.

INTRODUCTION

NAEP "is mandated by Congress to survey the educational accomplishments of U.S. students and to monitor changes in those accomplishments" (Ballator, 1996:1). Originally, NAEP surveyed educational accomplishments and long-term trends with a single assessment. Because of continual changes in the assessments, NAEP has evolved into a collection of state and national assessments. The main NAEP is designed to be flexible enough to adapt to changes in assessment approaches. The long-term trend NAEP is intentionally constructed and administered to be stable so that trends in student performance can be examined over time. Whereas both main NAEP and long-term trend NAEP focus on assessing achievement for the nation and for various subgroups of students, state NAEP, which is the most recent addition to NAEP, focuses on achievement of students by state. Main NAEP and long-term trend NAEP have distinct assessment exercises and administration procedures.

The National Assessment Governing Board (NAGB) oversees policy for the NAEP program and has called for NAEP to be redesigned (NAGB, 1996). One of NAGB's concerns involves the apparent inefficiency in continuing to maintain both main NAEP and long-term trend NAEP. To address this concern, NAGB (1996:10) has stated that "it may be impractical and unnecessary to operate two separate assessment programs. . . . A carefully planned transition shall be developed to enable 'the main National Assessment' to become the primary way to measure trends in reading, writing, mathematics, and science in the National Assessment program." Many individuals and committees have expressed concern that the transition suggested by NAGB might result in losing the currently available long-term trends (e.g., Jones, 1996; Glaser et al., 1996, 1997; National Research Council, 1996). In response to this concern, NAGB no longer plans to use main NAEP as the primary way to measure trends; however, there might be inefficiencies in having two programs.

This paper was commissioned by the National Research Council to discuss ways in which long-term trend NAEP could be phased out and replaced by the main NAEP assessments while still maintaining a long-term trend line. One significant question to be addressed is the following: How can a single assessment be developed that is stable enough to provide long-term trends while still being flexible enough to adapt to changes in assessment approaches? Another significant question is: How can such an assessment be implemented without losing the current long-term trend line?

The history of NAEP is considered with a focus on those aspects that led to separating long-term trend NAEP and main NAEP. Those aspects include changes to the NAEP purpose with the first redesign in the mid-1980s and problems that were encountered in measuring trends with the redesigned assessment, such as those involving the NAEP reading anomaly (Beaton and Zwick, 1990; Zwick, 1991). Relevant components of the current redesign effort are summarized, and characteristics of the current main NAEP and long-term trend NAEP assessments are compared on their content and administration procedures. This comparison facilitates a discussion of how the two assessments might be replaced by a single assessment.

Different designs for assessing long-term trends with NAEP are discussed next. These designs include ones that involve overlapping trend lines, such as those suggested by Glaser et al. (1997) and Forsyth et al. (1996). The evaluation of these designs includes considering how their implementation would affect the measurement of long-term trends as well as the effect on the main NAEP assessments. The paper concludes with recommendations for research to further evaluate the different design possibilities, along with recommendations about which designs should receive further consideration.

RELEVANT NAEP HISTORY

Jones (1996) presented a history of NAEP with a focus on procedural changes that occurred at various stages of its evolution. These stages include the original development of NAEP in the early 1960s, the first operational NAEP in 1969, the first redesign in the early 1980s, and the current redesign effort. The portions of Jones's discussion that are relevant to the relationship between main NAEP and long-term trend NAEP are summarized here. The original "goals of NAEP were to report what the nation's citizens know and can do and then to monitor changes over time" (Jones, 1996:15). From the beginning, NAEP was intended to be a group-level assessment in which scores were not reported for individuals. However, significant changes have occurred in the assessment over time.

Originally, performance was reported exercise by exercise, but by the time of the first redesign it was being reported on groups of exercises, often by objective. Following the first redesign, exercises were scaled using item response theory (IRT) procedures, and average scale scores were reported instead of percentages correct by exercise or groups of exercises.

In the initial assessments, matrix sampling procedures were used in which different sets of exercises were given to different examinees. With these procedures, exercises were read aloud using tape-recorded presentations that minimized the effects of reading ability and served to pace the presentation of exercises to examinees. With the first redesign, a more efficient sampling design was used in which examinees in a given room were administered different sets of exercises, which resulted in elimination of tape-recorded presentations.

In the initial assessments, nearly everyone of ages 9, 13, and 17 was included in the sampling frame, but by the time of the redesign only individuals who were in school and of ages 9, 13, and 17 were assessed. Following the redesign, school grades 4, 8, and 12 replaced ages 9, 13, and 17 as the primary basis for sampling and reporting. Also, the procedures used for classifying individuals into population groups differed considerably over time (Barron and Koretz, 1996).

Jones (1996:17) reported that the content of the assessments began to change after the redesign, and "as curricular reform took center stage, NAEP began to be viewed as an agent for change. Exercises began to focus on desired curricula rather than on curricula already in place." In addition, Jones speculated that the use of the IRT scaling procedures following the redesign affected the content of the assessments. Following the redesign, fewer extremely easy or extremely difficult exercises were chosen for the assessment, so that booklets did not necessarily contain some very easy and very difficult exercises. A greater proportion of exercises were multiple choice. Also, there was pressure to restrict exercises to those with unidimensional properties to meet the assumptions of IRT.

To help maintain trend lines, "special 'bridge samples' were maintained when operational changes were introduced [to NAEP in the 1982, 1984, and 1986 assessments]. For bridge samples, conditions deliberately were kept similar to those of earlier assessments to appraise change in achievement from earlier assessments" (Jones, 1996:17). With the 1985-1986 assessment the reading achievement of 9- and 17-year-olds appeared to decline more than a plausible amount from 1984 and 1986. Upon further study it was found that several changes in NAEP procedures, rather than actual changes in reading achievement, were responsible for the decline. The apparent decline in reading achievement is now known as the NAEP reading anomaly (Beaton and Zwick, 1990; Zwick, 1991).

Because of these problems, the main NAEP and long-term trend NAEP programs were separated following the 1985-1986 NAEP assessment. Main NAEP is allowed to adapt to changes in assessment approaches. Attempts are made to track short-term trends with main NAEP only when procedures are comparable from one assessment to the next. Since 1985-1986, long-term trend NAEP has been similar to those of earlier years, using the same booklets, administration procedures, and definitions of examinee groups. Long-term trend NAEP has allowed for tracking of important trends by "studiously maintaining conditions of assessment that are sufficiently comparable over time to provide valid evidence about achievement change" (Jones, 1996:18).

The main NAEP and long-term trend NAEP assessments are not designed to produce state-level data. In 1990, 1992, and 1994 voluntary *trial state* NAEP assessments were conducted that produced state-level data to compare states to one another and to the nation. These assessments were considered to be trial assessments because of concerns about their usefulness. Potential benefits of state-level NAEP data have been summarized by Phillips (1991) and potential problems by Koretz (1991). The National Academy of Education (1993) panel that evaluated trial state NAEP recommended that it be continued but with ongoing evaluation and congressional oversight. In 1996 the term *trial* was removed from the title, and the assessments are now referred to as *state* NAEP.

The state NAEP assessments use representative subsets of main NAEP booklets. The two programs differ in administration procedures and other operational procedures, such as who is included in the assessments. In addition, state NAEP assesses only fourth- and eighth-grade students. Although NAGB (1996) has considered combining the state NAEP and main NAEP assessments to increase efficiency, these differences make combining them challenging (Mullis, 1997; Rust, 1996; Spencer, 1996). The use of state NAEP likely will increase pressure for changing the assessment's content because a wider group of people in states and school districts have a stake in NAEP. For this reason and because of operational complexities, a decision to combine state NAEP and main NAEP would complicate combining main NAEP and long-term trend NAEP.

DIFFERENCES BETWEEN MAIN NAEP
AND LONG-TERM TREND NAEP

The main and long-term trend assessments administered between 1986 and 1997 and that are planned to be administered after 1997 are summarized in Table 7-1. As is evident from this table, main NAEP covers many more subject areas than long-term trend NAEP. From 1988 until the present, long-term trend NAEP has used nearly the same procedures and exercises in each assessment. In addi-

TABLE 7-1 Main NAEP and Long-Term Trend NAEP Assessments by Year Since 1986[a]

	Main NAEP	Long-Term Trend NAEP
1986	Reading. Mathematics, Science, Computer Competence	Reading, Mathematics, Science
1988	Reading, Writing, Civics, U.S. History	Reading, Writing, Mathematics, Science, Civics (ages 13 and 17 only)
1990	Reading, Mathematics, Science	Reading, Writing, Mathematics, Science
1992	Reading, Writing, Mathematics	Reading, Writing, Mathematics, Science
1994	Reading, U.S. History, Geography	Reading, Writing, Mathematics, Science
1996	Mathematics, Science	Reading, Writing, Mathematics, Science
1997	Arts (grade 8 only)	
1998	Reading, Writing, Civics	
1999		Reading, Writing, Mathematics, Science
2000	Mathematics, Science	
2001	U.S. History, Geography	
2002	Reading, Writing	
2003	Civics, Foreign Language (grade 12 only)	Reading, Writing, Mathematics, Science
2004	Mathematics, Science	
2005	World History, Economics	
2006	Reading, Writing	
2007	Arts	Reading, Writing, Mathematics, Science
2008	Mathematics, Science	

[a]Assessments administered from 1986 to 1994 were adapted from Allen et al. (1996); small special-interest assessments are not shown. Assessments administered from 1996 to 2008 are from NAGB (1997). Future assessments reflect plans.

tion, there has been sufficient stability in content frameworks and procedures for long-term trend NAEP to allow for reporting long-term trends as far back as 1970 (Campbell et al., 1997). In contrast, main NAEP assessments have been allowed to differ from administration to administration so that results on one administration of main NAEP often are not comparable to those from previous administrations. In addition, the main NAEP and long-term trend NAEP assessments in the same-subject matter areas differ considerably in assessment content and operational procedures. Thus, results from the main NAEP and long-term trend NAEP assessments for the same subject area are not directly comparable.

Barron and Koretz (1996) have summarized many of the differences between main NAEP and long-term trend NAEP in content, operational procedures, examinee subgroup definitions, analysis procedures, and results. Some of their major findings are discussed here. They reported that the content of the two assessments is different:

> The trend assessments are based on content frameworks that were developed for the 1983-84 assessments in reading and writing or the 1985-86 assessments in mathematics and science. Since the development of these frameworks, substantial changes have occurred in the objectives that content experts believe teachers should emphasize. The current practice is to make the changes in the main NAEP assessment called for by content experts and supported by the National Assessment Governing Board, but to leave the trend assessment frameworks undisturbed. (Barron and Koretz, 1996:215)

They also reported that the exercise formats for long-term trend NAEP are mainly multiple choice, whereas main NAEP includes a much larger proportion of constructed-response exercises.

They reported that there are also many differences between the two assessments in operational procedures and definitions of examinee subgroups. Main NAEP oversamples minority populations to allow for relatively precise subgroup comparisons. Oversampling of minorities is not done with long-term trend NAEP, which leads to "insufficiently precise" assessment of trends in minority-group performance (Barron and Koretz, 1996:214). In addition, main NAEP primarily uses grade-based sampling and reporting at grades 4, 8, and 12, whereas long-term trend NAEP primarily uses age-based sampling and reporting at ages 9, 13, and 17. Procedures for identifying minority groups differ in the two assessments. For example, for race "the variable used in the main assessment, called *derived race* because it combines information from multiple sources, gives priority to student-reported information about race and ethnicity. . . . The variable used in the trend assessment, called *observed race . . .* is simply the exercise administrator's judgment as to the racial-ethnic background of each student" (Barron and Koretz, 1996:226). In addition, the main NAEP assessments use a *focused* design, in which an examinee is administered exercises from a single subject area. In long-term trend NAEP an examinee is administered exercises from more than one subject-matter area. This difference in administration design leads to each student spending less time on a particular subject area in long-term trend NAEP than in main NAEP.

Similar analysis procedures are used for the two programs; however, "in recent years, the main assessment has used a far greater number of background variables in its conditioning (Barron and Koretz, 1996:220). Furthermore, different score scales are used, which can create difficulties in comparing the two assessments. Performance levels are used in reporting performance for main NAEP but not for long-term trend NAEP.

The many differences between the two assessments could influence conclusions about student achievement in the United States, both at a given time and in trends over time. For example, Barron and Koretz (1996:241-242) have speculated that "trends likely would have been somewhat different if the trend assessment had more closely resembled the current main assessment [in content]," that "the use of age-defined rather than grade-defined samples appears to be influencing both the overall trend line and the trends for specific population groups," that "differences in the method for grouping students into population groups . . . had major effects on the classification of Hispanic students," and that "overall trends for populations as a whole might be different if the trend assessment had a mix of formats more similar to that of the main NAEP assessment."

In certain situations main NAEP has given different results than long-term trend NAEP. In an example provided by Barron and Koretz (1996), the main NAEP assessments indicated greater relative gains in writing achievement in high school than did the long-term trend NAEP writing assessment.

To provide a more recent example, the difference between males' and females' scores on the 1996 main NAEP science assessment is compared to the difference on the 1996 long-term trend NAEP science assessment at selected percentiles. Tables 7-2 and 7-3 provide the results used to make this comparison. Because the two assessments are reported on different metrics, the differences were standardized using the semiinterquartile range for the total group, $Q = (P_{75} - P_{25})/2$. (The standard deviation could not be used to standardize the differences because it was not reported by O'Sullivan et al. (1997). In addition, Q may be preferable to the standard deviation for standardizing percentiles because it is a percentile-based statistic.) As shown in Figure 7-1, the standardized differences are larger on long-term trend NAEP than on main NAEP at all percentiles and grades. Although it is difficult to determine the cause of this difference, it is possible that the greater use of multiple-choice exercises on the long-term trend NAEP assessment than on the main NAEP assessment is partly responsible.

In summary, main NAEP and long-term trend NAEP differ in content, exercise types, subgroup definitions, operational procedures, and analysis procedures. Although these differences likely affect assessment results, it is difficult to tell exactly how.

TABLE 7-2 Differences in Selected Percentiles Between Males and Females in Main NAEP Science[a]

	All	Male	Female	Difference	Difference/Q
Grade 4					
P_{10}	105	105	105	0	.000
P_{25}	130	130	129	1	.046
P_{50}	153	154	152	2	.093
P_{75}	173	175	172	3	.140
P_{90}	190	191	188	3	.140
Grade 8					
P_{10}	104	103	104	−1	−.043
P_{25}	128	128	128	0	.000
P_{50}	153	154	151	3	.130
P_{75}	174	175	172	3	.130
P_{90}	192	194	190	4	.174
Grade 12					
P_{10}	104	103	105	−2	−.087
P_{25}	128	129	127	2	.087
P_{50}	152	155	150	5	.217
P_{75}	174	178	171	7	.304
P_{90}	192	196	187	9	.391

[a]Percentiles are from O'Sullivan et al. (1997); $Q = (P_{75} - P_{25})/2$.

TABLE 7-3 Differences in Selected Percentiles Between Males and Females in Long-Term Trend NAEP Science[a]

	All	Male	Female	Difference	Difference/Q
Age 9					
P_{10}	174.5	176.5	172.3	4.2	.146
P_{25}	201.3	202.9	200.0	2.9	.101
P_{50}	231.0	232.7	229.6	3.1	.108
P_{75}	258.9	262.1	256.2	5.9	.205
P_{90}	283.6	286.9	279.0	7.9	.274
Age 13					
P_{10}	105.3	208.9	202.4	6.5	.248
P_{25}	230.4	233.9	227.6	6.3	.240
P_{50}	257.7	262.4	253.6	8.8	.335
P_{75}	282.9	288.6	277.3	11.3	.430
P_{90}	304.4	309.3	298.4	10.9	.415
Age 17					
P_{10}	235.1	234.0	235.8	−1.8	−.059
P_{25}	265.9	268.9	263.3	5.6	.182
P_{50}	298.2	303.9	293.3	10.6	.345
P_{75}	327.3	333.2	321.7	11.5	.375
P_{90}	351.7	358.6	344.1	14.5	.472

[a]Percentiles are from Campbell et al. (1997); $Q = (P_{75} - P_{25})/2$.

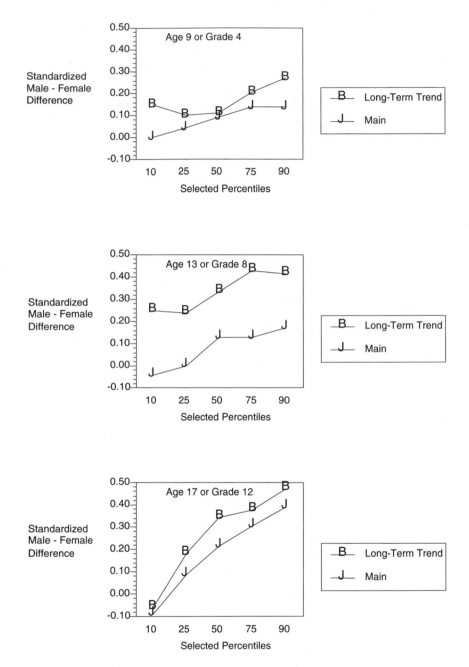

FIGURE 7-1   Standardized male-female differences in 1996 long-term trend NAEP and main NAEP selected percentiles.

ALTERNATIVE DESIGNS FOR MAIN NAEP AND
LONG-TERM TREND

The design for NAEP involves using main NAEP to assess current achievement and long-term trend NAEP to monitor trends. Main NAEP is allowed to change to reflect current thinking in education. Long-term trend NAEP has remained the same since the mid-1980s; even the same exercises are used from one long-term trend NAEP assessment to the next. In this section, alternative designs are discussed for the main NAEP and long-term trend NAEP assessments.

Design 1: Keep the Current Design

One possibility is to continue with the current design, which for long-term trend NAEP uses the same exercises and operational procedures from one assessment to the next. Even this tightly constrained design runs the risk, over time, that certain exercises will change in how they function. When such changes occur, the assessment of long-term trends in proficiency is threatened. As Zwick (1992:207-208) has pointed out, one "pitfall of preserving portions of the assessment is that, in the case of some items, the relation of item performance to overall proficiency . . . may be altered because of curricular and societal changes." She discussed an example from the NAEP science assessment on acid rain that was included on the 1978, 1982, 1986, and 1988 assessments. Presumably, because of the increased exposure of the problem of acid rain in the news media, rather than increases in science proficiency, this exercise became easier. Situations might also occur in which the content of certain exercises becomes dated, resulting in exercises becoming more difficult over time, even though the proficiency being measured by the assessment does not decrease. Zwick (1992:208) concluded that "an item that remains the same across assessments in a superficial sense may nevertheless function differently as a measure of proficiency."

In addition, the content of an assessment can become less relevant as a measure of achievement in current curricula. As curricula change, certain aspects that are reflected in a particular assessment might come to be emphasized less or not at all. In addition, new aspects may be introduced that could not possibly have been included in an earlier assessment. Presumably, these sorts of changes in curricular emphasis have been behind the frequent changes that have occurred in main NAEP, which often have made it difficult to measure even short-term trends with main NAEP.

Goldstein (1983) concluded that it is difficult to separate changes in particular exercises from changes in the proficiency being measured. He reasoned that, if certain exercises become easier over time and other exercises more difficult (which is likely to be the case with almost any assessment over a long enough period), measuring absolute trends in achievement might not be useful. Due to these difficulties, Goldstein concluded that, over time, focusing on relative comparisons would be more useful than focusing on absolute comparisons. For example, the differences between males and females in science achievement might be examined to ascertain if the gap is narrowing. Such a comparison could be made, even if the assessments given at different times are not directly comparable in their content.

Despite the concerns discussed by Goldstein, NAEP has continued to track what he refers to as absolute trends in achievement. Jones (1996:20) concluded that "the primary worth of NAEP has been as a monitor of changes in achievement for the nation." To maintain trend lines with long-term trend NAEP, the exercises have remained the same. However, for each assessment, analyses are conducted to ascertain whether the exercises are functioning in the same way as in previous assessments. Exercises are excluded from long-term trend assessments for reasons that include being very difficult, having poor fit to the IRT model, and showing large changes in parameter estimates from previous assessments (Allen et al., 1996). Although these procedures can help maintain trend lines, it can become difficult to separate actual changes in proficiency from changes in the functioning of particular exercises. Also, as stated previously, curricula might change so much that the relevance of the long-term trend assessment to current curricula becomes questionable. For these reasons, some changes in the long-term trend assessments are inevitable if the assessments are to provide educationally relevant information.

One other concern about long-term trend NAEP is that it does not take into account recent advances in data analysis procedures, such as the extensive use of conditioning variables and updated subgroup definitions. To maintain stability, long-term trend NAEP continues to use procedures developed in the 1980s. Zwick (1992:206) asked, "How can NAEP maintain continuity while staying current?" As suggested in this section, addressing Zwick's question should take into account the content of the assessments, the operational procedures for administering the assessments, and the societal context in which the assessments are made. This paper now explores alternative designs that might be used.

Design 2: Periodically Update Long-Term Trend NAEP While Maintaining Main NAEP

One possible change in the design of NAEP allows for relatively small modifications in the content of long-term trend NAEP while still maintaining both long-term trend NAEP and the main NAEP. With this design, main NAEP could continue to evolve to reflect curricular trends, unimpeded by the necessity to maintain long-term trends. However, unlike the current design, periodic modest changes are allowed in the content of long-term trend NAEP in an attempt to avoid problems associated with "the relation of item performance to overall proficiency . . . [being] altered because of curricular and societal changes" (Zwick, 1992:208). In this design the current long-term trend NAEP would continue to be used, with small modifications allowed, and the operational conditions of the long-term trend NAEP assessment would remain consistent over time. However, this design allows for replacement of some of the exercises used in the long-term trend NAEP assessment to avoid many of the problems identified by Zwick.

This design for long-term NAEP has many similarities to the designs of other large-scale assessment programs that use alternate forms of assessments for reasons of security. The ACT Assessment (ACT, 1997) and SAT (Donlon, 1984) which are used for college admissions purposes, are among the many assessments that use alternate forms. In these assessments, different exercises are used on each administration. Careful development procedures involving tight specifications are used to ensure that the alternate forms each measure the same constructs in similar ways. Although efforts are made to build alternate forms to be approximately equal in difficulty, equating procedures are used to adjust for the small differences in difficulty that are present (Kolen and Brennan, 1995). The procedures in these assessment programs are used to ensure that scores on the alternate forms can be used interchangeably regardless of the time at which the examinee is assessed or the particular alternate form that is administered. Used in tandem, the assessment development and equating procedures allow for comparing scores and assessing trends, even when completely different assessment exercises are used at different times. The general concepts of developing alternate forms of an assessment and equating could be used in a new long-term trend NAEP assessment design.

One difference between NAEP and assessments that routinely use equating processes is that NAEP uses a set of booklets, with different students administered different booklets. This type of design is made possible because group-level scores are reported, with no scores being reported to individual examinees. To consider equating processes with NAEP, an alternate form of NAEP assessment is defined as the set of booklets that are administered to examinees in an assessment. Using this idea, assessment specifications for NAEP are defined at the level of the set of booklets. To use an equating process with alternate NAEP forms (i.e., alternate sets of NAEP booklets), content specifications need to be developed and defined at the level of a set of NAEP booklets. Such specifications present the content, skills, and exercise types to be included in sufficient detail to ensure that the alternate NAEP forms measure the same educational constructs in the same way. Statistical specifications need to be developed so that the alternate NAEP forms are of nearly the same difficulty.

An equating process for long-term NAEP could involve randomly assigning students to take old and new assessments. Alternatively, a set of exercises from a previous assessment could be used as part of the new assessment. If used, this set of common exercises fully represents the content of the total assessment so that it serves to link one assessment to the next. By treating sets of NAEP

booklets as alternate forms, the procedures for designing equating studies discussed in Kolen and Brennan (1995) apply.

An equating process could accommodate removing exercises from a long-
term trend NAEP assessment when they become dated or when, as Zwick (1992)
has pointed out, the relationship of exercise performance to overall achievement
changes over time. Also, exercises could be removed if security concerns arise
pertaining to particular exercises on NAEP assessment. An equating process can
tolerate periodic updating of content as long as the updating does not affect the
constructs being measured. For example, with the ACT assessment, "curriculum
study is ongoing . . . . ACT assessment tests are reviewed on a periodic basis"
(ACT, 1997:4). ACT accommodates some changes to the content of the assessments within the context of the process of equating alternate forms.

The measurement of long-term trends in NAEP using an equating process
depends on developing tight assessment specifications that allow for the development of alternate forms of long-term trend NAEP. The specifications should
remain stable over time, with only modest updating of the specifications allowed.
The context in which the common exercises appear needs to be constant from one
assessment to the next, and the operational procedures used for the assessment
need to be preserved from one assessment to the next. In addition, with this
design, sample sizes for minorities should be increased to address the concern
expressed by Barron and Koretz (1996) that assessment of trends for minorities is
not sufficiently precise. One major limitation is that this design cannot directly
accommodate major changes in specifications or frameworks. For example, if
the frameworks for long-term trend NAEP were updated to be much more similar
to those for the current main NAEP, it would not be possible to equate the
resulting long-term trend NAEP to the previous one. In this event, special studies
would be required to link the two assessments if long-term trends were to be
followed from one long-term trend assessment to another.

Design 3: Eliminate Long-Term Trend NAEP and
Use Main NAEP for Trend Assessment

NAEP faces two formidable challenges if long-term trend NAEP is eliminated. First, the existing long-term trend comparisons for NAEP need to be
preserved. As described earlier, main NAEP has evolved substantially and now
is quite different from long-term trend NAEP. A study that links main NAEP to
long-term trend NAEP might be used to preserve trends. Second, if main NAEP
is used to assess trends in NAEP, it needs to be more stable than it has been in the
past. For long-term trends to be preserved when substantial revisions are made to
main NAEP, the revised assessment needs to be linked to the previous ones.
These linking studies are much more challenging to conduct than equating studies
because the assessments differ. In the Mislevy (1992) and Linn (1993) terminology, the processes of projection or statistical moderation would be used in these

linking studies. Suggestions for how the data might be collected to conduct these linkages are described later in this section. The linkages that result from these processes are considerably weaker than equatings because of the substantial differences in the content of the assessments.

The major differences between the current long-term trend NAEP and main NAEP assessments that were described by Barron and Koretz (1996) and summarized earlier in this paper present significant challenges to linking these assessments. Along with differences in content and exercise types, these include differences between the two assessments in operational and analysis procedures. For example, as discussed earlier, the main NAEP assessment uses "derived race," whereas the long-term trend assessment uses "observed race." Barron and Koretz (1996) suggested that differences in subgroup definitions could affect the classification of examinees to subgroups. Another related issue is that main NAEP assesses students at fourth, eighth, and twelfth grades, whereas long-term trend NAEP assesses individuals at ages 9, 13, and 17.

The first step in eliminating long-term trend NAEP using this design is to estimate the effect of subgroup and age/grade definitions on long-term trend NAEP. In a single year, long-term trend NAEP would be conducted using both the current long-term trend NAEP subgroup definitions and the current main NAEP subgroup definitions. Independent examinee samples could be used for this study. This linking study estimates the effect of changes in subgroup definitions on long-term NAEP trends. For example, this study estimates what the long-term trends would have been had "derived race" been used instead of "observed race" with long-term trend NAEP. Similar estimates are made of long-term trends for grade groups instead of for the age groups typically used with long-term trend NAEP.

In a second study, long-term trend NAEP is linked to main NAEP. In the same year as the first study, the main NAEP assessment could be conducted using a group of examinees that is independent of the group used in the long-term trend linking study. This study would be used to adjust for the effects of content differences, differences in exercise types, and differences in administration conditions (e.g., tape-recorded, paced, administrations in long-term trend NAEP as compared to main NAEP conditions that are self-paced).

The results of these studies could be analyzed in two ways. In one main NAEP is placed on the long-term trend NAEP scale, with trends continuing to be reported on the long-term trend NAEP scale. Following this process, main NAEP is reported on two scales: the main NAEP scale to report current NAEP performance and the long-term trend NAEP scale to report long-term trends. The other possibility is to place previous NAEP trend assessments on the current main NAEP scale. This second possibility involves reporting both long-term trends and current proficiency on a single scale, which might cause less confusion in assessment interpretation. This design is summarized in Figure 7-2, with the

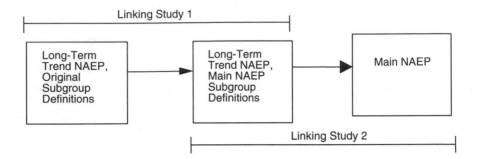

FIGURE 7-2 Studies for linking long-term trend NAEP to main NAEP.

arrows going from left to right to suggest that the long-term trend NAEP is placed on the main NAEP scale.

Even if these studies were conducted, certain conceptual issues need resolution. For example, effects of content differences between the two assessments are estimated using linking study 2. Implicit in this study is an assumption that the effects of content differences estimated in the year the study is conducted also hold for previous years (at least after controlling for year-to-year differences in distributions of examinees within subgroups). It is possible that substantive changes in education that occur between assessment cycles could affect the results of the linking. This assumption could be assessed only by repeating the design over multiple years. A decision needs to be made about whether interest is in estimating subgroup differences on main NAEP or subgroup differences on the previous long-term trend NAEP. If, as implied by Figure 7-2, all NAEP data are reported on the scale of the current main NAEP assessment, the trends are estimated for the current main NAEP assessment. Clearly, estimating such trends entails strong statistical assumptions, since main NAEP was not administered in previous years. As suggested by the results of Barron and Koretz (1996) and the NAEP science data results presented in Figure 7-1 here, the decisions that are made could affect the trends reported for various subgroups.

The analyses associated with these designs are complicated, methodology for analyzing the data and estimating trends needs to be developed, and an extensive research program is required. The research program might be initiated using data that already exist from years in which main NAEP and long-term trend NAEP were administered in the same subject-matter area in the same year. However, only preliminary studies of methodology could be conducted, unless data exist that allow for assessing the effects of changes in subgroup definitions, as would be investigated in linking study 1 of Figure 7-2.

For this design, linking studies 1 and 2 are conducted once. According to NAGB (1996:15), "test frameworks and test specifications developed for the National Assessment generally shall remain stable for at least ten years." When major changes are made, however, a linking study, similar to linking study 2 in Figure 7-2, is needed to link the new main assessment to the previous one. NAGB (1996:15) also stated that "in rare circumstances, such as where significant changes in curricula have occurred, the National Assessment Governing Board may consider making changes to test frameworks and specifications before ten years have elapsed." In such circumstances, linking studies are needed more often than every 10 years.

Linkings such as those described above are much weaker than equatings. Similar linkings have produced useful results in other assessment programs. For example, when ACT revised the ACT assessment in 1989, the new version was linked to the previous one (Brennan, 1989) for the English, mathematics, and composite scores. The linking was used to maintain trend lines and to help colleges update cutscores. However, linking studies require strong statistical assumptions, and it is always possible that the tracking of long-term trends could be disrupted if the assumptions fail to hold. An extensive research program that involves development of methodology and empirical research is needed before NAEP adopts this linking design.

Design 4: Eliminate Long-Term Trend NAEP and Maintain Two Main NAEPs for Trend Assessment

Zwick (1992) discussed maintaining an old and new main NAEP assessment for some time whenever the NAEP was substantially revised. Forsyth et al. (1996) and Glaser et al. (1997) expanded on Zwick's idea and suggested that at least two main assessments be used at a time so as not to lose trends developed with the previous assessment. In the design suggested by Forsyth et al., the different main assessments are linked in some way to help maintain long-term trends, although they did not describe how to conduct the linking. Compared to the previous design that uses a single main NAEP assessment, the use of overlapping assessments with overlapping trends provides some insurance against problems with links. If the linking methodology does not work properly, a few administrations could be used to establish the linkages.

In most other respects, however, this design has the same problems as the previous one. Main NAEP is still linked to long-term trend NAEP. New main assessments are still linked to previous main assessments whenever there is a major change in the assessments. The same sorts of conceptual issues remain, such as the reporting metric for trends, and how to estimate subgroup trends. As with the previous design, an extensive research program is needed to study procedures for conducting the linking. Unlike the previous design, this one requires that multiple assessments be maintained, and it has the potential to create confusion because multiple reporting metrics will be used at any given time.

CONCLUSIONS AND RECOMMENDATIONS

Regardless of which design is used, changes in the context of NAEP continue to threaten any long-term trend NAEP assessment. For example, if NAEP were to become a high-stakes assessment, widespread teaching to NAEP might threaten long-term trend assessment (Zwick, 1992). In a similar vein, Jones (1996:19) expressed concern that, with the adoption of state NAEP, "if NAEP materials were to be used for high-stakes assessment at the level of districts or schools within states, [could] threaten not only the comparability of national and state results with earlier findings, but also the integrity of findings from any current assessment." Jones also expressed concern that measurement of NAEP trends could be made impossible if ways were found to increase student motivation on NAEP. The proposed Voluntary National Test could have similar effects. These sorts of changes in the context of NAEP would directly affect main NAEP, but might not affect a separate long-term trend assessment. Therefore, designs that assess trends using a separate long-term trend NAEP (Designs 1 and 2 presented here) could be more robust to changes in the context of NAEP than are the designs that use main NAEP to assess long-term trends (Designs 3 and 4 presented here).

Two questions were posed in the first section of this paper: How can a single assessment be developed that is stable enough to provide long-term trends while still being flexible enough to adapt to changes in assessment approaches? How can such an assessment be implemented without losing the current long-term trend line? Only two of the four designs discussed address both of these questions: Design 3: eliminate long-term trend NAEP and use main NAEP for trend assessment, and Design 4: eliminate long-term trend NAEP, and maintain two main NAEPs for trend assessment.

Both designs require conducting complex linking studies, making strong statistical assumptions, and being supported by an extensive research program for developing linking procedures that work in the NAEP context. The outcome of this research program is difficult to predict. Possibly, procedures could be developed that allow for linking assessments as different as long-term trend NAEP and main NAEP or as different as new and old main NAEP. However, it is also possible that the results of the research will indicate that changes in main NAEP assessments need to be much more tightly constrained than is presently the case. A research program could begin with existing long-term trend NAEP data and main NAEP data for those years in which the two assessments were administered during the same year in the same subject areas. However, special data collections certainly are needed in the process of developing the necessary linking procedures. Although safer than Design 3 in that trends will not be lost as easily because of the use of overlapping assessments, Design 4 requires that two assessments be maintained.

Another potentially useful alternative is: Design 2: periodically update long-term trend NAEP while maintaining main NAEP. In this design, main NAEP is allowed to change, in small ways, to better reflect current curricula. The design requires that assessment specifications be developed to ensure that the alternate forms of long-term trend NAEP measure the same constructs in similar ways. It improves on current procedures by allowing for the introduction of new exercises but still provides stable estimation of long-term trends. No extensive research program is required to develop and evaluate new linking methodology. Instead, equating designs that have been used extensively in a variety of assessment programs are used to ensure that long-term trends can be maintained. As suggested earlier in this section, this design might be more robust than Designs 3 or 4 to changes in the context of NAEP assessments. For these reasons, even though it does not eliminate the separate long-term trend NAEP and though it requires maintaining the current long-term trend NAEP, Design 2 deserves further consideration.

ACKNOWLEDGMENTS

The author thanks Roderick Little and two anonymous reviewers for their comments on a draft of this paper.

REFERENCES

ACT
  1997   *ACT Assessment Technical Manual.* Iowa City, Iowa: ACT.
Allen, N.L., D.L. Kline, and C.A. Zelenak
  1996   *The NAEP 1994 Technical Report.* Washington, D.C.: National Center for Education Statistics.
Ballator, N.
  1996   *The NAEP Guide*, Revised Edition. Washington, D.C.: National Center for Education Statistics.
Barron, S.I., and D.M. Koretz
  1996   An evaluation of the robustness of the National Assessment of Educational Progress trend estimates for racial ethnic subgroups. *Educational Assessment* 3(3):209-248.
Beaton, A.E., and R. Zwick
  1990   *The Effect of Changes in the National Assessment: Disentangling the NAEP 1985-86 Reading Anomaly.* No. 17-TR-21. Princeton, N.J.: Educational Testing Service.
Brennan, R.L., ed.
  1989   *Methodology Used in Scaling the ACT Assessment and P-ACT+.* Iowa City, Iowa: ACT.
Campbell, J.R., K.E. Voelkl, and P.L. Donahue
  1997   *NAEP 1996 Trends in Academic Progress.* Washington, D.C.: National Center for Education Statistics.
Donlon, T., ed.
  1984   *The College Board Technical Handbook for the Scholastic Aptitude Test and Achievement Tests.* New York: College Entrance Examination Board.

Forsyth, R., R. Hambleton, R. Linn, R. Mislevy, and W. Yen
  1996   *Design Feasibility Team Report to the National Assessment Governing Board.* Washington, D.C.: National Assessment Governing Board.
Glaser, R., R. Linn, and G. Bohrnstedt
  1996   Letter to Roy Truby from the National Academy of Education panel on the evaluation of the NAEP trial state assessment project. February 23.
  1997   *Assessment in Transition: Monitoring the Nation's Educational Progress.* Stanford, Calif.: National Academy of Education.
Goldstein, H.
  1983   Measuring changes in educational attainment over time: Problems and possibilities. *Journal of Educational Measurement* 20(4):369-377.
Jones, L.V.
  1996   A history of the National Assessment of Educational Progress and some questions about its future. *Educational Researcher* 25(7):15-22.
Kolen, M.J., and R.L. Brennan
  1995   *Test Equating: Methods and Practices.* New York: Springer-Verlag.
Koretz, D.M.
  1991   State comparisons using NAEP: Large costs, disappointing benefits. *Educational Researcher* 20(3):19-21.
Linn, R.L.
  1993   Linking results of distinct assessments. *Applied Measurement in Education* 6:83-102.
Mislevy, R.J.
  1992   *Linking Educational Assessments: Concepts, Issues, Methods, and Prospects.* Princeton, N.J.: ETS Policy Information Center.
Mullis, I.V.S.
  1997   Optimizing State NAEP: Issues and Possible Improvements. Report commissioned by the NAEP Validity Studies Panel. American Institutes of Research: Palo Alto, Calif.
National Academy of Education
  1993   *The Trial State Assessment: Prospects and Realities.* Stanford, Calif.: National Academy of Education.
National Assessment Governing Board (NAGB)
  1996   *Policy Statement on Redesigning the National Assessment of Educational Progress.* Washington, D.C.: NAGB.
  1997   *Schedule for the National Assessment of Educational Progress.* Washington, D.C.: NAGB.
National Research Council
  1996   *Evaluation of "Redesigning the National Assessment of Educational Progress."* Committee on Evaluation of National and State Assessments of Educational Progress, Board on Testing and Assessment. Washington, D.C.: National Academy Press.
O'Sullivan, C.Y., C.M. Reese, and J. Mazzeo
  1997   *NAEP 1996 Science Report Card for the Nation and the States.* Washington, D.C.: National Center for Education Statistics.
Phillips, G.W.
  1991   Benefits of state-by-state comparisons. *Educational Researcher* 20(3):17-19.
Rust, K.
  1996   Sampling issues for redesign. Memorandum to Mary Lyn Bourque, NAGB, May 9.
Spencer, B.
  1996   Combining State and National NAEP. Paper prepared for the evaluation of state NAEP conducted by the National Academy of Education.

Zwick, R.
   1991   Effects of item order and context on estimation of NAEP reading proficiency. *Educational Measurement: Issues and Practice* 10:10-16.
   1992   Statistical and psychometric issues in the measurement of educational achievement trends: Examples from the National Assessment of Educational Progress. *Journal of Educational Statistics* 17(2):205-218.

8

Issues in Combining State NAEP and Main NAEP

Michael J. Kolen

Separate data collections are used in the main National Assessment of Educational Progress (NAEP) and the state NAEP. To address concerns that the separate data collections might place too large a burden on the states, this paper examines options for combining main and state NAEP designs. State NAEP is described, and important differences between main NAEP and state NAEP are highlighted. Designs are discussed that have been proposed for merging the two data collections. The focus of these discussions is on how the sample designs interact with operational and measurement concerns. Conclusions and recommendations are presented. Significant administration differences between main NAEP and state NAEP exist, which make combining difficult. These differences currently are addressed by adjusting state NAEP scores. It is argued that even with these adjustments contradictory findings and complications are apparent, especially when making the criterion-referenced interpretations of NAEP scores. The administration differences also make implementation of any of the designs for combining main NAEP and state NAEP questionable. Suggestions are made to consider using the same recruitment and administration conditions for main NAEP and state NAEP. The strengths and weaknesses of various designs for combining main and state NAEP are discussed.

INTRODUCTION

NAEP "is mandated by Congress to survey the educational accomplishments of U.S. students and to monitor changes in those accomplishments" (Ballator, 1996:1). Originally, NAEP surveyed educational accomplishments and long-term trends with a single assessment. Because of continual changes in the assessments, NAEP has evolved into a collection of state and national assessments. Main NAEP is designed to be flexible enough to adapt to changes in assessment approaches. Long-term trend NAEP is intentionally constructed and administered to be stable so that trends in student performance can be examined over time. Whereas main NAEP and long-term trend NAEP focus on assessing achievement for the nation and for various subgroups of students, state NAEP, which is the most recent addition to NAEP, focuses on achievement of students by state.

The National Assessment Governing Board (NAGB) oversees policy for the NAEP program and has called for NAEP to be redesigned (NAGB, 1996). NAGB has expressed concern about the burden placed on states involved in having separate state NAEP and main NAEP data collections. To address this concern, NAGB (1996:7) has stated that, "where possible, changes in national and state sampling procedures shall be made that will reduce [the] burden on states, increase efficiency, and save costs." As part of its evaluation of NAEP, the National Research Council commissioned this paper to examine options for combining main and state NAEP designs.

This paper starts by describing state NAEP and highlighting important differences between main NAEP and state NAEP. A discussion follows of designs that have been proposed for merging the two data collections—either by first selecting a national sample and then building state samples or by selecting state samples and then determining which subset of those data could serve as the national sample. The focus of these discussions is on how the sample designs interact with operational and measurement concerns. Finally, conclusions and recommendations are presented.

COMPARISON OF MAIN NAEP AND STATE NAEP

The main NAEP and long-term trend NAEP assessments were not designed to produce state-level data. To explore the possibility of NAEP providing data at the state level, in 1990, 1992, and 1994 voluntary *trial state* NAEP assessments were conducted that produced state-level data to compare states to one another and to the nation as a whole. These assessments were considered to be trial assessments because of concerns about their usefulness. Potential benefits of state-level NAEP data are summarized by Phillips (1991) and potential problems by Koretz (1991) and Jones (1996). The National Academy of Education Panel (1993) that evaluated trial state NAEP recommended that it be continued but with ongoing evaluation and congressional oversight. In 1996 the term trial was removed from the title, and the assessments are now referred to as state NAEP. Recently, others have discussed issues in combining state NAEP and main NAEP, including Forsyth et al. (1996), Glaser et al. (1997), Mullis (1997), Rust (1996), Rust and Shaffer (1997), and Spencer (1996).

Content of the Assessments

The state NAEP and main NAEP assessment administrations since 1986 and those planned through 2008 are listed in Table 8-1. The table indicates that, although main NAEP typically is administered in grades 4, 8, and 12, state NAEP typically is administered only in grades 4 and 8. In addition, main NAEP is administered in more subject-matter areas. The subject areas for the early state NAEP assessments were only loosely related to those for main NAEP. However, beginning in 1996 and in future plans, state NAEP mathematics and science assessments are to be given in the same years as the main NAEP mathematics and science assessments. A similar statement can be made about the reading and writing assessments.

TABLE 8-1 Main NAEP and State NAEP Assessments by Year Since 1986[a]

Year	Main NAEP (grades 4, 8, and 12 except where noted)	State (or Trial State) NAEP
1986	Reading. Mathematics, Science, Computer Competence	
1988	Reading, Writing, Civics, U.S. History	
1990	Reading, Mathematics, Science	Mathematics (grade 8)
1992	Reading, Writing, Mathematics	Mathematics (grades 4 and 8), Reading (grade 4)
1994	Reading, U.S. History, Geography	Reading (grade 4)
1996	Mathematics, Science	Mathematics (grades 4 and 8), Science (grade 8)
1997	Arts (grade 8)	
1998	Reading, Writing, Civics	Reading (grades 4 and 8), Writing (grade 8)
1999		
2000	Mathematics, Science	Mathematics (grades 4 and 8), Science (grades 4 and 8)
2001	U.S. History, Geography	
2002	Reading, Writing	Reading (grades 4 and 8), Writing (grades 4 and 8)
2003	Civics, Foreign Language (grade 12 only)	
2004	Mathematics, Science	Mathematics (grades 4 and 8), Science (grades 4 and 8)
2005	World History, Economics	
2006	Reading, Writing	Reading (grades 4 and 8), Writing (grades 4 and 8)
2007	Arts	
2008	Mathematics, Science	Mathematics (grades 4 and 8), Science (grades 4 and 8)

[a]Assessments administered from 1986 to 1994 are adapted from Allen et al. (1996); small special-interest assessments are not shown. Assessments administered from 1996 to 2008 are from National Assessment Governing Board (1997). Future assessments reflect plans.

In recent state NAEP assessments (Allen and Mazzeo, 1997; Allen et al., 1997) the assessment exercises used in state NAEP have been identical to ones used in main NAEP. In addition, the scores from state NAEP have been reported on the NAEP proficiency scale.

Administration Procedures

State NAEP and main NAEP differ in administration procedures. According to Allen et al. (1997:13):

> The state assessments differed from the national assessment in one important regard: Westat [NAEP contractor] staff collected the data for the national assessment while, in accordance with the NAEP legislation, data collection activities for the state assessment were the responsibility of each participating jurisdiction. These activities included ensuring the participation of selected schools and students, assessing students according to standardized procedures, and observing procedures for test security.

Linking State NAEP to Main NAEP

Recognizing that these differences in administration procedures might cause differences in assessment results, linking studies have been conducted by the National Center for Education Statistics (NCES) and its contractors to estimate the effects of administration differences and to adjust scale scores for any effects that exist. The rationale for these studies has been described by Yamamoto and Mazzeo (1992:168) and is summarized here:

> Because the assessment instruments for [trial state NAEP and main NAEP] were identical, one of the common-item approaches to linking the scales might have been considered. However, the rationale for such an approach is based on an assumption that the item response functions for the . . . items were the same under the [trial state NAEP and main NAEP] . . . test administration conditions. The aforementioned considerations [differences in administration conditions], as well as data from the assessment itself, suggest otherwise.

Thus, although the same items are used in state NAEP and main NAEP, concerns about the effects of differences in administration procedures led to the decision to independently scale the two assessments.

Linking studies that have been conducted use a common person design, in which a sample of examinees from main NAEP is matched to the state NAEP sample. These linking studies have not only estimated the size of the effects of differences in administration conditions but also attempted to adjust for them. Allen et al. (1997:16) described the linking study for the 1996 state assessment in mathematics, which is typical of these linking studies, as follows:

The results from the state assessment program were linked to those from the national assessment through linking functions determined by comparing the results for the aggregate of all fourth- and eighth-grade public-school students assessed in the state assessment with the results for public-school students of the matching grade within a subsample (the National Linking sample) of the national NAEP sample. The National Linking sample for a given grade is a representative sample of the population of all grade-eligible public-school students within the aggregate of the 45 participating states and the District of Columbia (excluding Guam and the two DoDEA jurisdictions). Specifically, the grade 4 National Linking sample consists of all fourth-grade students in public schools in the states and the District of Columbia who were assessed in the national mathematics assessment. The grade 8 National Linking sample is equivalently defined for eighth-grade students who participated in the national assessment. . . . Each mathematics content strand scale was linked by matching the mean and standard deviation of the scale score averages across all fourth- or eighth-grade students in the matching grade National Linking sample.

Thus, the linking sample for main NAEP is a subset of main NAEP that is matched as closely as possible with the state samples. Such linking studies appear to have been successful in adjusting for administration differences to the extent that the distribution of scale scores for the matched sample for state NAEP was found to be acceptably close to the distribution of scale scores for the main NAEP matched sample (see, e.g., Allen and Mazzeo, 1997, and Allen et al., 1997).

Magnitude of the Effects of Administration Differences

Because the main and state NAEP assessments used exactly the same exercises, the effects of the different administration procedures can be investigated directly by comparing the proportion correct on items from the two matched samples. If there were no administration differences between the two assessments, the proportion correct, apart from sampling error, for each item and on average, over all items, would be the same for the two assessments. However, when these linking studies have been conducted, it has been found repeatedly that the average proportion correct on state NAEP tends to be higher than the average proportion correct on main NAEP for the matched samples. This finding suggests that, on average, students can be expected to correctly answer more items when an assessment is administered under state NAEP administration procedures than when an assessment with identical questions is administered under main NAEP administration conditions. Yamamoto and Mazzeo (1992) reported that for the matched samples in the 1990 trial state assessment in mathematics the average proportion correct was .02 higher on the trial state NAEP than on the main NAEP assessment. In another example, based on linking studies for the NAEP reading assessment, Spencer (1996) reported nearly a .01 difference in average proportion correct in 1992 and a difference of .03 in 1994.

Administration Differences Responsible
for Differences in Assessment Results

Results of the linking studies indicate that some aspects of the differences in administration of the two assessments are resulting in systematic differences in the average proportion correct on the two assessments. Hartka and McLaughlin (1993) identified motivational differences as one possible explanation and speculated that:

> One condition that might lead to higher scores on the TSA [trial state NAEP] is higher motivation among students. In the TSA, quality control monitors recorded instances of local school personnel giving students incentives to participate. . . . Another possibility is that different personnel administering the assessments (Westat staff for national [main] NAEP and local school personnel for the TSA) created different climates in the schools and that this contributed to the difference in performance between the national and TSA samples.

Spencer (1996) reported that there may be differences in participation rates for the two assessments. He presented data for the 1994 trial state assessment indicating that the overall percentage of sampled schools that participated was lower than for main NAEP in 1994. For this assessment the percentage of students participating in school was higher for the trial state NAEP than for main NAEP. Hartka and McLaughlin (1993) found differences in some of the background characteristics of students participating in state NAEP and main NAEP. Although many possible reasons for the differences might exist, Spencer pointed out that it can be difficult to assess the importance of each aspect of these administration differences.

Implications of Differences for Score Interpretation

Apparently, the linking studies that adjust for differences in administration conditions have the following as their goal: the scale scores reported for a particular state should reflect the scale scores that state would have received had the state assessment been administered under the conditions used to administer the main NAEP assessment. Various assumptions are implicit in conducting these linking studies, and a single set of linking constants is applied for all jurisdictions. This procedure seems sensible insofar as administration differences between main NAEP and state NAEP are the same from state to state. However, it seems likely that administration conditions differ across states. If so, the assessments would be more accurate for some states than for others. The overall adjustment would be unable to correct for these differences in accuracy.

Consider the following hypothetical illustration. States 1 and 2 have the same mean scale scores as the nation if the assessment is administered under main NAEP administration conditions. This common average scale score is 270, and the average percentage of the exercises correct is 60 percent for the two states and the nation. When state NAEP is actually administered, state 1 carefully follows the prescribed administration conditions, and the average percentage of the exercises correct for state 1 is 60 percent. State 2 is not so careful in following the administration procedures, and its average percentage of the exercises correct is 64 percent. Also, over all states the average percentage of items correct in state NAEP is 62 percent.

State NAEP is then linked to main NAEP. Based on this study, a state with an average percentage of items correct in state NAEP of 62 percent will have an average scale score of 270. Following this linking study, state 1 earns an average scale score of below 270, which is below the average for the nation and below the average for state 2. State 2 earns an average scale score above 270, which is above the average for the nation and above the average for state 1. In effect, state 1 has been penalized for carefully following the administration procedures. State 2 has been rewarded for not taking as much care. This sort of situation, while presented in a hypothetical example, is bound to occur if there is variation across states in the effects of administration procedures on NAEP performance. An overall adjustment, like the one currently applied, is unable to remove these sorts of inequities that are a result of administration differences from one state to another.

The conditions that require a study for linking state NAEP to main NAEP can also lead to apparent contradictions in statistics that are reported with state NAEP. These contradictions are apparent when comparing the states to the nation on statistics that are based on percentages of items correct. Table 8-2 presents scale scores and percentages correct for the nation and for various states for the 1992 NAEP trial state assessment in mathematics for eighth grade. Statistics are presented for the nation and for the states of New York, Delaware, and Arizona. Scale scores are presented in the top portion of the table. New York has the same average overall scale score as the nation; the average overall scale score for Arizona is slightly below that for the nation; and the average overall scale score for Delaware is four points below that for the nation. Comparisons of the five subscales lead to similar conclusions about how the states compare to the nation. These scale score averages incorporate the adjustments from the study that linked state NAEP to the main NAEP scale.

Average percentages correct over multiple-choice and constructed-response items are given in the bottom portion of the table. On average, New York correctly answered 2 percent more of the items than were answered correctly in the nation. Thus, based on the bottom portion of the table, New York appears to be higher performing than the nation. Although Delaware performed more poorly than the nation based on scale scores, the state performed similarly based on average percentage correct. Some contradictory conclusions result from inspection of this table. Arizona is below the national average on scale scores but is, on average, able to answer more items correctly than answered in the nation. New York is at the national average based on scale scores but above the national

TABLE 8-2 Main NAEP and State NAEP Mean Scale Scores and Average Percentage Correct for the Nation and Three States in the 1992 State and Main NAEP Mathematics Assessments

Index	Nation	New York	Arizona	Delaware
Scale Score				
Overall	266	266	265	262
Numbers and operations	270	270	269	267
Measurement	264	262	264	258
Geometry	262	261	260	257
Data analysis, statistics, and probability	267	268	265	262
Algebra and functions	266	265	264	263
Percentage Correct (Multiple-Choice and Constructed-Response)				
Overall	54	56	55	54
Numbers and operations	62	64	63	62
Measurement	51	52	52	50
Geometry	52	54	53	52
Data analysis, statistics, and probability	48	51	48	48
Algebra and functions	51	53	51	50

Source: National Center for Education Statistics (1993:43, 126, 341).

average based on percentage correct. Delaware is below the national average on scale scores but at the national average based on percentage correct.

In National Center for Education Statistics (1993:46), of the 44 jurisdictions shown, 50 percent are above the national average in scale score. However, for these 44 jurisdictions, over 61 percent are above the national average based on percentage correct. These contradictions arise because scale score statistics reported for states are adjusted for administration differences, whereas percentage-correct scores are not adjusted. Such contradictions and other related issues that result from the need to conduct linking studies are particularly troublesome in the more criterion-referenced uses of NAEP. One of the related issues is that IRT (item response theory) parameter estimates for a given item could differ considerably from the main NAEP to the state NAEP assessment.

Implications of Differences for Item Maps and Achievement Levels

Item maps and achievement levels are two of the procedures used to help policy makers and the public better understand NAEP results. In item maps, various scale score levels are chosen and items found that discriminate between pairs of adjacent levels. The following example, based on the 1996 NAEP mathematics assessment, is taken from Reese et al. (1997:9):

> To better illustrate the NAEP mathematics scale, questions from the assessment are mapped onto the 0-to-500 scale at each grade level. These item maps are

visual representations that compare questions with ability, and they indicate which questions a student can likely solve at a given performance level as measured on the NAEP scale. . . . As an example of how to interpret the item maps, consider a multiple-choice question that requires students to identify cylindrical shapes and maps at a scale score of 208 for grade 4. . . . Mapping a question at a score of 208 implies that students performing at or above this level on the NAEP mathematics scale have a 74 percent or greater chance of correctly answering this particular question. Students performing at a level lower than 208 would have less than a 74 percent chance of correctly answering the question. . . . As another example, consider a constructed-response question that requires students to partition the area of a rectangle and maps at a score of 272 for grade 8. . . . Scoring of this response allows for partial credit by using a four-point scoring guide. Mapping a question at a score of 272 implies that students performing at or above this level have a 65 percent or greater chance of receiving a score of 3 (Satisfactory) or 4 (Complete) on the question. Students performing at a level lower than 272 would have less than a 65 percent chance of receiving such a score.

Reese et al. (1997:9, fn. 6) go on to say that:

> For constructed-response questions a criterion of 65 percent was used. For multiple-choice questions with four or five alternatives, the criteria were 74 and 72 percent, respectively. The use of a higher criteria for multiple-choice questions reflected students' ability to "guess" the correct answer from among the alternatives.

Main NAEP data are used to construct the item maps. Recall that students tend to score higher when using state NAEP administration than when using main NAEP administration conditions. So on state NAEP students at a particular ability would tend to have a greater chance of correctly answering particular multiple-choice items and a greater chance of receiving higher scores on constructed-response items than the item maps would imply. Alternatively, if the item maps had been constructed using state NAEP data, the items would have tended to have been mapped at a higher score level than they were mapped using main NAEP data.

Also, the parameter estimates for individual items on state NAEP differ from those on main NAEP. Therefore, if the item maps had been constructed using state NAEP item parameter estimates instead of main NAEP parameter estimates, the item mapping for particular items could differ considerably, possibly in either direction.

Achievement levels are another means used to enhance the interpretability of NAEP results. As stated in Reese et al. (1997:42), a judgmental process is used to set achievement levels:

> The result of the achievement level-setting process is a set of achievement level descriptions and a set of achievement level cutpoints on the 500-point NAEP scale. The cutpoints are minimum scores that define *Basic, Proficient,* and

Advanced performance at grades 4, 8, and 12. . . . . The results are based on the judgments of panels, approved by NAGB, of what *Basic*, *Proficient*, and *Advanced* students should know and be able to do in mathematics, as well as on their judgments regarding what percent of students at the borderline for each level should answer each question correctly. The latter information is used in translating the achievement level descriptions into cutpoints on the NAEP scale.

As with the item maps, achievement levels are set using main NAEP data. It is likely that somewhat different achievement descriptions and cutpoints would emerge from the achievement-level-setting process if state NAEP data were used instead of main NAEP data.

For score-reporting purposes, the percentage of examinees in a state who are reported to score at or above a particular achievement level are based on score distributions that have been adjusted in the study in which state NAEP was linked to main NAEP. To the extent that students earn higher scores on state NAEP than on main NAEP, the effect of this adjustment is to lower the percentages at or above each cutpoint for state NAEP. That is, on state NAEP there is a tendency for a greater proportion of students to score at or above each achievement level than the proportions reported in the state NAEP program.

To handle the effects on reported scores of the administration differences between state NAEP and main NAEP, a decision was made to adjust the state NAEP scores. While understandable and possibly the best decision given the circumstances, this decision can lead to potential misinterpretations and inaccuracies in interpreting scores from state NAEP. These problems seem most serious when attempting to make criterion-referenced interpretations of scores, such as those made with item maps and achievement levels.

DESIGNS FOR COMBINING STATE AND MAIN NAEP SAMPLES

In this section, issues in developing designs for combining state and main NAEP samples are discussed. Currently, sampling, administration, and analysis (other than the study used to adjust for administration differences) are done separately for state and main NAEP. Rust (1996) suggested three general approaches to combining state and main NAEP. In one approach the sampling and administration continue to be separate, but the analyses are based on pooled data. In another approach a national sample is drawn and supplemented as necessary to obtain an adequate state sample. Finally, samples are drawn from each state and supplemented as necessary to obtain an adequate national sample. Specific proposals presented by Rust and Shaffer (1997) and Spencer (1996) for implementing these general approaches are discussed here.

This discussion of sampling procedures relies heavily on work by sampling statisticians, including Rust (1996), Rust and Johnson (1992), Rust and Shaffer (1997), and Spencer (1996). The designs suggested in these papers are reviewed here. The designs are summarized and how they interact with various administrative and measurement issues is evaluated. The focus is on practical design issues; there is no intent to provide a sampling statistician's perspective on these issues.

Independent samples of schools are used in main and state NAEP, and different designs currently are used for selecting samples in the two programs. Efforts are made to ensure that no one school is included in both samples. In addition, as is discussed, the sampling designs used in the two programs have important differences.

In the schedule for future assessments, as shown in Table 8-1, more subject areas and more grades will be included in main NAEP than state NAEP. However, in the future main and state NAEP will assess grade 4 and grade 8 mathematics and science in the same years (e.g., 2000, 2004, and 2008) and grade 4 and grade 8 reading and writing in the same years (e.g., 2002 and 2006). The following discussion of combining the state and main NAEP samples pertains only to these combinations of grade, test, and year.

As stated by Rust and Johnson (1992:127), "the NAEP sampling and weighting procedures are designed to obtain sample data that permit estimates of subpopulation characteristics of reasonably high precision." The precision targets are stated ahead of time, and samples are designed to meet these targets.

Current Design for Main NAEP

The goal of the main NAEP sample design is to adequately represent the population of students in the United States in a particular grade as well as certain subpopulations. According to Rust and Johnson (1992), the main NAEP samples are drawn using a multistage probability sampling design with three stages of selection. The three stages are summarized as follows:

Stage 1. The United States is divided into approximately 1,000 geographical areas. A sample of these geographical areas is selected.

Stage 2. A sample of schools is selected from within the selected geographical areas.

Stage 3. A sample of students is selected from within the selected schools.

According to Rust and Johnson (1992:112), Stage 1 is used "to make feasible the task of recruiting and training staff to administer the tests in a cost effective manner" because the assessments will be given in only a small number of geographical areas (e.g., Rust and Johnson, 1992, reported that in main NAEP in 1990 only 94 of the geographical areas were selected). Stratification and weighting procedures are used to ensure that the sample is representative and that the desired levels of precision are attained. In addition, procedures are used to deal with schools that are selected but decline to participate. Recruiting of schools and test administration are done centrally by a single NAEP contractor. Data analysis for main NAEP is conducted using the national data only.

Current Design for State NAEP

The goal of the state NAEP sample design is to adequately represent the population of students in a given state in a particular grade as well as certain subpopulations. To reduce the burden on schools, efforts are made to ensure that schools chosen for state NAEP are not in main NAEP. The two-stage probability sample used in each state that participates in state NAEP is summarized as follows:

Stage 1. A sample of schools is selected from within the state.
Stage 2. A sample of students is selected from within the selected schools.

Stratification and weighting procedures are used to ensure that the sample is representative and that the desired levels of precision are attained. In addition, procedures are used to deal with schools that are selected but decline to participate. See Rust and Johnson (1992) for more detail. Recruiting of schools and test administration are conducted by personnel in the state.

As indicated earlier, a linking study is used to adjust state NAEP results for differences in administration conditions between state NAEP and main NAEP. Recall that a single set of linking functions is developed and used to adjust the results for all states. Apart from using main NAEP data to estimate linking functions, data analysis for state NAEP is conducted using the state data only. Some possibilities for combining the main and state NAEP sample designs and/or data analyses follow.

Spencer's (1996) Approaches

One way to combine the two assessments, referred to here as *Spencer's Approach 1*, uses the current designs and administration procedures for both assessments and then pools the data during analysis. The potential benefit of using this procedure is that sampling error could be reduced for national and regional statistics by including the state data along with the main NAEP data. In addition, the sampling error for the state statistics could be reduced by using main NAEP data from a state along with the state NAEP data from that state.

However, combining the main and state NAEP data relies heavily on the linking study used to adjust state NAEP scores for differences in administration conditions between main and state NAEP. As Spencer (1996) pointed out, the linking adjustment introduces error, and it would be necessary to ensure that the random error and bias due to linking are negligible; otherwise, this approach could increase error. Spencer also pointed out that there would be some additional costs associated with conducting the analyses, creating new weights, and estimating standard errors. He recommended further study of this possibility.

Spencer considered a second possibility, referred to here as *Spencer's*

Approach 2, intended to save money and increase precision by combining the sampling designs for main and state NAEP into one integrated design. He presented the following possibility: "Select the national sample and see how many schools fall in each state. Then draw an additional sample of schools in each state in state NAEP to meet the target precision for that state" (Spencer, 1996:54). In this design, therefore, the current main NAEP sampling plan is used, but the state plan is modified. For main NAEP, recruiting of schools and test administration are still done centrally by a single NAEP contractor. For the additional schools in each state that are selected, recruiting of schools and test administration are still done by state personnel. Spencer also suggested that, as with Spencer's Approach 1, sampling error for main NAEP might be reduced if data from main NAEP and state NAEP were pooled for main NAEP analyses.

Preliminary analyses conducted by Spencer suggested that Spencer's Approach 2 procedures leads to approximately a 6 percent reduction in the sample size for state NAEP, which results in significant cost savings in test materials, booklet processing, test scoring, and other administration costs. As with Spencer's Approach 1, there are some (relatively small) additional costs associated with conducting the analyses. Note that under this design, to meet target precision for the states, it is necessary to pool data from the state and main NAEP samples. These precision targets could be met only if the random error and bias due to linking are negligible. Spencer recommended that this design be studied further.

Spencer also considered a third possibility, referred to here as *Spencer's Approach 3*, that saves even more money and reduces the sample size for main NAEP. He suggested the following possibility: "Select the state NAEP sample first and then draw a supplemental sample to yield a national sample meeting the target levels of precision overall and for subgroups. These target levels of precision would be met both for the subjects and grades covered and state NAEP and also for those not covered" (Spencer, 1996:55).

Spencer demonstrated that this design leads to substantial savings, beyond those for Spencer's Approach 2. However, he pointed out that implementing this possibility requires that "decisions about what states will participate in state NAEP and what subjects will be covered must be made before combined NAEP can be designed. . . . Success would seem unlikely" (Spencer, 1996: 55). The concerns regarding linking error in this design are even more severe than they are for Spencer's Approach 2, because for Spencer's Approach 3 it is necessary to pool data from state and main NAEP samples to meet target precision for main NAEP.

Rust and Shaffer's (1997) Sampling Possibilities

Rust and Shaffer (1997) compared three sample designs. The first design, referred to here as *Rust and Shaffer's Approach 1*, involves combining the separate samples that are currently used in main and state NAEP. This design is essentially the same as Spencer's Approach 1. In their second proposed design, referred to here as *Rust and Shaffer's Approach 2*, they moved away from use of the 1,000 geographical areas that are currently used for main NAEP.[1] They proposed using the following procedures:

Stage 1. A sample of schools is selected from within each state that results in precision comparable to current state NAEP.

Stage 2a. Among the selected schools in each state, designate a subset as national schools (with a minimum of two schools per state). Over all states the results from just these schools would result in precision comparable to current national NAEP. The number of national schools selected in this way is comparable to the current number of national schools.

Stage 2b. Among the selected schools, those not designated as national schools are designated as state schools.

Stage 3a. A sample of students is selected from the selected national schools.

Stage 3b. Only if a state agrees to participate, a sample of students is selected from the selected state schools.

Stratification and weighting procedures are used to ensure that the sample is representative and that the desired levels of precision are attained. In addition, procedures are used to deal with schools that are selected but decline to participate. As is currently done, administration by national schools is conducted by an NCES contractor, and state administration is conducted by state staff. In a departure from current procedures, recruitment is done by staff in states participating in state NAEP.[2]

Rust and Shaffer (1997) suggested that the analyses for main NAEP be based on all participating schools (both national and state), although the designed precision could be obtained from national data. State NAEP analyses are based on all

---

[1] Recall that Rust and Johnson (1992:112) indicated that these geographical areas were used as a first stage of sampling to "make feasible the task of recruiting and training staff to administer the tests in a cost effective manner." Rust and Shaffer (1997) did not indicate why it is now possible to move away from the use of geographical areas as a first-stage sampling unit. Note that the use of these geographical areas as a first-stage sampling unit results in more sampling error than if schools were sampled at the first stage (ACT, 1997).

[2] Rust and Shaffer (1997) suggested that this change would enhance participation in main NAEP. However, they did not discuss how this enhanced participation, if it did exist, might affect the comparability of main NAEP scores between current main NAEP and main NAEP after the change in recruitment procedures was made. It seems, however, that who recruits schools is not really an integral part of their design in that the design could be followed with the NCES contractor continuing to recruit schools. Clearly, this issue would require further study before a change in recruitment procedures is made.

participating schools in the state (both national and state) to meet state precision targets. This design has some potential significant benefits. Preliminary analyses conducted by Rust and Shaffer suggested that these procedures lead to an approximate 10 percent reduction in the sample size for state NAEP, compared to current procedures, which leads to significant cost savings. The precision of national statistics is comparable to current precision if the national data are used alone. The national statistics are more precise if the state and national data are pooled for main NAEP. Rust and Shaffer (1997:6-11) also discussed the benefits to recruitment from the "synergism in the recruitment process for state and national components" if states do all of the recruitment.

As with the other designs that involve an integration of main and state NAEP data, a major issue concerning this design is that it requires a linking study to adjust state results for differences in state and national administration conditions. The gain in precision for main NAEP and the state precision targets likely could be achieved only if the random error and bias due to linking are negligible. In addition, this design requires considerable coordination of state and national NAEP.

The final proposed design, referred to here as *Rust and Shaffer's Approach 3*, dropped the requirement of Rust and Shaffer's Approach 2 that the target precision for the national statistics be attainable using only the national data. A major effect of dropping this requirement is to reduce the number of test administrations that are done by the NCES contractor. The stages provided earlier for Rust and Shaffer's Approach 2 would still be followed, except that Stage 2a would be replaced by the following:

Stage 2a. Among the selected schools in each state, designate a subset as national schools (with a minimum of two schools per state). Over all states the results from just these schools do *not* result in precision comparable to current main NAEP. The number of national schools selected in this way is around one-half of the current number of national schools.

As in Rust and Shaffer's Approach 2, stratification and weighting procedures are used to ensure that the sample is representative and that the desired levels of precision are attained; procedures are used to deal with schools that are selected but decline to participate; administration by national schools is conducted by an NCES contractor, whereas state administration is conducted by state staff; all recruitment is conducted by state staff.

Unlike Rust and Shaffer's Approach 2, the analyses for main NAEP to achieve target precision are based on all participating schools (both national and state). Like Rust and Shaffer's Approach 2, state NAEP analyses are based on all participating schools in the state (both national and state) to meet state precision targets.

Preliminary analyses by Rust and Shaffer (1997:6-10) indicated that this design has all the potential benefits of Rust and Shaffer's Approach 2, with the addition that the sample size that requires administration by the NCES administration contractor is reduced and the overall sample size is reduced even further. However, these analyses also indicated that benefits depend heavily on the degree of participation in state NAEP. In addition, this design requires use of the results of the linking study to achieve the desired precision for main NAEP. For these reasons Rust and Shaffer recommended further consideration of Rust and Shaffer's Approach 2 but not Rust and Shaffer's Approach 3 because the former design is "considerably more robust to the vagaries of the outcome of the state participation process."

Rust and Shaffer (1997:6-25) concluded that *Rust and Shaffer's Approach 2* should be considered because "this approach will lead to much more useful data at the national and regional levels. It will enhance participation in centrally administered schools. It will have little impact on cost. The approach is robust to the level of state participation in NAEP."

Discussion and Comparison of the Approaches

Spencer's Approach 1 and Rust and Shaffer's Approach 1 involve no changes in the sample designs. These approaches have the potential to increase precision. The additional costs associated with these approaches involve further analyses, which likely are small compared to the administrative costs. The major potential drawback of either of these approaches is that they rely on there being little random error or bias when adjusting state NAEP results for operational differences between state NAEP and main NAEP. The sources of these operational differences and their degree of stability should be thoroughly understood before these approaches are used.

Spencer's Approach 2 continues to use geographical area as the first stage in a multistage sampling procedure, whereas Rust and Shaffer's Approach 2 eliminates this first stage. This elimination might cause some operational difficulties in that administration of main NAEP would occur in more diverse geographical areas. However, if this first stage is eliminated, fewer schools would need to be sampled for main NAEP, which is true whether or not the samples are combined (ACT, 1997). Thus, if the first stage can be eliminated, at least in this aspect, Rust and Shaffer's Approach 2 seems preferable to Spencer's Approach 2. However, it is unclear why the first stage can be eliminated, whereas it was deemed necessary in the past. This issue needs to be addressed before further consideration of Rust and Shaffer's Approach 2.

A major issue with both Spencer's Approach 2 and Rust and Shaffer's Approach 2 is that both rely heavily on there being little random error or bias in adjusting state NAEP results for operational differences between state NAEP and main NAEP. The sources of these operational differences and their degree of stability should be thoroughly understood before these approaches are used.

Forsyth et al. (1996) also indicated that it will be important to design the approaches so that last-minute withdrawals of states do not affect the main NAEP samples.

Given problems that accrue from the need for the linking study, Forsyth et al. suggested it might be possible to design NAEP so that the same administration conditions are used for main and state versions. In particular, they suggested using local administrators for main NAEP (as well as for state NAEP), with an increase in the monitoring and degree of training of the administrators. If this approach is considered, however, they suggest that the effects of such a change be monitored on participation rates among schools selected for main NAEP in states not participating in state NAEP. In addition, such a significant change in main NAEP could affect comparability of national statistics before and after the change is made.

Combining main and state NAEP sampling has the potential for a modest reduction in the number of schools involved in NAEP. However, much more work is needed to detail and evaluate the approaches before they are implemented. A significant problem in each approach arises from the operational differences between main and state NAEP that cause complications potentially difficult to overcome. Unless the operational procedures for main NAEP and state NAEP can be made much more similar to one another, the potential complications caused by these approaches might lead to severe problems in combining NAEP samples.

CONCLUSIONS

Future plans are for state NAEP to be administered at approximately the same time as main NAEP and for the content of state NAEP to be a subset of the content of main NAEP. These plans suggest that now there might be a greater chance of combining main and state NAEP samples than in the past. However, current plans still result in significant administration differences between main and state NAEP. These differences currently are addressed by adjusting state NAEP scores. Even so, contradictory findings and complications are apparent, especially when making the criterion-referenced interpretations of NAEP scores that seem to be gaining prominence through the use of item maps, achievement levels, and now market basket reporting (Forsyth et al., 1996; National Center for Education Statistics, 1996). The conditions that make the linking studies necessary create confusion when attempting to make criterion-referenced interpretations with state NAEP.

The administration differences also make implementation of any of the designs for combining main and state NAEP questionable. Much more needs to be known about the effects of the administration differences. A starting point for further investigation would be to address the following questions:

Question 1: To what extent are the linking constants equal across states? Differences among states in ability, participation rates, and recruitment procedures should be investigated as variables that might influence linking constants.

Question 2: How large is the random error component in estimating the linking constants?

Question 3: To what extent does bias or systematic error influence the linking constants?

Question 4: To what extent would results from state NAEP be affected if the administration and recruitment conditions for state NAEP were changed to be consistent with those for main NAEP?

Question 5: Do the differences in administration and recruitment conditions affect the constructs that are being measured by the NAEP assessments?

These questions should be thoroughly addressed before any design for combining the state and main NAEP samples is implemented under current recruitment and administration conditions. Note that even after conducting the extensive research that addressing these questions entails, the analyses presented in Spencer (1996) and Rust and Shaffer (1997) suggest that combining the samples for state and main NAEP would result in only a modest decrease in sample size.

Another approach is to use administration and recruitment procedures that are the same for main and state NAEP, such as those suggested by Forsyth et al. (1996). One possibility is to use the centralized administration and recruitment procedures currently used with main NAEP. Using these procedures for both main and state NAEP is optimal from the perspectives of combining samples, of having comparable results for the two assessments, for combining reporting and analyses, and for being able to compare main NAEP results from before and after changes were made in recruitment and administration procedures. Although these procedures might be prohibitive from a cost perspective, they should be thoroughly investigated.

Another possibility suggested by Forsyth et al. is to use the current state administration procedures for main NAEP but possibly with more central oversight and standardization than is currently used with state NAEP. This type of change in recruitment and administration procedures would require a study to link main NAEP under these new administration conditions to main NAEP under the previous administration conditions. Conducting this study could be costly and difficult to implement.

If the issues regarding linking and administration conditions are addressed sufficiently, Spencer's Approach 2 and Rust and Shaffer's Approach 2 would be good places to start in developing a combined sampling plan. Spencer's Approach 2 might be preferable if the first-stage sampling is by geographical area. Rust and Shaffer's Approach 2 might be preferable if, from an operational perspective, this first stage is unnecessary.

ACKNOWLEDGMENTS

The author thanks Karen Mitchell and two anonymous reviewers for comments on a draft of this paper.

REFERENCES

ACT
  1997 *ACT's NAEP Redesign Project: Assessment Design Is the Key to Useful and Stable Assessment Results.* Final Report. Iowa City, Iowa: ACT.
Allen, N.L., and J. Mazzeo
  1997 *Technical Report of the NAEP 1996 State Assessment Program in Science.* Washington, D.C.: National Center for Education Statistics.
Allen, N.L., D.L. Kline, and C.A. Zelenak
  1996 *The NAEP 1994 Technical Report.* Washington, D.C.: National Center for Education Statistics.
Allen, N.L., F. Jenkins, E. Kulick, and C.A. Zelenak
  1997 *Technical Report of the NAEP 1996 State Assessment Program in Mathematics.* Washington, D.C.: National Center for Education Statistics.
Ballator, N.
  1996 *The NAEP Guide*, Revised Edition. Washington, D.C.: National Center for Education Statistics.
Forsyth, R., R. Hambleton, R. Linn, R. Mislevy, and W. Yen
  1996 *Design Feasibility Team Report to the National Assessment Governing Board.* Washington, D.C.: National Assessment Governing Board.
Glaser, R., R. Linn, and G. Bohrnstedt
  1997 *Assessment in Transition: Monitoring the Nation's Educational Progress.* Stanford, Calif.: National Academy of Education.
Hartka, E., and D.H. McLaughlin
  1993 *A Study of the Administration of the 1992 National Assessment of Educational Progress Trial State Assessment Program.* Palo Alto, Calif.: American Institutes for Research.
Jones, L.V.
  1996 A history of the National Assessment of Educational Progress and some questions about its future. *Educational Researcher* 25(7):15-22.
Koretz, D.M.
  1991 State comparisons using NAEP: Large costs, disappointing benefits. *Educational Researcher* 20(3):19-21.
Mullis, I.V.S.
  1997 Optimizing State NAEP: Issues and Possible Improvements. Paper commissioned by the NAEP Validity Studies Panel.
National Academy of Education
  1993 *The Trial State Assessment: Prospects and Realities.* Stanford, Calif.: National Academy of Education.
National Assessment Governing Board (NAGB)
  1996 *Policy Statement on Redesigning the National Assessment of Educational Progress.* Washington, D.C.: NAGB.
  1997 *Schedule for the National Assessment of Educational Progress.* Washington, D.C.: NAGB.
National Center for Education Statistics
  1993 *Data Compendium for the NAEP 1992 Mathematics Assessment of the Nation and the States.* Washington, D.C.: National Center for Education Statistics.

1996   *An Operational Vision for NAEP—Year 2000 and Beyond.* Washington, D.C.: National
         Center for Education Statistics.
Phillips, G.W.
1991   Benefits of state-by-state comparisons. *Educational Researcher* 20(3):17-19.
Reese, C.M., K.E. Miller, J. Mazzeo, and J.A. Dossey
1997   *NAEP 1996 Mathematics Report Card for the Nation and the States.* Washington, D.C.:
         National Center for Education Statistics.
Rust, K.F.
1996   Sampling Issues for Redesign. Memorandum to Mary Lyn Bourque, NAGB, May 9.
Rust, K.F., and E.G. Johnson
1992   Sampling and weighting in the national assessment. *Journal of Educational Statistics*
         17(2):111-129.
Rust, K.F., and J.P. Shaffer
1997   Sampling. In *NAEP Reconfigured: An Integrated Redesign of the National Assessment
         of Educational Progress*, E.G. Johnson, S. Lazer, and C.Y. O'Sullivan, eds. Working
         Paper No. 97-31. Washington, D.C.: National Center for Education Statistics.
Spencer, B.
1996   Combining State and National NAEP. Paper prepared for the evaluation of state NAEP
         conducted by the National Academy of Education.
Yamamoto, K., and J. Mazzeo
1992   Item response theory linking in NAEP. *Journal of Educational Statistics* 17:155-173.

9

Difficulties Associated with Secondary Analysis of NAEP Data

Sheila Barron

The National Assessment of Educational Progress (NAEP) has tracked academic achievement for over a quarter of a century, providing some of the best data available on the academic performance of students in America's schools. NAEP began as a relatively simple assessment of student achievement that reported the percentage of students who could correctly answer individual questions. It has evolved into a set of complex assessment systems designed to serve a variety of purposes.

One purpose of NAEP is to provide a rich database that can be used by secondary analysts to address important educational issues. There are a number of challenges associated with this function of NAEP. First, the research questions of interest are not set out in advance of the development of the assessments and accompanying questionnaires. Thus, the developers of NAEP must try to anticipate what data will be most useful to secondary analysts and the level of precision needed. Second, providing data for secondary analysis is only one function of NAEP. Thus, the developers of NAEP must try to balance the anticipated needs of secondary analysts with other, sometimes competing, NAEP functions. Third, the data must be provided to researchers in a useable form along with adequate documentation and support.

NAEP data are used by researchers with varied backgrounds and interests. Content-area specialists, sociologists, economists, and psychometricians have all wanted to use NAEP to answer important questions in their respective fields. The data each of these groups would like NAEP to provide differ, sometimes dramatically. Their knowledge of measurement issues important in understanding the NAEP data also varies considerably as well as their background in statistical analysis and their ability to use large and complex databases. Thus, it is clear that the challenges to developers of NAEP are considerable.

Those responsible for the NAEP assessments have tried to meet these challenges by listening to the concerns of secondary analysts and, when possible, making changes to the questionnaires and assessments, the means by which the data are provided, and the NAEP documentation. In addition, they have developed training and special materials for helping researchers use NAEP data. Despite these considerable efforts, researchers continue to have significant problems conducting secondary analyses of NAEP data.

This paper addresses the difficulties that researchers encounter when they attempt to use NAEP data and the means by which the National Center for Education Statistics (NCES) and the Educational Testing Service (ETS) have tried, and are trying, to improve the usability of the data. The problems of secondary analysts who use secure NAEP data as well as researchers who use other NAEP data (e.g., published statistics, public release data) were of interest. The information presented in this paper was collected through informal interviews with a number of NAEP secondary analysts as well as a number of staff members at NCES and ETS. This paper provides an overview of the potential difficulties one may encounter when using NAEP data and makes recommendations for improving the usability of NAEP data for secondary analysis in the future.

LITERATURE REVIEW

Although this is a topic researchers involved with NAEP talk—and commiserate—about often, very little has been written about the difficulties secondary analysts confront. Kenney and Silver (1996) discuss lessons they learned as content experts working with NAEP data. They concluded that the way in which NAEP findings are organized and reported may discourage researchers from using the data—specifically, researchers who know little about the complex structure of the assessment but who are experts in curriculum and pedagogy. In addition, they found that the actual student responses to the extended constructed-response questions, a potentially rich source of information, were useable only by investing amounts of time and money that would be prohibitive to most researchers.

Although few articles have been written that specifically address the difficulties of using NAEP data, information about these difficulties can occasionally be found in papers in which analyses of NAEP data are reported. Lee et al. (1997) used NAEP data to look at the effect of high school course offerings on equity and student achievement. They included a candid summary of the difficulties they encountered using NAEP data. Specifically, they did not find many of the relationships between background variables and student achievement that are routinely observed in data on student achievement. They concluded that the outcome variable of interest in their study—students' mathematics achievement—was flawed in that particular iteration of the NAEP survey because of the conditioning model used to scale the data. However, this was not initially apparent, and Lee et al. reached this conclusion only after poring over detailed technical documentation of the NAEP scaling procedures.

OVERVIEW OF NAEP

NAEP is not a single assessment but a system of assessments. The main NAEP assesses students in a small number of subjects approximately every two years. The contents of the various assessments reflect current thinking about what students should know and be able to do. Samples of students in grades 4, 8, and 12 from across the country are tested using both multiple-choice and constructed-response questions. In a given subject area, not all students respond to the same set of questions. A large number of test booklets are constructed in which test questions are grouped into blocks and blocks are assembled into booklets. The main NAEP assessment is divided into a national administration and a state-level administration. In the state-level administration, students are sampled from participating states at rates that allow for accurate estimates of the distribution of proficiency at the state level.

The long-term trend NAEP assesses students in reading, mathematics, science, and writing approximately every two years. The content of the assessment has been the same since the mid-1980s. Samples of students ages 9, 13, and 17 from across the country are tested using primarily multiple-choice questions in all subjects except writing. As in the main NAEP, in a given subject area, not all students respond to the same set of questions. However, the structure of the trend NAEP is less purposeful than that of the main NAEP. The trend NAEP came into being after problems resulted from trying to link the 1986 assessment in reading to the 1984 assessment. The anomalous results were concluded to be due to changes in the measurement conditions (i.e., timing and item order) across the two assessments (Beaton and Zwick, 1990). The decision was made to create a trend assessment in which consistency over time was rigidly maintained. A small number of booklets from the 1984 or 1986 administration (depending on the subject area) were chosen for use in the trend assessment, and these booklets have been used in all subsequent administrations of the trend assessment.

Scaling and reporting of the data are similar for both sets of assessments. Item response theory (IRT) procedures are used to estimate item characteristics (e.g., difficulty, discrimination). The resulting item parameter estimates are used along with the item responses and background information collected on the examinees to estimate the distribution of student proficiency. Because it is the distribution of student proficiency that is of interest rather than estimates of proficiency for individuals, individual scaled scores are not generated. Rather, five plausible values are generated that are based on the distribution of possible scaled scores for the individual.

NAEP periodically reports the results of its main, state, and trend assessments. The primary results that are presented are averages for the population as a whole and for important subgroups (i.e., Hispanics) as well as the percentage of students reaching various performance standards. In addition to asking students to respond to test questions, students are asked a number of background questions. Data are also collected on schools and teachers.

METHODS

This paper has three objectives: (1) to outline the difficulties secondary analysts have in using NAEP data; (2) to discuss the means by which NCES and ETS have attempted to address these problems; and (3) to develop recommendations for improving the usability of NAEP data.

To outline the difficulties that secondary analysts have using the data, interviews were conducted (either by phone or e-mail) with researchers who have conducted secondary analyses of NAEP data or who have received training on secondary analysis of NAEP data but have not used the data outside the training. The pool of potential interviewees came from a number of sources: a list of members of the American Educational Research Association's (AERA) Special Interest Group on Research Using NAEP Data; researchers who have received secondary analysis grants from NCES; a list of attendees at a 1996 NAEP training session sponsored by NCES; first authors of papers involving secondary analysis of NAEP data presented at the 1997 AERA national conference; and referrals from other researchers.

It is difficult to identify the total number of researchers in the pool of potential interviewees because the names provided by these various sources overlapped to a degree. In addition, a small number of the people on these lists were employees or former employees of NAEP contractors, who likely would have greater familiarity with the data than a typical secondary analyst and thus may not have encountered the same problems using the data as the typical secondary analyst. A rough estimate of the number of potential interviewees in the resulting pool is 80 to 90.

Only a subset of the researchers in the pool of potential interviewees were contacted. Time did not permit a full-scale mail survey. In addition, phone numbers or e-mail addresses were not provided for most of the people. A total of 43 researchers were contacted by phone or e-mail and asked to respond to a series of questions about their experiences with NAEP data. Fourteen researchers provided answers to the questions. Some went into great detail about their experiences and the strengths and weaknesses of the NAEP data, whereas others provided more cursory responses. The researchers varied widely in the depth of their experience with NAEP data. Several researchers could be called repeat users, but only two were involved in studies that delved into a number of different issues.

The researchers came from a variety of backgrounds and differed in their research objectives. The largest proportion was interested in using NAEP data to model the effects of various student and school characteristics on student proficiency. Typical of this type of research was a study that sought to explain group differences in performance using information provided in the NAEP background variables. The types of analyses conducted by these researchers were typically regression based. Hierarchical linear modeling (HLM) was mentioned by most researchers. For the most part, these analysts used data from the background variables and the plausible values.

A number of the researchers interviewed for this paper were involved in research that looked at measurement issues. Two researchers were interested in the validity of background variables; two were interested in linking state NAEP data to data from a state testing program; two were interested in the dimensionality of the data; another conducted research looking at the impact of motivation on performance. The data used and the types of analyses conducted by these researchers varied widely.

There were only a couple of researchers who were interested in the content of NAEP in a particular subject area. One was a content expert who was interested in extracting information about what students can do in different areas of mathematics; the other was interested in the content validity of the science assessment. The data of interest to these researchers differed substantially from other researchers. It was not necessary to run any analyses on the data files to obtain the information needed for this research. What was needed was access to the NAEP items and student responses as well as information about item-level performance that could be obtained from the published statistics. In addition to secondary analysts, five researchers who underwent training to use NAEP data but who had not yet done any NAEP analyses were interviewed. These researchers were asked about the training they attended and about why they had not used NAEP data following the training.

In addition to collecting information from secondary analysts, three people who work on NAEP—two from ETS and one from NCES—and are knowledgeable about issues concerning secondary analysis of NAEP data were interviewed. They were asked about training opportunities and other assistance available to secondary analysts as well as other efforts NCES and ETS have made to facilitate NAEP research. Because redesign of NAEP is currently being considered, special attention was given to the implications that possible changes in NAEP could have for secondary analysts. Recommendations were developed based on the comments by secondary analysts and NAEP staff. Some of the recommendations came directly from secondary analysts; others were developed by looking for practical ways to ameliorate the problems that secondary analysts reported.

RESULTS

Overall, NAEP secondary analysts were very positive about the training they attended, special computer programs written to facilitate use of the data, and the helpfulness of ETS and NCES staff. Secondary analysts had positive and negative things to say about NAEP documentation. Comments about getting access to the data and the complexity of the data were largely negative. All but one of the researchers interviewed described at least one problem that he or she encountered when trying to analyze the NAEP data. This researcher said that the NAEP system is very complex and takes a lot of effort to understand. He went on to say that he encountered many challenges with the data but no problems. The median number of problems reported was three, and the maximum was seven.

Discussions with NAEP secondary analysts identified six areas of concern: (1) obtaining the data, (2) timing of the availability of data, (3) complexity of the methodology used in NAEP, (4) form and organization of the data, (5) documentation, and (6) getting help. These six areas are not completely independent— that is, difficulties in one area often impact other areas.

Obtaining NAEP Data from NCES

Researchers who wanted data that are only available on secure data files reported difficulties obtaining data in the first place. NAEP data come in several forms: published reports and data compendiums, public-release data files (for assessments before 1990), and secure data files. To obtain secure NAEP data, a site license is needed. The procedure for obtaining a license can be arduous, especially in large organizations such as universities and state government agencies. For example, one researcher needed the signature of the state attorney general in order to obtain the data at the university where she was a graduate student. This proved especially difficult as it was an election year and the attorney general was busy campaigning.

Several researchers who attended training seminars on NAEP but who had not done any research using the data said that, although the NAEP data are very relevant to their research interests, they have not used the data because of how difficult it is to obtain a site license. One researcher said that the reason his university did not have the data was because the procedure is so complicated and takes an overwhelming amount of paperwork and nobody was willing to get involved in it. The difficulties associated with obtaining a site license stem from concerns the government has that the information provided to researchers about schools and students be used properly and not released to the public. The potential exists when using secure data for a researcher to use information provided about schools to identify individual schools and to use these data to the detriment of the school. Researchers commented that they felt these security precautions are "far too extreme" and that the risks have been "overdramatized." In addition, one researcher indicated that the data he required did not need to be secure but because the data were available only on the secure files he had to go through the whole process of getting secure data.

There do not appear to have been any efforts by NCES to make the process of getting a site license easier. However, because of the way the law is written, there may be little that NCES can do to change the process. According to NAEP staff, efforts are currently under way to explore, once again, providing public-use files that would not require a site license. These files would have the information that makes districts and schools individually identifiable removed. However, to make these files available to secondary analysts, the law authorizing NAEP would need to be changed.

Although no problems concerning getting access to the published data were reported, NCES is making efforts to make it even easier to obtain those types of data. The NCES Web site (www.nces.ed.gov/NAEP) currently has many reports and data compendiums available for downloading. In addition, there is an extensive catalog of NAEP publications and data products with information for placing orders.

Timing of the Availability of NAEP Data

Several researchers were unhappy about the long lag between the administration of NAEP and the data being available for secondary analysts. It takes about a year from the administration of NAEP for the results to be released to the public. It takes much longer for the data and the accompanying technical documentation to be available for secondary analysts. According to the NCES Web site, the technical report for the 1996 science assessment was released in January 1998, almost two years after the assessment was administered. When researchers were interviewed for this paper in January 1998, several complained that they were still waiting for data from the 1996 NAEP assessment. One researcher commented that he did not understand why it took so long—that commercial test publishers, albeit with simpler systems, get results out in six weeks.

According to NAEP staff, their current priority is to make assessment results available to the public in as timely a fashion as possible. Other data (e.g., questionnaire data, special studies data) and technical documentation are not an initial priority. NCES and ETS have been making efforts to decrease the time between administration of NAEP and the release of results. These efforts, if successful, would conceivably have a positive impact on the timing of data availability for secondary analyses. However, these efforts have not been very successful. Because of the complexity of NAEP and the need for hand scoring of constructed-response questions, a great deal of work must be done before results can be reported. In addition and largely because of the complexity of NAEP, problems have occurred in scaling the data. These problems cause additional delays or, in the worst cases, reanalysis of the data and a modification of results that have already been released.

Complexity of the NAEP Data

Issues stemming from the complexity of NAEP permeate many people's statements about using the data. A number of researchers made remarks that speak to the complexity of NAEP as a whole. For example, one researcher commented on how difficult it is to make sure one is doing the analyses correctly. He pointed out that with NAEP data there are many opportunities to make mistakes. Another researcher reported obtaining anomalous results and not being able to discover why. He commented that NAEP is so complicated that even with top-notch psychometricians working on the project they could not figure out whether the anomalous results were real or were an artifact of the NAEP data. Researchers commented about a number of specific aspects of the NAEP design and methodology that they thought contributed to its complexity. Aspects of NAEP that researchers discussed were clustered sampling, BIB (balanced incomplete block) spiraling, conditioning student achievement on background information, and plausible values.

Clustered Sampling

Clustered sampling is often an issue in research involving education. Because students are grouped into classrooms and schools, the students in a given group usually look more alike than a random sample of students. This issue impacts NAEP analyses because examinees are chosen for NAEP by first drawing a sample of schools and then a sample of students from within the chosen schools. Thus, the assumption of most standard statistical tests—that instances of measurement be independent—is violated. Because this assumption is violated, special methodology is required to compute estimates of sampling error in NAEP. There are two methods recommended in the NAEP documentation: design effects and jackknifing.

Using design effects is relatively simple but gives only crude estimates of the standard errors. In this method, standard errors computed by using formulas for independent observations are inflated using a design effect. This design effect is an estimate of how large the impact of clustering (and other sources of dependency among the observations) is on the sampling error variance. Estimates of the design effects are provided to the secondary analyst in the NAEP documentation.

Jackknife estimates of standard errors are much more precise but historically have been difficult for many secondary analysts to compute. Using NAEP data, computing jackknife standard errors is accomplished by repeating the analysis of interest once for each set of jackknife weights—typically there are 62 sets. The variance of the jackknife estimates is the estimate of the sampling error variance.

Several researchers thought that the need to use a special procedure to compute standard errors was a hindrance to their research. One reported not undertaking analyses because of the lack of an easy way to compute standard errors. Design effects were thought to be too imprecise and jackknifing too labor intensive—requiring that each analysis be repeated 63 times (once to get the statistic of interest and 62 times to get the statistics that go into computing the jackknife standard error).

There is little chance that sampling for NAEP will change to eliminate the need for special computational procedures for computing standard errors—clustering effects are inherent in educational settings and designing NAEP so that it does not take advantage of the grouping of students into schools, and larger aggregations would be prohibitively expensive. In addition, there are many types of analyses in which the clustered nature of the sample is desirable (e.g., examining school effects). However, there are other ways to facilitate analysis of NAEP data, and this is one example of how NCES and ETS have listened to the problems of secondary analysts and worked to find solutions. There is now SPSS and SAS code included with the data that can be used to compute jackknife standard error estimates.

BIB Design

Most traditional assessments involve either all students taking a single form of the test or students taking one of a small number of forms of the test where the different forms are designed to be as parallel as possible. These designs, either a single form or multiple parallel forms, have important advantages when the purpose of measurement is to provide precise estimates of achievement for individuals.

The purpose of NAEP is quite different—to provide precise estimates of the distribution of achievement in important populations rather than estimates for individuals. Thus, there are other designs that could optimize measurement efficiency. Assessment designs that increase measurement efficiency when individual scores are not the goal of the assessment generally involve having different students take different samples of items without trying to make the sets parallel.

NAEP takes this approach. Items are bundled into blocks and blocks are then assigned to booklets, creating a large number of "forms" of the assessment or booklets. Each block is bundled with every other block in at least one booklet, allowing for the entire item covariance matrix to be calculated. (Some NAEP assessments use a variation on this design.) In this design, called a balanced incomplete block (BIB) design, no effort is made to make booklets parallel in the traditional measurement sense. What is important is that, given the same testing time and number of students, greater coverage of the content domain can be achieved using a BIB design than traditional designs.

The advantages of a BIB design for measurement efficiency are thought by the designers of NAEP to outweigh the disadvantages. The main disadvantage of a BIB design is that scores for individuals generated by using standard methods (either IRT or classical test theory methods) are likely to have more error in them than is tolerable.[1] For this reason, NAEP does not report traditional estimates of student proficiency. The implications of this decision for secondary analysis will be considered in the next section, which covers the statistical technique of conditioning.

A second disadvantage of the BIB design is that analyses based on the item data are made more complicated and more error prone than would be the case with a more traditional design. Several researchers reported that it can take a great deal of effort to understand the structure of the item-level data and to reorganize such data to fit statistical programs that use item-level data. In addition, because only a fraction of the examinees are administered each item, the item-level statistics are not estimated precisely.[2] This is especially true if the item statistics of interest are based on a subgroup of the population.

NAEP staff reported trying to facilitate secondary analysts by providing information in the NAEP documentation about booklet and block codes needed to understand which items a specific examinee was administered. However, this appears to be the extent of the efforts made to address secondary analysts' concerns about the BIB design. Fundamental changes to NAEP have not been made because the advantages of the BIB design for measurement efficiency are widely thought to outweigh the disadvantages. The NAEP redesign will examine this issue and may come up with new alternatives.

Conditioning

The aspect of the methodology that appears to cause secondary analysts the most concern is conditioning student achievement on background information. The process of conditioning on student background information in NAEP is also called "multiple imputations" or "plausible values methodology." For the purposes of this paper the scaling methodology and the resulting plausible values will be discussed separately. This distinction reflects how many secondary analysts look at NAEP: secondary analysts commented on the process by which the

---

[1]For the most part, increased error is not technically caused by the BIB design. A BIB design allows adequate content coverage while using less testing time, and it is the decrease in testing time (thus a decrease in the information collected from individual students) that causes an increase in error variance.

[2]This depends, of course, on the number of examinees and the number of blocks of items. In some years and on some assessments, the total number of examinees has been high enough and the number of blocks low enough that the sample size for individual items was quite large.

data are scaled, the conditioning, and the "scores" that result from that process, the plausible values.

Conditioning is a Bayesian approach to scaling. It uses the information available from the assessment along with other information known about examinees to create estimates of proficiency. For example, if a student comes from an advantaged suburban school and reports other things that are associated with high performance but performs poorly on the assessment, his or her estimated proficiency (i.e., plausible values) will be higher than an unconditioned estimate of proficiency would be. The assumption is that this student was a victim of measurement error and his or her "true proficiency" is more like that of similar students with the same background characteristics. Likewise, a student who did well on the assessment but comes from a disadvantaged school and has other characteristics correlated with low performance would have an estimated proficiency lower than an unconditioned estimate would be.

According to *The NAEP Technical Report* (Allen et al., 1996), conditioning on background information results in better estimates of the distribution of proficiency for important groups.[3] However, it also results in biased estimates of achievement for individual students. This requires researchers to take special precautions to ensure that their analyses and conclusions are not affected by this bias.

Conditioning can cause problems for secondary analysts who are interested in modeling the effects of student characteristics on achievement. The problem most widely discussed is a downward bias in the estimates of effects for variables that were not used in conditioning when they are included in an analysis with variables that were used in conditioning. Two researchers reported getting anomalous results when modeling the effects of student and school characteristics on student achievement. In addition, other researchers reported being concerned that their results were impacted by this bias.

ETS has made efforts to minimize these problems. The 1994 technical report (Allen et al., 1996) states that "the set of variables used [in conditioning was] defined with the aim of holding to low levels secondary biases in analyses involving a broad range of variables not included in the conditioning model." Thus, the problems that researchers reported pertaining to bias in estimates of the effects of variables not included in the conditioning model should be less of an issue in the more recent NAEP assessments. Another problem that conditioning causes for secondary analysts is more fundamental. Researchers with years of experience with NAEP and strong backgrounds in statistics said that they still do not understand the methodology used to scale NAEP in anything more than general terms

---

[3]Another advantage of conditioning is that is allows estimates of proficiency to be obtained for individuals who answered all of the items either incorrectly or correctly—something that is problematic with traditional scaling methods.

and are unsure of the impact the scaling procedures have on analyses they have conducted or wish to conduct. They widely reported being uncomfortable using data in their research when they do not understand the scaling methodology used to generate the data.

The NAEP Technical Report (Allen et al., 1996) states that "when the underlying model is correctly specified, plausible values will provide consistent estimates of population characteristics." The impact of the model not being correctly specified has not been well researched and needs to be addressed. The technical report also states that conditioning allows key population features to be estimated consistently even when item booklet composition, format, and content balance change over time (Allen et al., 1996). However, it is not known to what degree changes to the item booklet composition, format, and content balance also change the degree to which the model has been correctly specified. Such changes may impact the results in unknown ways. There have been enough anomalies in the results to make this a serious concern.

ETS has tried to assuage people's concerns about conditioning but has failed, in the opinion of a number of researchers, to provide an adequate explanation of how conditioning impacts the data. ETS has not based its statements about conditioning on research using real data or data simulated to have characteristics similar to NAEP data.[4] One researcher went so far as to say that she thought that ETS staff were patronizing and that they used overly abstruse statistical arguments. Another analyst characterized ETS's standard response to people's concerns about conditioning as "Trust me. It works."

Plausible Values

Instead of each student being given a score that is the best estimate of his or her "true score" given the information available from the assessment, students taking NAEP are given five plausible values. The plausible values are random draws from each individual's posterior distribution obtained using the information available on the assessment as well as background information.

The advantage of using plausible values is that error due to giving students only a sample of items is incorporated into standard error estimates reported for NAEP. A second advantage is that measurement error is apparent to researchers using the data—if you do the analyses once for each plausible value, the results will be slightly different each time and that difference is due to measurement error, whereas with the type of scores given on most assessments, it is possible for researchers to forget that this type of error is present to some degree in all assessments.

---

[4] The theoretical underpinnings of conditioning are spelled out in papers by Rubin (1987) and Mislevy (1991).

Plausible values are handled in secondary analyses in the following way: (1) the analysis of interest is performed five times—once for each of the five plausible values; (2) the standard deviation of the estimates resulting from the five repeats of the analysis is computed; and (3) this standard deviation provides an estimate of the error in the statistic that is due to sampling of items. For most analyses the use of plausible values means more work for the analyst but what needs to be done is straightforward and, though tedious, relatively easy to accomplish. One researcher commented on this aspect of NAEP by saying simply that it would be nice not to have the plausible values.

There are some types of analyses however, where a single best estimate of each student's achievement is really needed. In these cases the use of plausible values by NAEP is a very real barrier to analysis of the data. One example of this is when the purpose of the analysis is to evaluate the scaling methodology used in NAEP. Two researchers reported wanting to do this type of research and being stymied by the lack of a single best estimate of student proficiency.

NCES and ETS have made efforts to make computation using plausible values easier for secondary analysts. The data extraction program that accompanies the data will automatically handle the plausible values. In addition, software for handling plausible values in HLM analyses was developed using an NCES grant. However, NAEP staff have been less responsive to researchers who need a single optimal proficiency estimate for each examinee, and ETS has not made its software available so that secondary analysts could produce their own estimates of proficiency.[5]

Form and Organization of NAEP Data

Several problems were reported concerning the form and organization of NAEP data on the data files from researchers interested in item-level data. One researcher was frustrated because scored item data are not available on the data files. He reported that the file contained the item responses and a scoring key but, because of the use of blocks of items contained in different booklets, applying the scoring key to the data was a time-consuming process. Since scored data are needed for many types of analyses, making secondary analysts repeat the scoring appears to be an unnecessary and error-prone burden.

Another aspect of the item-level data that was troublesome to some secondary analysts was the order in which the items are listed on the file. Because of the BIB design, the order of presentation of items differs across examinees. A particular block may be administered first in one booklet and last in another.

---

[5] This author was told by NAEP staff that the first plausible value could be used for analyses requiring a single optimal estimate of proficiency. However, this clearly was not the understanding of the NAEP researchers who encountered this problem.

However, items are presented in only one order on the data files. Thus, the data files present the item responses in an order unrelated to the order in which the items were administered to examinees. If a researcher needs a dataset that has items listed in the order they were administered, it is necessary for him or her to construct it using information about the order in which blocks were presented in different booklets.

At this time, ETS does not provide scored item-level data. However, ETS does provide SAS and SPSS code for scoring the data and has reported being interested in adding the ability to score the data to the data extraction program. This is not a case where researchers are asking ETS and NCES to eliminate one way of doing things and go with a different way. Rather, researchers would like multiple presentations of the data to be available so that, depending on the purpose of their research, they could use the presentation most suited to their analysis. Providing both scored and unscored data to researchers would cost money by increasing the size of the data files. It would save money for secondary analysts (some of which comes through NCES in the form of research grants). Thus, this is an area where the tradeoffs need to be explored further.

Documentation

Issues related to NAEP documentation were mentioned frequently. Researchers rely heavily on the NAEP data reports (e.g., Mullis et al., 1993) and technical manuals (e.g., Johnson and Allen, 1992) to understand the data. Both positive and negative comments about documentation were common. On the positive side, a number of researchers said that NAEP is well documented. One researcher said the technical reports were her "bible" and that she relied on them heavily in doing her analyses. Another researcher said that, compared to the documentation he had seen for other large-scale assessments, NAEP documentation was very good.

On the negative side, researchers reported spending a great deal of time "slogging" through the technical manuals trying to understand the data and make sure they were doing the analyses correctly. Two researchers with a great deal of experience with large databases indicated that NAEP technical documentation was much more difficult to use than documentation for other NCES databases. One researcher reported that it was the descriptions of the actual data, not the technical information, that was not as clear as in other NCES programs. Several researchers indicated that they would like the documentation to provide more examples of how data analysis should be conducted. As one researcher put it "I think [researchers] can generalize from examples better than they can from abstract recommendations."

One researcher was concerned about the usability of the documentation by content experts who may not be using the data files but who need to get item information directly from the NAEP documentation. She thought that information about items in the NAEP documentation is not well organized and that the documentation is difficult for content experts to use because information is scattered in many different places. NCES and ETS are continually trying to improve their documentation, and it seems clear that over time there have been improvements. One researcher pointed out that because of the complexity of NAEP it is more difficult to explain the methodology and data than is the case for other assessments.

Getting Help

The researchers I spoke with had very positive things to say about the staff of NCES and ETS. One researcher called the people from NCES, ETS, and other organizations who conducted the NAEP training seminars "wonderful, helpful, and knowledgeable." However, several researchers reported that it is often difficult to get answers to questions about NAEP, especially answers to questions that are technical in nature or that relate to assessments other than the main NAEP or the state assessment.

Two difficulties mentioned were related to getting help with NAEP analysis problems. First, it is often not clear who one should contact in order to get a question answered. One researcher recommended there be a staff person whose job it is to understand the data and answer secondary analysts' questions or at least be able to route a caller to someone who would be able to answer the question. Second, the system is so complex that it is difficult to fully understand it or keep track of what has been done, even for people who work on NAEP full time. Thus, even though NCES and ETS staff try to be helpful, there are questions that arise that are not familiar to most NAEP staff.

Because of the complexity of NAEP data and the special procedures needed to properly analyze the data, NCES and ETS offer training seminars to people interested in conducting research using NAEP data. Overall, researchers thought the training they received was very helpful. They liked the opportunity to meet and interact with NAEP staff. They liked getting hands-on experience with the data and being able to try out special software written to help secondary analysts with the special features of NAEP. One researcher reported that the training was most helpful in describing the data and identifying the problems one would likely encounter.

Most but not all comments about training were positive. On the negative side, one researcher reported that the least helpful aspect was providing a model for how to correctly analyze the data. The same researcher thought that the training he received was insufficient to allow researchers to conduct methodologically sound research. Another researcher wanted training to be more geared to specific audiences; because of the varied backgrounds of the researchers in his training seminar, the leaders did not go into the depth about technical issues that he would have liked.

Overall, NAEP staff should be applauded for their efforts to help researchers deal with the complexity of the data. Many of the researchers I spoke with had benefited from training programs offered by NCES and ETS. Also, including SPSS and SAS code along with the data has improved the usability of the data. In addition, two researchers I spoke with received funding from NCES to develop special software for secondary analysts to use—software that would automatically handle things like plausible values and jackknife weights.

Summary of Results

The comments of secondary analysts ran the gamut from high praise to severe criticism. Only one researcher reported having no problems conducting secondary analyses of NAEP data. At the other extreme, there was one researcher whose experience with the data was so negative that she swore she would never use NAEP data again. In addition, there were researchers who had not used NAEP data due to the complexity of the data and/or difficulties associated with getting a site license. The comments differed among types of researchers—the comments of content experts differed somewhat from those of sociologists, and sociologists' concerns differed to some extent from those of psychometricians. In addition, comments tended to reflect the time when the research was conducted. Over the years a number of changes have been made to the NAEP assessments, and software has been developed to help secondary analysts use the data. Thus, some concerns raised by secondary analysts would be less problematic if the research were conducted today. Several researchers commented that some of the difficulties they encountered may be unavoidable in an assessment like NAEP, whereas others were adamant that there is no reason for the system to present such difficulties.

RECOMMENDATIONS

Before making recommendations it is important to highlight that there are tradeoffs involved in almost any decision that is made regarding NAEP. Creating data that secondary analysts can use to address important issues in education is only one of the purposes of NAEP. Thus, where these recommendations conflict with what is best from the perspective of another purpose of NAEP, only the policy makers charged with balancing these purposes can judge what is best for the overall program.

If early reports about the NAEP redesign are true, use of NAEP data by secondary analysts is at risk of becoming a low priority in the new NAEP assessment system. Obviously, secondary analysts are opposed to this. NAEP data are currently a unique resource for addressing important questions in education. The primary analyses of NAEP data are generally restricted to descriptive statistics (e.g., means and percentages), and thus it is generally up to secondary analysts to more deeply mine the data. NAEP has the potential, with changes designed to facilitate secondary analysis of the data, to be an even more important resource for addressing issues in education.

There are a number of recommendations to facilitate secondary analysis of NAEP data that resulted from interviews with NAEP secondary analysts and NAEP staff at NCES and ETS. Several of them would be relatively easy to implement. Others involve simplifying the NAEP design and scaling procedures.

Relatively Easy-to-Implement Changes

Improve Communication Between NAEP Staff and Secondary Analysts

First, better communication should be established between NAEP staff and secondary analysts. A number of researchers commented that, although NAEP staff are very helpful, there are no automatic lines of communication to help researchers and it is often difficult to get in touch with NCES staff. For example, one researcher commented that NAEP staff should be more proactive about providing researchers with information. She said that when there was an error in the data from one year—data that NCES had records of her obtaining—she was not notified of the error. It was up to her to find out about the error and request that NAEP send revised data files. A couple of researchers wanted more advertising of NAEP training opportunities.

Some of the comments made by secondary analysts illustrate the poor communication lines. One researcher requested there be an 800 number that secondary analysts can call to have questions answered. There is, in fact, an 800 number for reaching the NAEP staff at ETS (800-223-0267). However, that number is not included in any of the NAEP documentation I have seen, so it is not surprising that many researchers are not aware of it. Another researcher recommended that there be a staff member who understands the NAEP data designated to help secondary analysts. ETS and NCES do have staff members for whom part of their job is to help secondary analysts. However, who these people are is not widely publicized. I was directed to Al Rogers at ETS (800-223-0267) for questions about the data files, accompanying program modules, and special software and Alex Sedlacek (202-219-1734) at NCES for questions about NAEP grants.

The NAEP Web site could help implement this recommendation. The Web site's address could be included with all NAEP reports, including pamphlets like the NAEP facts series. At the Web site, contact information for NAEP staff could be included, such as phone numbers and e-mail addresses. The Web site could also provide information about available training. A second way in which open communication could be facilitated is with a newsletter geared toward secondary analysts that informs researchers about data releases, known problems with the data, available training, NAEP contact staff, the NAEP 800 number, the address of the Web site, and any changes to NAEP that are being made that might affect secondary analyses.

Create Differentiated Data Files

The second recommendation is that ETS create data files geared to different types of researchers. For example, for analysts who want to analyze item data, scored data should be available as well as unscored data. There are undoubtedly other special files that would facilitate secondary analysis, and better communication between NAEP staff and researchers would be helpful in identifying them.

Provide Guidelines and Examples for Specific Types of Analyses

The third recommendation involves changes to the documentation. Researchers asked for more examples of analyses using NAEP data. They also asked for more guidelines on how to conduct specific types of analyses. This may be an area that NAEP staff are wary to enter. For many types of analyses (e.g., how best to compare performance on NAEP at the state level), experts do not agree. Thus, for ETS or NCES to advocate a specific method could be controversial. However, it may be possible for NCES to either fund secondary analysts who are interested in documenting the pros and cons of different methods of conducting specific types of analyses or bring together panels of experts to write a report on the issue.

Implementing this recommendation would also require that better communication be established. NAEP staff, specifically ETS staff who write the NAEP technical documentation, currently reported knowing little about the specific interests of secondary analysts. They reported trying to make documentation as general as possible to allow for a wide audience of potential users. This is certainly a worthy goal and should be continued. However, researchers would like to see the general guidelines supplemented with examples of how the guidelines can be put into practice in specific situations.

More Ambitious Changes

Change the Requirements for Obtaining NAEP Data

The fourth recommendation is to make the data easier to obtain. Although this may not be easy to implement because it requires changes in the legislation authorizing NAEP, it seems apparent to many researchers that the security precautions related to NAEP are overly strict and as such are an impediment to broad use of the data by secondary analysts.

Simplify NAEP

Simplifying NAEP has the potential to ameliorate a number of the concerns voiced by secondary analysts: (1) simplifying NAEP could result in making NAEP results and data available in a much more timely fashion; (2) it could lessen confusion about the data; (3) it could reduce the amount of documentation needed to explain the data and result in documentation that is easier for secondary analysts to use; and (4) it could reduce the amount of help that secondary analysts need as well as make it easier to obtain help because more people would understand the data and be able to help others. There are many ways in which NAEP could be simplified. Several are considered below: changes in the information collected, changes in sampling, and changes in scaling.

The Information Collected. One way to simplify NAEP would be to reduce the amount of information that is collected. For example, much, if not all, of the background and school-level information that is collected now could be eliminated or the constructed-response questions could be eliminated so that hand scoring and polytomous scoring are not necessary. However, researchers who use the NAEP data clearly did not want changes that would reduce the amount of information available on students and schools. In fact, a number of researchers were concerned that a redesign of NAEP would reduce the background and school information collected and they vocally opposed such a change.

Sampling. There are other changes that would be of interest to many NAEP researchers but that would add prohibitively to the cost of the program. For example, the cost of obtaining samples of students who are not affected by clustering would facilitate some types of analyses but would dramatically increase the cost of administering the assessment.

Scaling. Changes in assessment design that would eliminate the need for conditioning (also called "multiple imputations" or "plausible values methodology") have the potential to simplify many aspects of NAEP. Conditioning is the aspect of NAEP that the most secondary analysts voiced concern about. Although conditioning is based on sound theoretical work (Rubin, 1987), it is far from clear that its advantages (i.e., that using conditioning means that the item booklet composition, format, and content balance can be changed over time without adversely impacting the comparability of the results from different years) hold up using real data.

Is it feasible to redesign NAEP in such a way that conditioning is not required? Conditioning serves two purposes. The first is the one that is most commonly discussed: conditioning allows fewer items to be administered to each examinee. When conditioning was first used in NAEP, the combination of limited testing time (50 minutes) and testing in multiple subjects (as well as asking a number of background questions) meant that students frequently spend as little as 15 minutes on a particular subject. Clearly, estimates of an individual's proficiency in a broad content area cannot be precisely estimated in that short a period of time. However, later administrations of NAEP changed from assessing individuals in multiple subjects to testing individuals in a single subject. Thus, a student now generally spends about 45 minutes being assessed in a single subject area.[6] This amount of time is similar to the amount of time students are given on many tests used to generate individual scores. Thus, it is reasonable to at least explore whether conditioning is still needed because of limited numbers of items administered to individuals.

One argument for the continued need for conditioning is that NAEP has changed from reporting a proficiency for a single broad content area such as mathematics to reporting proficiencies for more narrowly defined subareas such as geometry. Thus, even though enough items might be administered to an individual to report unconditioned scaled scores in mathematics, not enough items are administered in each content area to accurately estimate unconditioned scaled scores in the subareas. Other ways to handle the additional error in the estimates of the distribution of performance on the subareas need to be explored.

The second, and possibly more important reason, for conditioning is its potential to allow changes in the assessment over time that would not be advisable otherwise. The NAEP technical report states that conditioning allows key population features to be estimated consistently even when item booklet composition, format, and content balance change over time (Allen et al., 1996).[7] However, even though, theoretically, conditioning allows such changes over time, not even the designers of NAEP believe it to the degree that they would rely on it with the long-term NAEP trend assessment.[8] The mantra of the long-term trend assessment is "when measuring change, don't change the measure." And even though the content balance of the long-term trend assessment is widely thought to be outdated and the content balance is uneven, that is exactly what has happened for 15 years—the exact same set of items has been administered in every assess-

---

[6]It is important to note that more of this time is used to administer performance items (large items) than was the case in earlier NAEP assessments.

[7]Questions about the advisability of making such changes to an assessment that is used to measure change are important but beyond the scope of this paper. What does the trend mean if what is assessed over time has changed? Such changes occur because, over time, the content experts have changed what they believe students should know and be able to do. Pressure for the NAEP frameworks to reflect what is currently considered important for students to know and be able to do means that the frameworks change as current thinking changes. Thus, NAEP is subject to all of the shifts that occur in current thinking, such as the relative importance of teaching, and assessing, basic skills versus higher-order thinking skills.

[8]As noted in the overview of NAEP, the long-term trend assessment is a separate assessment from main NAEP and state NAEP. When results are presented that track achievement in reading, mathematics, science, and writing since the late 1960s, those results come from long-term trend NAEP.

ment cycle in order to accurately maintain long-term trend lines. Although Zieleskiewicz (Chapter 6, this volume) found that the items on long-term trend NAEP are relevant and important in today's classrooms, there are important differences in the content balance on the long-term trend and main NAEP frameworks—differences that reflect shifts in what experts believe is important for students to know and be able to do (e.g., more emphasis on algebra and functions in mathematics in main NAEP). There has also been a shift toward greater use of alternative-item formats on the main assessment. Conditioning is used because the long-term trend booklets are from the early administrations when individuals were assessed in multiple subjects.

Does conditioning allow accurate measurement of trends when the item booklet composition, format, and content balance change over time? In other words, are the assumptions of the conditioning model adequately met with real data? Is the conditioning model robust when the assumptions are not met? Under what conditions is the model robust? Under what conditions is it not? These questions have not been addressed in the measurement literature. Conditioning is not widely used outside NAEP, and the programs that carry out NAEP conditioning are not available outside ETS. Thus, it is very difficult for anyone outside ETS to carry out research on conditioning as it is used in NAEP. Without a better understanding of the degree to which the purported benefits of conditioning hold up using real data and simulating these types of changes, it is impossible to judge the necessity of using conditioning in NAEP. Also important would be a comparison of the results using conditioning and not using conditioning to examine its practical impact.

Reported "Scores." Eliminating the plausible values would also simplify secondary analysis of NAEP data. Plausible values are used to make apparent to researchers that the estimates of student proficiency are just that—estimates. They contain measurement error as a result of asking students only a sample of questions. This is true of all assessments from the SAT to the licensure examines for health care professionals. It is perhaps more important in NAEP because conditioning results in biased estimates of individuals' proficiency, and thus a side benefit of plausible values is that they help analysts remember that individuals' scores are not calculated to be "best" in the same way they are in other assessments. Plausible values also allow for this measurement error to be estimated and used in establishing the significance of comparisons. However, measurement error is small in comparison to sampling error, and its omission from estimates of standard error is likely to have little practical impact on the reported results.

Consequences of a simpler NAEP design, allowing for the elimination of the conditioning and plausible values, potentially include (1) quicker turnaround for NAEP results and NAEP data for secondary analysis, (2) less confusion about the data, (3) less documentation needed to explain the data and documentation that is easier for secondary analysts to use, (4) a reduced need for secondary analysts to receive extensive help in order to analyze the data, and (5) a greater confidence in the validity of the results of secondary analysis of the data.

Conditioning and plausible values are fundamental aspects of the NAEP scaling procedures and may be considered by some to not be open to discussion, especially discussion focused on secondary analysis of NAEP data. The importance of producing data that are useable to secondary analysts with a wide variety of backgrounds is an issue for policy makers. It was the purpose of this study only to propose ways in which secondary analysis of NAEP data could be facilitated given that providing data for secondary analysis is currently part of the program's mission.

Although eliminating conditioning would increase the amount of upfront work that goes into test development, would require more discipline on the part of the people who decide the content of NAEP, and would mean other changes to the assessment, these changes may be feasible and not prohibitively expensive. In addition, added expense in terms of upfront work may well be made up by savings in the scaling and reporting phases. Clearly, a study of the feasibility of these changes would need to be made by independent researchers in order to empirically address the issue.

Summary of Recommendations

NAEP is a unique and rich source of information about the student population in the United States. Currently, much of NAEP's potential is not realized, however, because of the complexity of the data. The changes outlined above—clearer communication between NAEP staff and secondary analysts, documentation and data files geared toward different types of secondary analysts, and a simpler NAEP design—have the potential to dramatically increase the amount of research that is conducted using NAEP data, research that could be used to improve education and help students achieve to their potential.

ACKNOWLEDGMENTS

The author thanks all of the NAEP secondary analysts who shared their NAEP experiences; Larry Ogle from NCES and John Mazzeo and Al Rogers from ETS for providing information about NAEP; and Dean Colton, Dan Koretz, and Kris Waltman for reviewing drafts of the paper.

REFERENCES

Allen, N.L., D.L. Kline, and C.A. Zelenak
  1996   *The NAEP Technical Report: 1994.* Washington, D.C.: U.S. Department of Education, National Center for Education Statistics.

Beaton, A.E., and R. Zwick
  1990   *The Effect of Changes in the National Assessment: Disentangling the NAEP 1985-86 Reading Anomaly.* Princeton, N.J.: Educational Testing Service.
Johnson, E.G., and N.L. Allen
  1992   *The NAEP Technical Report: 1990.* Washington, D.C.: U.S. Department of Education, National Center for Education Statistics.
Kenney, P.A., and E.A. Silver
  1996   Interpretive Reports for the Fifth, Sixth, and Seventh NAEP Mathematics Assessments: "Lessons learned" from Year One of the Project. Paper presented at the annual conference of the American Educational Research Association, New York, April.
Lee, V.E., R.G. Croninger, and J.B. Smith
  1997   Course-taking, equity, and mathematics learning: Testing the constrained curriculum hypothesis in U.S. secondary schools. *Education Evaluation and Policy Analysis* 19(2):99-121.
Mislevy, R.J.
  1991   Randomization-based inference about latent variables from complex samples. *Psychometrika* 56:177-196.
Mullis, I.V.S., J.A. Dossey, E.H. Owen, and G.W. Phillips
  1993   *NAEP 1992 Mathematics Report Card for the Nation and the States: Data from the National and Trial State Assessments.* Washington, D.C.: National Center for Education Statistics.
Rubin, D.B.
  1987   *Multiple Imputations for Nonresponse in Surveys.* New York: John Wiley & Sons.

10

Putting Surveys, Studies, and Datasets Together: Linking NCES Surveys to One Another and to Datasets from Other Sources

George Terhanian and Robert Boruch

"Relations stop nowhere. . . .The exquisite problem is eternally but to draw . . . the circle within which they happily appear to do so."

Henry James, *Roderick Hudson,* 1876

This paper examines ideas about combining different datasets so as to inform science and society. It was prepared at the invitation of the National Research Council's (NRC) Board on Testing and Assessment so as to inform the board's deliberations about policy on education surveys in the United States. The surveys of paramount interest are those sponsored by the National Center for Education Statistics (NCES).

The research reviewed here and the implications that are educed from it are directed first to the NRC. They are dedicated in the second place to the interests of the NCES. The third target is the social sciences community more generally. Examples given here are drawn from a variety of sciences inasmuch as data linkage issues transcend academic disciplines. They are taken from different institutional jurisdictions because the issues cross geopolitical boundaries.

Two studies are used to provoke discussion and to frame some issues: Hilton's (1992) *Using Data-bases in Educational Research* and Hedges and Nowell's (1995) paper on national surveys of the mathematics and science abilities of boys and girls. We also depend heavily on other materials generated by NCES, the NRC, and others. This includes work, for example, on teacher supply, demand, and quality (National Research Council, 1992) and on integrating federal statistics on children (National Research Council, 1995). The minutes of the

NCES Advisory Council on Education Statistics reflect periodic interest in the way NCES surveys can be linked to one another or to data generated by other federal agencies (Griffith, 1992) and we exploit these also.

In what follows we begin with the two illustrations that help frame discussion. The pedigree of linkage is considered briefly, and the ubiquity of linkages in contemporary surveys is then discussed. Inasmuch as the meaning of words such as *linkage, merging,* and so on are used differently in the research literature, the next section covers ways to clarify the language. Distinctions are further drawn between statistical policy for making surveys connectable in contrast to de facto policy in which post facto connections are difficult. Evaluating the products of any variety of linkages is important, and this topic is covered also, based on suggestions about mapping and registering linkage studies. In the next to last section of the paper we suggest exploring some new kinds of linkage. The paper concludes with a summary of the implications of this work.

TWO INTRODUCTORY ILLUSTRATIONS

The origin of Hilton's (1992) book was in a project undertaken by the Educational Testing Service (ETS) to understand whether different sources of statistical information, each based perhaps on a national sample, could be combined to produce a "comprehensive unified database" of science indicators for the United States. Sponsored by the National Science Foundation, the project's general goal was to improve the way we capitalize on data that bear on educating scientists, mathematicians, and engineers. The book's implications, inadvertent and otherwise, are important for designing NCES surveys, among others.

Twenty-four education databases were reviewed by the project, including the Survey of Doctoral Recipients, national teacher examinations, and at least four massive longitudinal databases. Only 8 of the 24 were deemed worthy of deeper examination. That is, the eight could be "linked" in some sense with others, given the resources available. They included the National Longitudinal Study of the Class of 1972 (NLS:72) and the National Education Longitudinal Study of 1988 (NELS:88), the Equality of Opportunity Surveys (1960s), cross-sectional systems such as the Scholastic Assessment Test (SAT), and the NCES National Assessment of Educational Progress (NAEP).

As Hilton made plain in the preface to his book, the project was "not feasible." Put more bluntly, the ETS effort to combine datasets was a flop despite competent and thoughtful efforts. The databases chosen for examination could not be used for the purpose considered (i.e., to produce a comprehensive science database). It was, nonetheless, a project noble in aspiration and diligent in its execution.

The questions posed in the Hilton project about the available databases and which are relevant to linking any datasets seem important for designing new NCES surveys. Put in modified terms, the questions are as follows:

- What variables are common to various databases?
- What ways of measuring each variable, ways of sampling, and administration are common, making comparison (or linkage) among datasets
  easy?
- What differences in ways of measuring, administrating, and sampling
  make comparison (or linkages) dubious or difficult?
- What can be done to fix different datasets so they are "comparable" (or
  linkable) in some way and therefore make it sensible to put them together?

The Hilton book contained no detailed catalog of why the databases failed to
meet one or more of the criteria implied by these questions.

Hedges and Nowell (1995) attacked a different but related topic—understanding gender differences in mental abilities of various kinds based on disparate surveys. These authors chose to depend only on studies based on samples of
roughly the same target populations and that purportedly measured the same
abilities (e.g., reading). That is, they selected only studies that approached the
first three questions above in similar ways. Their final selections included NCES-
sponsored work, notably NELS:88, NLS-72, High School and Beyond (HS&B),
NAEP (trend data only), Project Talent, and the National Longitudinal Youth
Survey sponsored by the U.S. Department of Labor, among others. These are
summarized in Table 10-1. We rely periodically on its contents in what follows.

There was sufficient commonality in what was measured on whom in the
target populations in the Hedges-Nowell (1995) ambit to produce an informative
analysis. It is a fine illustration of combining different datasets so as to learn
whether males and females really differ on mental abilities and how they might
differ. For instance, the authors' dependence on well-defined national probability
samples avoided the inferential problems encountered in earlier studies, notably
depending on self-selected samples (as in SAT/ACT testing), idiosyncratic
samples (e.g., in test norming), and distributional assumptions (to get at characteristics of extreme scores). A main product of the Hedges and Nowell's work is
learning that males are more variable than females in their tested intellectual
achievement. This finding helps to elevate substantially the scientific conversation about the purported differences in the mean levels of math and science
abilities of boys and girls. It helps to show how more variability among boys may
produce specious claims about their ability relative to girls.

THE PEDIGREE OF EFFORTS TO PUT DIFFERENT
DATASETS TOGETHER

The idea underlying any linkage effort undertaken by NCES or by others is
that combining data from different sources can help us learn something new.
More to the point, the combination permits us to learn something that cannot be
learned from individual sources. The idea has fine origins. Alexander Graham

TABLE 10-1 Summary of Characteristics of the Six Datasets Considered by Hedges and Nowell (1995)

Characteristics	Project Talent	NLS-72	National Longitudinal Survey of Youth	High School and Beyond	NELS:88	NAEP
Year of assessment	1960	1972	1980	1980	1992	1971-1992
[Sample size (N)]	73,425	16,860	11,914	25,069	24,599	Varies
Population	All 15-year-olds	Twelfth-grade students	Noninstitutionalized 15 to 22 year olds	Twelfth-grade students	Eighth-grade students as of 1988	17-year-olds in school
Abilities measured						
Reading comprehension	◆	◆	◆	◆	◆	◆
Vocabulary	◆	◆	◆	◆		
Mathematics	◆	◆	◆	◆	◆	◆
Perceptual speed	◆	◆	◆	◆		
Science	◆		◆	◆	◆	◆
Social studies	◆			◆		
Nonverbal reasoning	◆	◆				
Associate memory	◆	◆				
Spatial ability	◆		◆	◆		
Mechanical reasoning	◆		◆	◆		
Electronics information	◆					
Auto and shop information	◆					
Writing						◆

Bell, for instance, exploited the notion in his study of genetic transmission of deafness. In the late 1880s he depended on completed Census Bureau interview forms found strewn in a government building basement and linked these to genealogical records from other sources (Bruce, 1973).

One can also trace the theme to John Graunt's effort in the seventeenth century to learn how to use records in the Crown's interest. Graunt exhorted the King to understand his empire through a lens consisting of compilations of records in statistical form: the counts of soldiers at arms, for instance, from one source and the numbers of births, deaths, and so on from other sources. Scheuren (1995), similarly thoughtful and exhortative, has reviewed and refreshed our thinking about how to augment administrative records and understand them better through surveys.

The pedigree of linkage studies is also reflected in contemporary efforts to evaluate social programs. In studies of manpower training and employment, for example, it has become common to link the employment records on specified individuals to their program records and to link these data in turn to research records on individuals (Rosen, 1974). In agriculture, health, and taxation, there have been fine studies of why and how one ought to couple data from different sources in a variety of ways (Kilss and Alvey, 1985).

From papers by Scheuren (1995) and others we learn about contemporary history of record linkage algorithms (developed by Tepping and Felligi-Sunter, among others), the construction of matching rules and the information exploited in matches, the idea of linkage documentation, and various approaches to adjusting for mismatches. We can learn about the role of privacy issues and statistical analysis implications from a related body of work (e.g., Cox and Boruch, 1988). We learn about appraising the benefits and costs of linkage of administrative records or the difficulty of doing so on account of sloppy practice, from aggressive investigatory agencies such as the U.S. General Accounting Office (1986a, 1986b).

The title of Hilton's book, *Using National Data-bases in Educational Research*, may suggest to some readers that they can learn something about whether, why, and how massive studies are combined and used. In fact, recent work on how to enhance the usefulness of statistical data is pertinent. Some of it has been economically oriented—for instance, Spencer's work (1980) on cost-benefit analysis to allocate resources to various data collection efforts and the follow-up papers by Moses, Spencer, and others. Scholarly papers on why and how social research data, including educational and health research data, are used are also relevant. Kruskal's volume (1982) is a gem on this account.

The analyses in Hilton's book were not burdened by the history of linkage. That is, the authors failed to put the ETS linkage studies into the larger context of such studies or the still larger context of design and exploitation of databases and survey. We learn about attempts to link the Armed Services Vocational Aptitude Battery to tests given in the longitudinal HS&B survey and to SATs, but we are not told about how this would enhance science indicators or inform decisions or, more importantly, improve the design of surveys. Similarly, the Hedges and Nowell (1995) paper does not consider implications of the work for the design of better surveys that can be linked in any respect, despite the fact that the authors are sensitive to the implications of their work on other accounts.

THE UBIQUITY OF PUTTING DIFFERENT DATASETS TOGETHER AND FUNCTIONAL CATEGORIES

Some varieties of linkage are common, even pedestrian. So frequently do they occur that they are taken for granted. Other varieties of linkage are not encountered often. They may be undertaken for reasons that seem obviously important or, to the lay public, obscure or trivial. This section provides illustration of linkages, pedestrian and otherwise. The examples are put into categories that have meaning for scientists and an informed public: national probability sample surveys, longitudinal studies, studies of the quality of data, intersurvey consistency, and hierarchical studies.

National Probability Sample Surveys

Virtually all national probability sample surveys in this country and elsewhere are an exercise in combining information from different systems. Telephone surveys often draw on a population listing of telephone numbers. A population census may draw on an address list for dwellings. The NCES Schools and Staffing Survey, for instance, depends on lists of schools identified as administrative units or locations. List information is used to construct the sample. Listed information is often combined in the same microrecord with the information provided by the respondent.

Longitudinal Studies: Tracking Change

Any longitudinal survey involves linkage at a basic level. Microrecords obtained on individuals or institutions at one point in time are linked to those obtained subsequently, as in NELS:88, NLS:72, and HS&B. The organization responsible for each wave of the survey may vary, of course, as when NCES used different contractors. Target populations, variables, and their measurement may also differ somewhat between waves.

Studies of the Quality of the Data

Any postenumeration survey of a national census and most post facto studies of the quality of a large survey employ linkage. Microrecords in the main initial survey, for instance, are compared to those generated in a more intensive, smaller, and presumably more accurate study of a subsample of the original target population. Efforts to estimate reliability of achievement tests focus on stability of individual scores over time; individual scores must be linked across time. Finally, many if not most studies of the validity of respondent reports in surveys rely on two or more sources of information on the trait or characteristics of interest. Enrollment records in colleges may be compared to self-reported enrollment information in a sample of students receiving subsidized loans.

In the federal statistics arena, most studies of response quality or measurement error require linkage and are described regularly in the professional literature. Scholarly reports usually appear, for instance, in the annual *Proceedings of the Section on Survey Methods of the American Statistical Association* and in reports issued by the federal agency that sponsored the work. It is disconcerting to see little representation of municipal statisticians in these *Proceedings* and reports. It is not clear why their contribution is sparse, and the matter deserves a bit of researchers' attention.

Intersurvey Consistency

The NCES has conducted a Private School Survey (PSS) independent of a special supplement to the Schools and Staffing Survey (SASS). SASS has depended on the PSS for a sampling frame of schools, using a basic form of linkage. More generally, both the supplemented SASS and PSS have provided estimates of the numbers of schools, teachers, and students in the private sector. Each survey is normally run at different times and measures some of the same variables. On at least one occasion each was run in the same year (Holt et al., 1994).

The results of each survey may or may not agree, differences in time frame being one possible reason for discordance. The occasion of a PSS and a SASS supplement in the same year permitted NCES to investigate the consistency between them. At times then NCES depends on applying algorithms to SASS that reweigh subgroups' totals of schools, teachers, and students in various categories so as to produce overall group totals that are consistent with PSS group totals. A "group" here might be a type of private school (e.g., Catholic).

"Linkages" here are of two kinds. First, the PSS is used as the sampling frame for SASS. Second, the memberships of schools in subgroups are supposed to be identical in PSS and SASS, and a linkage between the two is required for estimating new sampling weight.

Consider next the problem of assuring that a school's locale is properly identified as a large city or as midsized, as urban or suburban, and so on. Each year NCES attempts to record every school and its locale through the annual Common Core of Data (CCD) survey. Census Bureau data are used in the CCD to identify locales, using seven well-defined locational categories used by the bureau. Every two to five years SASS is run, targeting a sample of schools. In this effort SASS also elicits information on locales using a simplified question involving eight categories or responses. A challenge lies in reconciling the two sources of information about school locale (Johnson, 1993; Bushery et al., 1992). Reconciliation of the SASS and CCD files then involves linkage. Such studies reveal, for instance, that roughly 70 percent of SASS reports on locales are correct, that 87 percent of Census classifications are accurate, and that the most common discordance lies in the suburban categories. More important, note that both data sources are imperfect in different ways. This makes linkage-based reconciliation studies essential to assuring the quality and interpretability of the survey results.

Reconciliation studies that illuminate the discrepancies that might be found between two or more independent surveys are important. It would be dis-comfitting to find a 10 percent difference in the number of teachers in the United States based on one NCES survey, for example, in contrast to another NCES survey undertaken independently and within a year or two of the first survey. The differences between results of two independent surveys may be a matter of sampling error. Or they may be substantial and attributable to differences in questionnaire wording, definitions, and sampling frame. Being able to link records so as to understand the discrepancies is essential. Linkages may be at the entity level, such as a school, school district, or state. Or they may be at the individual level, as when teachers respond to a questionnaire about their career in teaching.

Consider the following examples based on Kasprzyk et al. (1994) and Jenkins and Wetzel (1994). Discrepancies between independent surveys of institutions, such as "schools," occur for a variety of reasons. For instance, some commercial firms define schools in terms of their physical locations. The CCD defines schools in terms of administrative units, two or more of which may be lodged in the same location. These differences are relevant to sampling frames and to results of surveys, of course. Careful analyses are done to assure that discrepancies and their implications are understood.

Furthermore, estimates of the number of teachers in each state may be based on SASS or on state-generated counts for CCD. The estimates may and do differ at times for some states. For instance, overestimates of 15 percent in nine states appeared in the 1990 to 1991 SASS for a variety of reasons. One such reason was the questionnaire wording used in each survey. A respondent in the CCD would report on a unit involving grades kindergarten through 6; the SASS respondent might report on kindergarten through 6 *and* on grades 7 and 8. Postprocessing edits helped reduce discrepancies.

Hierarchical Studies

Once said, it is obvious that any survey of schools, teachers in schools, and students assigned to particular teachers must involve a basic linkage of microrecords to be useful as a hierarchical study. That is, one must be able to link each child to his or her teacher and each teacher to the school that the teacher serves.

Research on the problem of doing such work in the context of SASS has been conducted since at least the early 1990s (King and Kaufman, 1994). Partly because such work often involves ex-ante design, rather than ex-post facto record linkage, difficulties in linkage appear to be ordinary. Rather, estimation issues appear to be difficult. Of course, many more levels of linkage are possible. The Third International Mathematics and Science Study (TIMSS) is an obvious example. It involves no temporal linkage of the kind that longitudinal studies require. It does involve sampling test items in each child, sampling classrooms in schools, sampling schools in each nation, and a nonprobability sample of nations. Thousands of instances of linkage of diverse kinds are entailed in such a study.

WHAT DOES "LINKAGE" MEAN?

Vernacular in the sciences is not as uniform as one might expect. Recall, for instance, debates over what constitutes a gene or genome in the Human Genome Project. Discussions about integrating or linking data in the social sciences also are affected by dialect differences. We discuss illustrations below and then dimensionalize the idea of linkage. The focus is on units whose records are to be linked, the populations from which units are sampled, and the variables that are measured on these units and other matters. All in what follows depends on learning from others about what linkage has meant in the context of work sponsored by NCES and others.

Vernacular and Definitions in Education Statistics

The Hilton (1992) book's vernacular is sufficiently different from technical parlance in related areas to confuse some readers. For instance, there are repeated references to "linking" and "merging" of different databases, but these terms are undefined. Further, the book's use of these words is at times not the same as is customary in contemporary statistical work. For instance, linkage is defined, in effect and occasionally, as combining microrecords based on a common identifier for the same person or entity. At times the book's use of the word *link* is to imply an intention to "put together." At other times the word *link* means to stratify the units in each database in the same way (e.g., high ability, Hispanic, and so on) in order to look at how frequencies in these strata change over time on a dimension such as persistence in studying science. The word *merge* is also used to describe putting different records together, records that may or may not have a common source.

The phrase "pooling data" was used by Hilton (1992) and has been used by others in the sense of doing a side-by-side comparison of statistical results from each of several different datasets. This phrase is not used in a way that some readers would expect. For some analysts "pooling data" means combining the data from two or more samples of the same population into one that can be analyzed as a complete sample. For others it means combining the results from samples of different populations. Finally, consider another more recent example. Bohrnstedt (1997) uses the words *link, integrate,* and *connect* in a thoughtful essay entitled "Connecting NAEP Outcomes to a Broader Context of Educational Information." His use of these terms, at first glance, is instructive. The conscientious reader might observe, for example, that Bohrnstedt makes a careful distinction between *link* and *integrate.* He refers, for example, to the "integration" of CCD information with NAEP data, and he discusses the possible "linkage" of NELS:88 and NAEP data. The reader who also possesses some knowledge of what these datasets contain might then conclude that two datasets can be linked, at least in the context of education, if both involve the assessment of achievement or performance. This reader would be mistaken, though. As Bohrnstedt concludes, he uses the term *link* when referring to CCD/NAEP integration: that is, he substitutes *link* for *integrate.* The word *connect* does not reappear in the paper's prose. What are the implications of this example? Especially in creative efforts such as Bohrnstedt's, the precise meanings of such words as *link, integrate,* and *connect* ought to be made plain.

Vernacular in Other Sciences

Work on genes and genomes engenders problems of differences in labeling the object of their attention in context. For instance, a gene for one species may be called something different from the same gene in another species. Given the remarkable growth in genetic research, including the number and size of genome sequence databases, this is not a trivial matter (Williams, 1997). Similarly, scientists have begun to build a World Wide Web-oriented database on gene mutations as a part of the Human Genome Project effort. A feature of the design problem is to agree on what to call mutation. "The nomenclature is nearly agreed on . . . (with) the systematic name . . . based on the nucleic acid change and . . . the common name based on the amino acid change" (Cotton et al., 1998:9). The Internet will be used to further explicate and debate.

The vernacular problem is not confined to the life sciences. It extends to mathematics. "Computation," for instance, was heralded in a recent *Science* piece on bridging databases. In fact, basic statistical analyses, rather than computations, were the main topic: understanding how to estimate relationships when there are many errors attributable to sampling and measurement (Nadis, 1996). The lead on an interesting letter to *Science* was entitled "Bioinformatics: Mathematical Challenges" (Grace, 1997). Yet the letter concerns what is now regarded as a conventional statistical analysis approach to understanding the structure underlying data (i.e., analysis of variance), developed by two scholars who admired and exploited mathematics, R.A. Fisher and O. Kempthorne.

Science has also carried excellent articles with headings such as "Digital Libraries" (e.g., Nadis, 1996), "Letters" (Cotton et al., 1998), and "Bioinformatics" (Williams, 1997). They all deal with the names of things. But such papers are not easily found in any Web or library-based search based on a single keyword. One of us had to review the articles published over a five-year period to get the connection.

Implication: Understanding and Standardizing Nomenclature

One of the implications of this vernacular problem for NCES is that discussion, analysis, and agreement on terminology are in order. Because there has been little standardization in educational statistics produced at the state level, in recent years NCES has played a leadership role in getting state education agencies to agree to common definitions in statistical reporting. Witness the rough consensus on using two or three definitions of "dropout," for example. Witness also the NCES surveys of how public schools ask about student's race and ethnicity and the stupefying variety in measurement that then impedes better thinking. NCES can play a related role here and to refresh the roles taken at times by the Internal Revenue Service's Statistics of Income division, the Census Bureau's methods division, and others. That is, NCES can help make plain what we mean by "combining" datasets or surveys; "connecting" them; "linking" microrecords, datasets, or surveys; "pooling" datasets or surveys; "integrating" surveys or statistical systems; "unified databases; and "merging" files. In other words, putting things together. Absent explicit definitions of what these words mean, reaching mutual understandings in the statistical and political communities will be difficult or impossible. Most importantly, designing surveys so that they can be linked, compared, merged, and so on will be impossible. NCES can be a leading agency in this effort.

Dimensions of Linkage

One way of arranging the way we think about linkage is to depend on the elements used in designing conventional statistical surveys. Consider then the ideas of units of sampling, populations, and variables in this context and extensions of the ideas.

Units: Individuals, Entities, or Both

Records on an individual may be linked, as when a child's school transcript is linked to the child's responses to a survey questionnaire, as in High School and Beyond. Or responses on one wave of the HS&B may be linked to responses on subsequent waves, as in any longitudinal study. Similarly, a child or parent's response to an education survey may be linked to responses to a survey, as in the education component of augmented National Health Interview Survey.

Records on institutions or other entities may be linked, as in NCES's planned longitudinal surveys of schools. Or records on a school may be linked in the sense that school responses to the SASS questionnaire may be linked to responses to the annual CCD survey. The linkage may be hierarchical in that a child's record may be linked to his or her teacher's response to a survey. These in turn are linked to archival records on the school, school district, or state in which the child and teacher work. TIMSS is an example. For deterministic linkage the individual or entity in one survey or survey wave must be identical to the entity in the second survey or wave. In other words, the records on the same identifiable entity appear in two places.

Populations and Sampling Frames

The totality of units of interest constitutes the target population. Overlaid on this is the sampling frame, design, and method to determine who or what is in the sample at hand in any given survey. For deterministic linkage to be possible, there must of course be some overlap in the target populations defined for each survey or archive. For instance, records on schools in SASS may be linked to records in CCD because the target populations overlap. Nonoverlap may occur because each survey is run at a different time in a different school. Some schools, for example, disappear: they may be closed or merged with other schools, for example.

Sampling frames must be defined similarly, if not identically, for linkage to be easy. For example, a change in sampling frame from one that is entity based to location based led to the need for reconciliation studies in SASS. These would not have been possible without linkage.

Variables and Their Measurement

Different surveys or archives may measure the same variable, as when NLS elicits information on gender in repeated waves of a longitudinal survey. Or the variables may differ, as when early surveys measure an individual's academic ability and later ones elicit information about the person's job acquisition.

Linkage is facilitated by some redundancy in measurement of a variable. For instance, gender should remain the same across repeated waves in a longitudinal survey even if the full name changes somewhat with deletion of a middle name or a change in surname with marriage. Linkage is arguably productive when different variables are measured in different ways. NAEP, for example, gets at the broad socioeconomic characteristic of each student. If it were possible to link NAEP to independent tax return information, studies of the relationship between achievement and parental resources would be far more informative.

Suggestions: A More Orderly Vernacular

The language of linkage is, as we have suggested, as promiscuous as is the use of certain words in other sciences. The language will change as the science changes, of course. Nonetheless, a perspective on standardization is desirable and possible. The National Research Council, NCES, or Office of Management and Budget (OMB) might be the vehicles for obtaining agreement on nomenclature. Our suggestion is as follows. First, focus one's attention on one study or sample survey dataset as primary. When two studies are equally important and must be put together, arbitrarily designate one as primary. View any linkage between this primary study and other studies or datasets as a linkage that involves augmentation of the primary study. Last, build on contemporary practice and some familiar vernacular to define the following eight kinds of linkage:

1. Sample augmentation. A different sample of the same target population is put together with the primary sample.

2. Variable augmentation. New variables, generated by different sources and observed on the primary sample, are added to the primary sample dataset. For instance, transcripts generated by schools on the courses that students take were added to a primary study that elicits information from students such as HS&B.

3. Time augmentation. New measures are put together with earlier measures of the same variables on the same sample. Longitudinal studies such as HS&B and NELS:88 involve this kind of linkage.

4. Family (kin) augmentation. Measures taken from relatives of units in the primary sample are added to the primary sample datasets. For instance, teachers' data are added to student data in TIMSS; the teachers' information bears on the students whose achievement levels are also measured and constitute the primary dataset.

5. Levels augmentation. Measures taken on units at a higher level than the units in the primary sample are added to the primary sample dataset. For example, nation-level policy variables may be observed and added to TIMSS datasets on schools and students in schools in each nation covered by TIMSS. The primary TIMSS dataset did not include observations at the national level, but new studies will.

6. Mode augmentation. New ways of measuring roughly the same variables on roughly the same units are added to a primary sample dataset. For instance, digitized videotape data may be added to teacher and student records in the same schools in TIMSS in two countries as a different way of measuring what is taught and how.

7. Population augmentation. New populations having been surveyed using the same measures are put together in a file with the primary sample dataset, the primary sample having been drawn from a different population. For instance, a new Chinese version of TIMSS might be added to the TIMSS data that heretofore had no Chinese data.

   8. Replicative augmentation. A different sample of a different or the same population using identical measures is put together with a primary sample dataset. The studies combined by Hedges and Nowell (1995) constitute a replicate augmentation.

   Eight kinds of linkage (augmentation) were just identified. To make their memorization easier, let us invent a mnemonic. Recall the musical scale: doh re me fah soh lah te doh? Change a couple of letters and we get:

   Voh: Variable augmentation
   Re: Replication augmentation
   Me: Mode augmentation
   Fah: Family augmentation
   Soh: Sample augmentation
   Lah: Level augmentation
   Te: Time augmentation
   Po: Population augmentation

This is miserable music but a possibly helpful way of arranging songs about linkage.

LINKAGE POLICY: EX-ANTE, EX-POST FACTO, OR BOTH

   Planning disparate studies so as to permit their combination at a later time is, we believe, important. Understanding how to combine studies after the fact, when we have been unable or unwilling to plan, is no less important. At the national, regional, or local levels, no planning is possible absent an institutional vehicle for enhancing cooperation among the organizations that sponsor statistical surveys. In what follows we make more clear what is meant by ex-ante and ex-post facto policy, present an illustration, and briefly discuss the institutional vehicles that might actualize such policy.

   Apropos of ex-ante linkage policy, there appears to be a fine opportunity to plan the combination of data generated by federal agencies with different *missions*. In this context the example we discuss concerns a federal agency that is authorized to generate national education data and a federal organization dedicated partly to generating data on the effects of education programs in the United States.

Definition and Analogy

   In principle it is possible to construct a national policy that facilitates putting datasets together in the interest of science and society. Such a policy might emphasize long-term planning for periodic linkage, that is, an ex-ante approach to the topic, or it might stress an ex-post facto perspective. The latter recognizes that the scientific or policy questions that invite putting different datasets together are often posed *after* particular studies are designed and data generated, rather than in advance of the studies' design and execution.

This distinction is analogous to that made in the specific context of a longitudinal study that itself entails linkage. Such a survey is planned so as to follow individuals or organizations over time. Information that permits follow-up is routinely obtained at the start of the survey and often in each follow-up wave of the survey. This "forward tracing" information includes, for instance, the names of relatives or organizations that might be helpful in locating the individuals who were sampled in the first wave at later points in time. Where a longitudinal study is not planned, rather it is constructed after the fact, resources for "backward tracing" are brought to bear. In the survey arena these have typically included post offices, telephone books, and credit bureaus.

A similar compartmentalization of tactics is implicit in ex-ante versus ex-post facto linkage initiatives. Ex-ante requires that one anticipate and obtain the kinds of information that will foster future linkages. This information may be basic. For instance, obtaining data on the same background variable, such as age, gender, education, race, or ethnicity, and collecting data on these in the same way, for instance, is one such forward linkage tactic. Ex-post facto linkages may require other resources. Among the latter we might include probabilistic matching algorithms that, in different ways, help determine that the same persons or entities appear in two independent sample surveys and administrative records systems. See, for instance, the *Proceedings of the Survey Research Methods Section of the American Statistical Association* for articles on this topic.

Questions and Modes of Response: An Illustration

Hilton's (1992) book provides ample evidence for the United States that questions about a survey respondent's economic status, race/ethnicity, or other important topics, have been asked differently across surveys and datasets. Such differences in questions prevent straightforward comparison of the results of independent surveys directed toward the same population. That is, they prevent linkage of a particular kind. The book, however, offered no recommendations about whether and how to standardize such questions.

Learning how to address an ostensibly simple question about race well, indeed figuring out what "well" means, is not easy. NCES has done work in this area, notably in discovering the variety of ways that schools ask related questions (see the citation in Evinger, 1997). The problem is, of course, general. Consider, for instance, recent federal efforts to determine how questions about racial and ethnic origins ought to be asked in surveys (Evinger, 1997). The Federal Interagency Committee for the Review of Racial and Ethnic Standards spent four years on the problem. Nearly 60,000 respondents were involved in randomized field experiments using seven variations on such questions embedded in the Current Population Survey. The study's objectives included learning more about whether and how to ask about multiracial self-identification and categories of race and ethnicity. The committee's recommendations based on this evidence and revised by OMB resulted in, among other things, a directive requiring standard use of five racial categories: white; black or African American, American Indian or Alaskan; Asian; and native Hawaiian or other Pacific Islander (see OMB Directive 15, 10/30/97, http://www.access.gpo.gov).

This kind of work helps avoid a major limit on the value of any linkage in at least one respect. Asking about race and ethnicity in roughly the same way, dictated by standardization of measurement, enhances linkage opportunities. Further, one major lesson of the work is that at times putting datasets together often engenders fundamental issues. For instance, a "simple" question that is put to a respondent is not always simply put or interpreted. A second lesson is that some problems in the arena transcend federal (and state) agency boundaries and require methodological research. To put the matter bluntly, it took the cooperation of 60,000 citizens to figure this out. They were engaged in large-scale field trials on how to ask questions, a nontrivial exercise in a country as diverse as the United States. Neither the NRC committee nor NCES needs a reminder of this, but others might.

We also know that embedding different forms of the same question in the questionnaire, for a subsample at least, is a decent vehicle for learning about relationships among questions. More general tactics might be invented, based perhaps on the test-equating strategies that have been explored by Holland and Rubin (1982), among others. Certainly the matter is pertinent to NCES's investments in learning how to integrate (and in what senses to integrate) the longitudinal and cross-sectional surveys that it sponsors (Griffith, 1992).

An implication of all this is that survey questions need to be designed with linkage in mind. NCES often does this implicitly and in an ad hoc fashion. We are unaware of an explicitly written standard for doing so as part of NCES's survey design strategy, nor does it appear to be a systematic program of empirical side studies or pilot work by NCES that regularly takes linkage seriously.

Organizational Vehicles

A national ex-ante strategy requires that an institutional vehicle be exploited to plan for linkage of surveys or other research projects across branches, dimensions, or units in an agency and to plan similarly across independent agencies. In the United States the Interagency Council on Statistical Policy is one vehicle for planning across statistical agencies. The council was created under the Paperwork Reduction Act. A section of the enabling legislation (Sec. 3504) gives authorization "to improve the efficiency and effectiveness . . . to coordinate the activities of the Federal Statistical System ((e)(1)), and promote the sharing of information" and so forth. Each of these elements of the statute bears on linkage, including the diverse kinds of linkage discussed in this paper.

The Interagency Council on Statistical Policy is one of several possible organizational vehicles. Other options may be more attractive, feasible, or appropriate. Consider, for instance, that a broad research theme and set of questions might drive a de facto data linkage policy in the United States. One such theme, suggested by Pallas (1995), is better alignment of economic statistics with education statistics. Putting relevant datasets together ex-post facto requires cross-agency cooperation, which in the United States is a complicated matter. Pallas (1995) suggests the invention of an interagency working group. Regardless of the merits of the particular theme, economics, and education, there are good precedents for the vehicle he suggests. They include the Interagency Task Force on Child Abuse and Neglect, to judge from recent conferences of the NRC's Board on Children, Youth and Families and the Committee on National Statistics.

Federal Statistical Agencies and Federal Agencies with Other Missions

In the United States and some other countries, considering ex ante policy on putting datasets together invites thinking about the institutional separation of passive statistical surveys from actively controlled experiments for planning and evaluation programs. At the political level, such separation may be essential. Federal statistical agencies such as the NCES, the Bureau of Justice Statistics, the National Center for Health Statistics, and the Bureau of Labor Statistics are supposed to be free of political influence, for example. Federal agencies that sponsor controlled experiments in education, crime, and so forth focus scientific attention on innovations that at times are politically sensitive. In education, for instance, the Planning and Evaluation Service of the U.S. Department of Education is responsible for medium- to large-scale evaluations of federally sponsored education programs in the United States. The staff of this Office of the Under Secretary have initiated high-quality randomized trials on dropout prevention programs, among others.

This political and statutory separation of these two kinds of institutions is not necessary on intellectual grounds. In particular, when the object of a study is to produce unbiased and generalizable estimates of the relative effectiveness of a program, combining the survey data with controlled field trials data is sometimes sensible. Estimates of effects based on the surveys are often generalizable because they are based on national or large probability samples, but they are suspect because they depend so heavily on specification of models that underlie the analysis. On the other hand, the controlled experiments usually must be localized, limiting generalizability. But they are more trustworthy on account of the randomization they use and the consequent lower vulnerability to violations of model-based assumptions.

Ex-post facto approaches to combining such data have been laid out in reports of the U.S. General Accounting Office. Specific applications of this "cross-design synthesis" approach include estimating the relative effect of mastectomy versus lumpectomy on five-year survival rates of women with breast cancer. Ex-ante approaches based on these ideas are given by Boruch and Terhanian (1996, 1998). Their hypothetical examples include coupling NAEP to controlled field experiments so as to learn about the relative effects of grouping students in schools by ability.

MAPS, DISPLAYS, REGISTRIES, AND EVALUATION

Consider the problem of how to make orderly our thinking about productive linkages of diverse kinds. This section considers two related topics. The first bears on the idea that it is possible to better map survey questions and response categories, this being crucial to understanding what variables (and ways of measuring them) are common or unique across different surveys. The second topic concerns the visual display of information on the contents of surveys. The third topic, inventing registries of linkages, has implications for enhancing understanding of the first two topics and for evaluating the products of any linkage effort or policy.

Mapping Questions and Response Categories

We are aware of no comprehensive effort to develop intellectual maps of the specific questions asked in surveys mounted by NCES or other federal statistical agencies in the United States. Nor are there maps of the variables that the questions are supposed to address. Quite apart from this it is difficult to conceive of definitions for a map, much less to specify how to construct one or to imagine the forms that such maps might take. Nonetheless, we present some ideas on the topic here. The premise is that intellectual maps, like contemporary geographic maps and genome representations, can be important to the development of the field.

Raw Material

What is the raw material for such a map? For any given survey it includes the basic element of a specific question and its associated response categories. A summary question and response of the sort often found in code books generated for statistical records, the labels for a table or chart in an academic research journal or government publication, and so forth are insufficient.

Marginal tabulations of the distributions of response are commonly available. These, along with reports on methodological studies of the item where they exist, also might be included as ingredients for map making. It is well understood that context counts, and so the block of questions into which a particular item is embedded and the entire protocol ought to be included as raw material. And, of course, structural information on a survey's sponsorship and timing are fundamental.

An Electronic Form of Map: Web Based

In principle it is possible to put a question and response onto a Web page with hypertext links to other raw material or distillations of the latter. Linkage levels might be based on one or more natural search propensities. For instance, links to a block of questions into which a specific question is embedded is natural. A second-level hypertext connection to the questionnaire is also natural. Or the search propensities of inquirers might be empirically based, so as to identify what types of links would be most helpful. That is, they might be designed so as to get at what inquirers prefer first, then proceed to what they want second, and so on. The map then is tailored to their needs, just as contemporary geographic maps are tailored.

Regardless of the particular search mechanism, it seems sensible to exploit the opportunities presented by hypertext linkage in this context. That is, the technology permits easy lateral connections. We can then learn how questions about (roughly) the same variable are addressed in different surveys. It makes easy the task of connecting vertically so as to get at target samples or sponsors, marginal distributions, and so on.

Precedent and Form: ZUMA

As we have said, we are unaware of a U.S. precedent for mapping. However, a potentially useful model is embodied in work on cross-nation surveys in Europe. In particular, Mannheim's Zentrum fur Umfragen, Methoden und Analysen (ZUMA) has undertaken to consolidate and analyze information on background variables, how they are asked, and how they might be "harmonized." The multicountry surveys of primary interest in this context are the Eurobarometer (European Commission), the International Social Survey Programme (29 member countries), the European Community Household Panel (ECHP, Eurostat), and the surveys falling within the purview of the European Society for Opinion and Marketing Research (ESOMAR).

ZUMA began the effort by focusing on background variables and learning which ones commonly used in analyses and commonly asked about in the surveys. Such variables are often measured in NAEP, TIMSS, and other education surveys and have been the subject of considerable discussion. ZUMA classifies them into broad categories: A.G.E.: age, gender, education; CIEOV: class, income, employment status, occupation, vote; and RHEMMR: religion, household, ethnicity, marital status, group membership, etc. Each variable is defined broadly. The specific wording of items and response categories is given across surveys. Each is summarized in tabular form exemplified by the next exhibit. The hard-copy ZUMA report at hand (McCabe and Harkness, 1998; Harkness and Mohler, 1998) is densely packed with information. A Web-based system for its display, one that exploits hypertext connections and vertical and horizontal links, is likely to be more user friendly.

Software

A partial precedent for automated mapping lies in contemporary software developed for linking different kinds of administrative records. For example, Austin's school district may have 3,000 courses on its books because this district, as others, reports all courses approved by the Texas State Department of Education in its course portfolio. The district, however, has only 1,000 course categories or elements. A method to "map" one set of information to the other has been created to facilitate the linkage. This "Success Finder Mapper" (www.evalsof.com) is automated in the sense of making the mapping easier. It does depend on human judgment, of course, to set parameters and rules (Ligon, 1998). The product appears interesting enough to justify exploring its utility in a survey context in contrast to an administrative record context.

Visual Representations

Developing visual representations of such information seems important given its potential density. For instance, multiple displays or maps might be constructed for each variable, with the questions' "distance" from one another plotted on a line or in a two-dimensional space. The distance might be based on some index of semantic differential or difference on cluster analyses or some other approach. Or it might be based on a simple count of common features. Consider, for instance, the crude number of response categories for a simple question about whether the respondent works in the four tabulated surveys:

Survey Number	1	2	3	4
Number of response categories	5	7+	10	11

They might be displayed so as to emphasize common features—for example,

	ISSP	ESOMAR	EURO	ECHP
Self-employed	Y	Y	Y	Y
Never employed	N	N	Y	N

Note: ISSP = International Social Survey Programme. ECHP = European Community Household Panel.

We are aware of no serious research on this topic of displaying different questions about the same variable and response categories. The work by Tufte (1990) and others seems pertinent. Learning about how to exploit multiple n-dimensional displays, "escaping flatland" in Tufte's vernacular, is a tantalizing prospect. Because the features of questions and response categories may themselves be of categorical character, recent developments in the visual display of categorical information also are relevant. (See also Blasius and Greenacre, 1998, for a provocative if numbing array of options discussed at a conference convened by the Zentralarchiv fur Empirische Sozialforschung in Cologne.)

Analyses

Analyzing how questions about the same variable differ from one another across surveys, how response categories differ whether and how marginal distributions of responses differ, and so on is a complex matter. Scholars can exploit registries or maps of questions in analyses, thereby adding value to the maps and increasing our understanding of how to measure well and how to link different surveys. (See Braun and Miller, 1997, for a nice illustration of subtle and not so subtle traps in asking about "education level" across different cultures, languages, and geopolitical jurisdiction, based on the ZUMA mapping project.)

Printed Displays

How do we better display information on multiple surveys so as to make plain what is common to two or more of them and what is unique? Commonness of some elements is fundamental to putting datasets together. Learning then how to fabricate a two-dimensional display to characterize commonness succinctly is likely to be helpful. Displays with this intent are helpful, in some respects, to judge from those given in Hedges and Nowell (1995) and an NRC (1995) report on integrating statistics on children. From these one can learn how difficult it is to construct informative displays and some lessons about how to improve them.

First, nonuniformity in displays is discomfiting. The NRC volume displays surveys down the left margin in rows; the columns are variables or topics considered by one or more of the surveys. Hedges and Nowell arranged their display in the opposite way. Further, measured variables such as "family background" are identified as a broad category in some displays but not in others. Broad categories appear in some displays or the same study but not in others. For instance, Brooks-Gunn et al. (1995) identify studies that measure "family context" and others that do not. Some papers in the NRC volume classify variables as inputs or outputs, while others use a different classification. Some of this variation is trivial and unnecessary. What ought to be rows and what ought to be columns is easily standardized, for instance. Arranging the variables vertically and the studies horizontally often works well. A rectangular standard is adequate, but the complexity of surveys and the poser of hypertext invite one to think in more than two dimensions for displays or maps.

A second lesson of the NRC volume and the Hedges and Nowell paper is that the usefulness of displays, at least for their authors, lies partly in the particular question, theory, or perspective embodied in their essay. Hofferth (1995), whose interest lies in evaluation, tailored her display to recognize inputs and outputs. Brooks-Gunn et al. (1995), whose theoretical work emphasized contextual variables, made a point of recognizing these variables explicitly rather than as inputs and outputs. All of this implies there is a deep need to develop a capacity for flexibility in the composition of displays, to permit or facilitate the fabrication of multiple different displays, each of which may be standardizable. The hypertext feature of Web sites, a potential n-dimensional analog to tinker toys, provides the feasibility.

Third, printed displays often do not get to the level of specific question and response. Consequently, we do not know whether questions concerning family resources, such as income, are asked identically in the Panel Study of Income Dynamics, NELS:88, and others (Brooks-Gunn et al., 1995). Similarly, recall that Pallas (1995) recognized the family background variables appear in NLS-72, HS&B, NELS:88, BPS, and the Beginning Post Secondary Study. Without a deeper and more burdensome search, we have no idea whether the questions that address these variables are the same or whether response categories are the same from one question to the next. Nor do we know whether question and response categories are the same as those in surveys cataloged by Brooks-Gunn et al. as "family material resources." Mapping questions in the ways suggested earlier can help reduce uncertainty in this respect.

Registry of Analyses and Linkages

It is important to understand the consequences of putting datasets together. Little research, however, appears to have been done to advance this understanding. In developing this paper we lacked the resources (or did not have the wit to ask for them) to mount a full-blown empirical study of the value of earlier linkages or to guess at the value of future linkages. One can infer some of the value, of course, from the work we described here, but this is not entirely satisfactory.

Two related topics then invite our attention: a registry of linkage and evaluating the uses of linkage. The handling of both topics carries the implication that the NRC committee, NCES, or both can take action. No federal agency or private foundation, including NCES, has an excellent system for tracking the uses to which the datasets that it sponsored are put. *Uses* here means the formal statistical analyses of either a stand-alone dataset or datasets that have been put together. The absence of a tracking system makes it difficult to periodically evaluate and improve any given survey. More to the point of this paper, assessing the value of linked datasets and building linkage policy would be difficult without such a system.

Consider, for instance, that in the Hilton (1992) book there are few references to independent analysis of the datasets that are in the book's ambit. The Hedges and Nowell (1995) paper is a bit more conscientious on this account. In particular, there is a literature review, but it is perforce brief. Both resources reflect a symptomatic lack of a good registry on which scholars analyzed what dataset and, further, on which scholars educed what implications for the datasets' improvement. Linkage often constitutes one option for improvement.

A broad implication is that NCES might consider creating registers of the use of datasets in the interest of improving surveys, including linked datasets. More conscientious efforts by authors, professional journal editors, and systems such as ERIC could facilitate this. Certainly, exploiting Internet-based Web sites is feasible for this and related efforts. See the Terhanian Web site for a registry of analysis of NELS:88, for example (http://dolphin.upenn.edu/~terhania/index.html), and Boruch and Terhanian (1998) more generally.

Evaluating the Products of Linkage

Evaluation, regardless of its style or method, would have to take into account the purposes of putting datasets together. The purposes and dimensions outlined earlier might be used to organize the effort. Each of these purposes or dimensions, of course, can be examined with respect to its value for various audiences—scientist, policymakers, intermediary organizations that interpret public statistics for particular constituencies, and so on.

To begin such an evaluation, one might study the production process. Linkage is no easy matter in many studies, to judge from the papers reviewed here on research in this arena. For example, merely assuming that an individual or entity is the same and can be identified as such in a record-linkage effort can be complicated. In a society as inchoate as the United States, names of individuals and institutions change or are altered for a variety of reasons. Their locations and other characteristics are often thought to be durable, but they also change often. Errors in understanding a question about identity or characteristics are not uncommon and are not trivial.

Certainly, the value of the products of linkage can be studied and understood. What do the products add to understanding? How? How do we know? Estimating the value added to a scientific body of knowledge in this, as in other arenas, is not always easy. So-called paradigm shifts, involving a remarkable and obvious change in the way science is done, are rare. More important, they come about only with industrious adherence to conventionally conscientious research standards and incremental advances that are discernable.

Much of the recent scholarly work on understanding the incremental value of scientific work depends on the system of peer-reviewed publications. Citation counts are a stereotypical device for characterizing value, but other approaches can be exploited. For instance, the *Proceedings of the American Statistical Association* is not viewed by some as a scholarly journal. Nonetheless, the work products published therein are fundamental to our understanding of what goes on at NCES and other statistical agencies. NCES's planned journal, and other peer-reviewed journals, may publish works that appeared earlier in the *Proceedings*. But it would be as foolish to rely on the latter alone as it would be to ignore the *Proceedings*.

SOME LINKAGE OPTIONS IN EDUCATION STATISTICS

There is no formal, well-articulated "linkage policy" at NCES or any other statistical or research agency in the United States. We are aware of no such policy in Sweden, Israel, France, the United Kingdom, Japan, or Germany. Absent formal policy, identifying viable and interesting examples of what is desirable is a dubious objective. In what follows we suppress our ambivalence and discuss what might be desirable. Each suggestion for the future ought to be considered in light of our earlier suggestions in this paper about evaluation and vernacular.

Linking NCES Surveys

Several of the NCES datasets mentioned earlier, including NAEP, SASS, NELS:88, and CCD, contribute in distinct ways to the research and policy-making communities' understanding of a variety of important educational issues. NAEP for example, generates national and subnational estimates of achievement in core subject areas on a regular basis. SASS, on a somewhat less regular basis, produces a wealth of information concerning teacher supply, demand, quality, and, more generally, conditions in schools. NELS:88 allows researchers to test myriad hypotheses bearing on how, and how well, students learn over time. And the CCD provides general information on the nation's universe of school districts and schools, respectively, on an annual basis.

Are These Datasets "Puzzle Pieces" that Fit Together Neatly?

Despite their unique contributions, these NCES surveys are not pieces of an education puzzle that fit together neatly. On the contrary, certain pieces seem broken, several duplicate pieces exist, some pieces are inexplicably missing, and a few new pieces are produced so slowly that they appear to be altogether lost. Examples are given in what follows.

Broken Pieces: Example 1

Terhanian (1997) analyzed 1994 NAEP data in the interest of developing a deeper understanding of the relationship between school expenditures and student reading proficiency. To obtain school expenditure information for his analysis, Terhanian linked CCD district information (which he then converted to per-pupil values) with NAEP district, school, teacher, and student information. The task of linking CCD and NAEP data was by no means straightforward or seamless, however, because the NAEP dataset did not include the CCD unique identification code for participating school districts or schools. Yet, as Terhanian discovered inadvertently, the NAEP dataset did include the two "broken" pieces (i.e., separate variables) of the unique district code. By simply concatenating the two, Terhanian was able to create the one variable that was necessary to augment the NAEP data with CCD data.

A Peculiar Irony

NCES does not provide researchers with instructions on how to "fix" the "broken" pieces in the NAEP user's manual. Nor do NCES representatives actively publicize the presence of these pieces. It is perhaps for these reasons that scholars who focus on NAEP's improvement often recommend linkage with the CCD. They simply do not realize that the two datasets are already linkable, albeit with difficulty.

Duplicate Pieces: Example 2

Several NCES datasets, including NELS:88, SASS, and NAEP, include questions about school quality, teacher experience, and other common areas that concern policy makers and researchers. In some cases the exact same questions, or very similar ones, appear on different surveys. In other cases, however, questions about the same topic are phrased so differently across surveys that it is impossible to compare responses. Understanding NCES's rationale here is not as complicated as it seems. No one at NCES is charged with the responsibility of coordinating the various surveys, many of which run during the same year, at the microlevel. That is, no one really knows which questions are on which surveys, much less how they got there. We believe there is a better way.

Missing Pieces: Example 3

Linkage efforts are less successful than planned at times because puzzle pieces are missing. In the 1992 NAEP eighth-grade national math assessment, for instance, only about 60 percent of 8,300 math teachers could be linked correctly to their students. Data were completely missing for 35 percent of the total sample of teachers and partly missing for another 5 percent. Attempts by researchers to shed light on the relationship between teacher characteristics and student achievement, then, could only flop. NCES and its contractors seem to have corrected the within-school linkage problem—the teacher/student match rate improved appreciably for the 1994 and 1996 NAEP assessments. The ability of NCES and its contractors to learn from such failures certainly bodes well for the future.

Lost Pieces: Example 4

NCES datasets are not always produced expeditiously. Instead, some datasets, notably the CCD, are produced so slowly that they appear to be altogether lost. This not only diminishes the usefulness of the CCD to researchers and others but also adds to their frustration. Consider, as an example, the case of the JASON Foundation for Education. In 1997 the foundation developed a promising method to deliver science instruction via the Internet to middle school students. At the same time, it developed a simple registration process for potential participants that exploited the interactive nature of the Internet and relied on information from the 1992 to 1993 CCD.

In order to register for the pilot program, participants had to first identify their school district from a menu of districts and then their school from a menu of all schools in their district. After they did so, additional information about the district and the school populated several data fields on the registration page. JASON then asked potential participants to complete the registration form by confirming or editing the CCD information that populated the data fields. From start to finish, the entire process should have taken less than five minutes.

The registration process turned out to be flawed, however, because a nontrivial percentage of CCD information was either obsolete or missing (i.e., it seemed "lost"). For this reason about 10 percent of the first several hundred JASON registrants could not find their school districts or schools listed among those on the registration Web site menu. Others who were able to find their school districts or schools often felt obligated to correct dated information (e.g., number of students in the school). The registration process turned out to be a burden for respondents despite the good intentions of the folks at JASON.

What does this example of a "lost piece" imply for NCES? If researchers and others are to rely on the CCD, NCES must ensure that data are collected and compiled more expeditiously. Comparing the pace of the current collection and compilation process to that of the movement of a glacier, regardless of the cause (e.g., state officials possess no obvious incentive to provide NCES with information in a timely manner), seems fair.

What Combination of NCES Data Is Available and at What Linkage Level?

For any randomly chosen public school in the United States, the CCD is likely to be the only NCES information source available to researchers and policy makers. Absent a change in how NCES designs its surveys, there is little reason to expect some nontrivial combination of CCD, SASS, NAEP, and NELS:88 data to be collected during the same year for a meaningfully representative sample of schools. This is despite the fact that some combination of these data would, in our opinion, better serve the research and policy-making communities.

Table 10-2 displays crudely the current linkages among and between the NCES datasets mentioned here. It also describes the level at which these datasets are currently linkable. What are the *current* research implications of these potential linkages on analysis? It is possible to link some combination of CCD (e.g., core per-pupil expenditures of the Amarillo Independent School District), SASS, NAEP, and NELS:88 information at the district level in a given year. See Terhanian (1997), Wenglinsky (1997), and Taylor (1997) for recent examples of analyses that have exploited some combination of these linkage opportunities. It is also possible, in some cases, to link CCD, SASS, and NELS:88 at the school level in a given year. About 23 percent of the schools in which the sample of NELS:88 students were enrolled in both 1990 and 1992, for instance, also participated in the 1990 to 1991 wave of SASS. CCD information, then, is also available for these schools during these years.

The value of linkage may seem trivial to researchers who wish to carry out analyses of student or school samples that are representative of the nation or states. The implications for the design of future surveys, however, are perhaps less trivial. Just as we recommended that NCES or some other thoughtful federal agency develop a map or maps of variables across surveys, we also suggest that they consider doing so for the actual surveys they sponsor. The object of mapping is to better understand how the education puzzle pieces fit together, what pieces are missing, and what pieces are needed to better complete the puzzle.

Linkage and Augmentation of NCES Data and Non-NCES Data

At times, states, other federal agencies, and government contractors produce information that can be linked to NCES datasets, including NAEP. For instance, the Pennsylvania Educational Policy Studies Project, which is affiliated with the

TABLE 10-2 Linkages Between and Among NCES Datasets

Level	Data Source			
District	SASS	NELS:88	CCD	NAEP
School	SASS	NELS:88	CCD	

University of Pittsburgh, maintains a database that provides general descriptive data on the universe of Pennsylvania's school districts. These data include valuable information that is not available through other sources such as the CCD, notably each school district's Equalized Subsidy for Basic Education (ESBE) revenue (which is the largest source of state aid to school districts) and the ratio the state uses to determine ESBE revenue.

States such as Pennsylvania, then, are in a position to exploit linkage opportunities. For instance, the Pennsylvania state department of education might compare NAEP results with results from its own state assessment. Or Pennsylvania might undertake a large-scale satisfaction survey of the sample of schools participating in NAEP or SASS in the interest of understanding the effect of school quality, measured more broadly than it is currently measured, on school and perhaps even student achievement. Instances of states capitalizing on NCES's efforts are hard to find, however.

An example of a government agency capitalizing on and augmenting NCES's work is not so hard to find. The General Accounting Office (GAO) used the SASS sample in its recent work to investigate the quality of school facilities across the United States. GAO did not, however, return an augmented dataset to NCES for analysis because no arrangement had been made with NCES in advance. To us this seems quite shortsighted on the part of either NCES, GAO, or perhaps both.

The American Institutes for Research, a government contractor, has produced a Teacher Cost Index (TCI) to which NAEP or other NCES datasets might be linked. The TCI is a district-level index that accounts for factors that underlie differences in the cost of living among school districts (Chambers, 1995). Developed in part on the basis of an analysis of the 1993 to 1994 SASS, the TCI provides researchers with an arguably important tool for adjusting expenditure data to make expenditure effectiveness comparisons more fair. It enables researchers to estimate, for instance, the annual salary that school districts across a state would have to pay a similarly qualified teacher.

Private Organizations

At a high level of analysis, private organizations often link their efforts to a dataset generated by public agencies. Louis Harris and Associates, for instance, periodically surveys nationally representative samples of teachers, students, and parents. The sampling frames on which the organization relies include the CCD. Harris's efforts do not usually engender individual privacy issues because data are reported only in the aggregate. Moreover, the issues that concern Harris are not necessarily those that NCES and other federal agencies are able to focus on. Rather, Harris consciously seeks to fill missing information gaps and therefore focuses on certain important issues in far greater depth than NCES. These issues include parental involvement; safety and violence in schools, neighborhoods, and cities; and gender equity in schools.

There is no great reason why Louis Harris and Associates or other private organizations could not cooperate with NCES (or other statistical agencies) to enhance understanding of the value of sample augmentation linkage of the sort described earlier. Harris could have used the NCES Schools and Staffing Survey or any of the recent NAEP samples, for example, to inform or improve the design of the 1997 Metropolitan Life surveys that investigated gender equity and parental involvement in schools from the perspectives of students, teachers, and parents. And the organization might have provided NCES with resultant datasets as well as suggestions for improving future surveys and/or linkage.

Organizations such as Louis Harris and Associates are sensitive to the idea that linkages of various kinds can advance the company's mission in the public interest. They also recognize that linkage of datasets may be useless and that linkage engenders both naive and subtle privacy issues. More important, such organizations can be encouraged to develop more creative and innocuous approaches to policy on putting datasets together. This effort could be made for national samples of schools, local education agencies, sampling frames, and so forth. The information that comes about as a result ought to become a part of the knowledge base for NCES and other statistical agencies.

SUMMARY

Implication: Electronic Mapping

NCES, and perhaps other statistical agencies, can invent a Web-based system for mapping the variables measured in each survey sponsored by the agency (and other studies), the questions that address the variables, and the question response categories, exploiting hypertext to facilitate the acquisition of deeper information and wider searches. This would make easier the task of understanding what is common and unique to diverse surveys in education and perhaps other areas. Such a system is a natural extension of NCES's work on data warehousing and electronic code books and can adopt software that meets open database connectivity standards.

Implications: Nomenclature

NCES can play a leadership role in clarifying and standardizing the semantics of linkage. This would help make plainer and more uniform words such as *merging, pooling, connecting* datasets and so forth and fostering sensitivity to definitions of these in statistical policy, activity, and publications. NCES has been vigorous in related respects in the past, to judge from the agency's work with state education agencies on, for example, determining what dropout means and how a dropout is counted.

Implications: Dimensionalizing Linkage

NCES can explore ways to make plainer the functions of linking surveys, in effect dimensionalizing linkage activity. This might be done, as suggested earlier, by hinging dimensionalization on the ideas of augmenting a primary survey with two or more secondary ones, focusing on what is augmented: samples, populations, variables, modes of measurement, replication, and so on. The rationale is that we need to learn how to better arrange our thinking about very complex linkage efforts.

Implication: Linkage Policy

NCES can explore at least two approaches to linkage policy. Ex-ante policy stresses the idea that all surveys can be planned so as to be more connectable in specific senses. Ex-post facto policy recognizes that not all linkage can be planned and that unplanned linkage must be planned for. Further, institutional vehicles for developing policy can be identified and explored, such as interagency councils and statistical agency task forces. In the continued absence of coherent policy, we are unlikely to make much progress in productively exploiting diverse surveys or in better understanding the benefits and costs of linked studies.

Implication: Registries, Displays, and Evaluation

Developing a registry of each study that depends on linkage and developing new ways of displaying linkable or linked studies is possible. These are essential to understanding the linkage landscape and, moreover, to evaluating the value of linkages of various kinds. No such registries exist. Partly for this reason, perhaps, few formal and comprehensive evaluations of linkage efforts have been published.

Implication: Broken Pieces, Missing Pieces

NCES can consider approaching linkage issues productively by using a "broken pieces, missing pieces" theme. That is, one tries to understand how a study could be more informative had the possibility of linkage actualized through better planning. This perspective is kin to the idea underlying good postmortems in medicine and good crash investigations in the aviation and nuclear sciences, engineering, and other disciplines. It can be exploited by statistical agencies in the linkage context as it is, in effect, in individual survey efforts and formalized.

Implication: Cross-Agency and Cross-Institution Initiatives

NCES can play a leadership role in understanding whether, how, and how productive certain kinds of linkage studies that cross institutional and geopolitical jurisdiction lines have been and could be done. In principle, for example, some surveys sponsored by the public might easily be linked in one or more dimensions with privately sponsored surveys. In principle a survey mounted by a federal statistical agency such as NCES can be designed so as to permit easy connection to a study designed by a federal agency with another mission, such as program evaluation. What is possible in principle is not always possible in practice, but unless we explore the former, we will not improve the latter.

To return to the general topic of this essay, recall the quotation from Henry James at the start of this paper. It says, in other words, that everything is related to everything else. To make this manageable, NCES and the statistical and social sciences community have to draw circles around the more connectable things. In this respect the work reviewed in this paper and the implications educed here can help NCES and the research community do better in the future. This requires resources, of course, not the least among which is the political and scientific will to make data work harder to serve the public interest.

ACKNOWLEGMENTS

Research for this paper was sponsored by the National Center for Education Statistics, the National Science Foundation, and the U.S. Department of Education. We are grateful to colleagues at the Planning and Evaluation Service of the U.S. Department of Education, the U.S. General Accounting Office, and the Education Statistical Services Institute for conversations that helped clarify our thinking on the topic.

REFERENCES

Blasius, J., and M. Greenacre
1998   *Visualization of Categorical Data.* New York: Academic Press.
Boruch, R.F., and G. Terhanian
1996   So what? The implications of new analytic methods for designing NCES surveys. Pp. 4.1-4.118 in *From Data to Information: New Directions for the National Center for Education Statistics*, G. Hoachlander, J. Griffith, and J.H. Ralph, eds. Washington, D.C.: U.S. Department of Education.
1998   Controlled experiments and survey-based studies on educational productivity: Cross-design synthesis. Pp. 59-85 in *Advances in Educational Productivity, Volume 7*, A. Reynolds and H. Walberg, eds. Greenwich, Conn.: JAI Press.
Bohrnstedt, G.W.
1997   Connecting NAEP Outcomes to a Broader Context of Educational Information. Paper presented at the annual meeting of the American Educational Research Association, Chicago.

Braun, M., and W. Miller
 1997 Measurement of education in comparative research. *Comparative Social Research* 16:163-201.
Brooks-Gunn, J., B. Brown, G.J. Duncan, and K.A. Moore
 1995 Child development in the context of community resources: An agenda for national data collection. Pp. 27-97 In *Integrating Federal Statistics on Children: Report of a Workshop*. Board on Children and Families and Committee on National Statistics, National Research Council. Washington, D.C.: National Academy Press.
Bruce, R.V.
 1973 *Bell: Alexander Graham Bell and the Conquest of Solitude*. New York: Little Brown.
Bushery, J., D. Royce, and D. Kasprzyk
 1992 The Schools and Staffing Survey: How re-interview measures data quality. In *1992 Proceedings of the Section on Survey Research Methods*. Alexandria, Va.: American Statistical Association.
Citro, C.F.
 1997 Editor's postscript. *Chance* 10(4):31.
Chambers, J.
 1995 *Public School Teacher Cost Differences Across the United States*. Washington, D.C.: National Center for Education Statistics.
Cotton, R.G.H., V. McKusick, and C.R. Scriver
 1998 The HUGO Mutation Database Initiative. *Science* 279:10-11.
Cox, L.H., and R.F. Boruch
 1988 Emerging policy issues in record linkage and privacy. *Journal of Official Statistics* 4(1):3-16.
Evinger, S.
 1997 Recognizing diversity: Recommendations to OMB on standards for data on race and ethnicity. *Chance* 10(4):26-31.
Grace, J.B.
 1997 Letter. *Science* 275:1862-1863.
Griffith, J.
 1992 Presentation to the National Advisory Council on Education Statistics (March 12-13, 1992): Draft Paper on a Proposal for an Integrated Longitudinal Studies Program. Washington, D.C.: National Center for Education Statistics.
Harkness, J., and P. Mohler
 1998 *Towards a Manual of European Background Variable: Part I, Appendix II: Report on Background Variables in a Comparative Perspective*. Mannheim, Germany: Zentrum fur Umfragen, Methoden und Analysen.
Hedges, L.V., and A. Nowell
 1995 Sex differences in mental test scores, variability, and numbers of high scoring individuals. *Science* 269:41-45.
Hilton, T., ed.
 1992 *Using National Data-bases in Educational Research*. Hillsdale, N.J.: Lawrence Erlbaum Associates.
Hofferth, S.L.
 1995 Children's transition to school. Pp. 98-123 in *Integrating Federal Statistics on Children: Report of a Workshop*. Board on Children and Families and Committee on National Statistics, National Research Council. Washington, D.C.: National Academy Press.
Holland, P.W., and D.B. Rubin, eds.
 1982 *Test Equating*. New York: Academic Press.

Holt, A., S. Kaufman, F. Scheuren, and W. Smith
    1994   Intersurvey consistency in school surveys. Pp. 105-110 in *Volume II: 1994 Proceedings of the Section on Survey Research Methods*. Alexandria, Va.: American Statistical Association.

Jenkins, C.R., and A. Wetzel
    1994   The 1991-92 teacher follow-up survey reinterviewer and extensive reconciliation. Pp. 821-826 in *Volume II: 1994 Proceedings of the Section on Survey Research Methods*. Alexandria, Va.: American Statistical Association.

Johnson, F.
    1993   Comparisons of school locale settings: Self-reported vs. assigned. Pp. 689-691 in *1993 Proceedings of the Section of Survey Research Methods*. Alexandria, Va.: American Statistical Association.

Kasprzyk, D., K. Gruber, S. Salvucci, M. Saba, F. Zhang, and S. Fink
    1994   Some data issues in school-based surveys. Pp. 815-820 in *Volume II: 1994 Proceedings of the Section on Survey Research Methods*. Alexandria, Va.: American Statistical Association.

Kilss, W., and W. Alvey, eds.
    1985   *Record Linkage Techniques: Proceedings of the Workshop on Exact Matching Methodologies*. Washington, D.C.: U.S. Department of the Treasury.

King, K.E., and S. Kaufman
    1994   Estimation issues related to the student component of SASS. Pp. 1111-1115 in *1994 Proceedings of the Section on Survey Research Methods*. Alexandria, Va.: American Statistical Association.

Kruskal, W.H., ed.
    1982   *The Social Sciences: Their Nature and Use*. Chicago: University of Chicago Press.

Ligon, G.
    1998   Success Finder Mapper. Available at: www.evalusoft.com.

McCabe, B., and J. Harkness
    1998   *Towards a Manual of European Background Variable: Part I, Appendix II: Report on Background Variables in a Comparative Perspective*. Mannheim, Germany: Zentrum fur Umfragen, Methoden und Analysen.

Nadis, S.
    1996   Computation cracks semantic barriers between data-bases. *Science* 272:1419.

National Research Council
    1992   *Teacher Supply, Demand, and Quality: Policy Issues, Models, and Data-bases*, E.E. Boe and D.M. Gilford, eds. Committee on National Statistics. Washington, D.C.: National Academy Press.
    1995   *Integrating Federal Statistics on Children*. Board on Children and Families and Committee on National Statistics. Washington, D.C.: National Academy Press.
    1999   *Grading the Nation's Report Card: Evaluating NAEP and Transforming the Assessment of Educational Progress*, J.W. Pellegrino, L.R. Jones, and K.J. Mitchell, eds. Committee on the Evaluation of National and State Assessments of Educational Progress, Board on Testing and Assessment. Washington, D.C.: National Academy Press.

Pallas, A.
    1995   Federal data on educational attainment and the transition to work. Pp. 122-155 in *Integrating Federal Statistics on Children: Report of a Workshop*. Board on Children and Families and Committee on National Statistics, National Research Council. Washington, D.C.: National Academy Press.

Rosen, S., ed.
  1974   *Final Report of the Panel on Manpower Training Evaluation: The Use of Social Security Earnings Data for Assessing the Impact of Manpower Training Programs.* Washington, D.C.: National Academy of Sciences.

Scheuren, F.
  1995   *Administrative Record Opportunities in Educational Survey Research.* Report prepared for the National Center on Educational Statistics. Washington, D.C.: George Washington University.

Spencer, B.D.
  1980   Conducting benefit cost analysis. Pp. 38-59 in R.W. Pearson and R.F. Boruch, eds. *Lecture Notes in Statistics: Survey Research Designs.* New York: Springer-Verlag.

Taylor, C.
  1997   The Effect of School Expenditures on the Achievement of High School Students: Evidence from NELS and the CCD. Paper presented at the American Educational Research Association annual meeting, Chicago.

Terhanian, G.
  1997   School Policies and Practices, Student Proficiency, and Racial Differences in Proficiency: Evidence from a Multilevel Analysis of the Reading Proficiency of 4th Graders from Pennsylvania and New York. Paper presented at the Summer Data Conference of the National Center for Education Statistics, Washington, D.C.

  1999   Homepage. Available at: http://dolphin.upenn.edu/~terhania.

Tufte, E.R.
  1990   *Envisioning Information.* Cheshire, Conn.: Graphics Press.

U.S. General Accounting Office
  1986a   *Computer Matching: Assessing Its Costs and Benefits.* Washington, D.C.: U.S. General Accounting Office.

  1986b   *Computer Matching: Factors Influencing the Agency Decision Making Process.* Washington, D.C.: U.S. General Accounting Office.

Vogel, G.
  1997   Publishing sensitive data: Who calls the shots? *Science* 276:523-526.

Wenglinsky, H.A.
  1997   *When Money Matters: How Educational Expenditures Improve Student Performance and When They Don't.* Princeton, N.J.: Policy Information Center, Educational Testing Service.

Williams, N.
  1997   How to get databases talking to one another. *Science* 275:301-330.

11

Developing Classroom Process Data
for the Improvement of Teaching

James W. Stigler and Michelle Perry

Of the many factors that determine student academic achievement, classroom instruction is but one. Yet it is surely an important one. Indeed, all attempts to improve education must of necessity at some point be mediated through the classroom. This is obvious because classroom practice represents the most direct means for affecting student outcomes. However, there has been surprisingly little research on this link in the chain in affecting student outcomes.

As a nation, we collect very little data on what happens inside classrooms. As Mandel (1996:3-29) wrote, "The national conversation about teaching has always been compromised by a dearth of information about the quality of practice and practitioners. . . . When dismal or promising results about student performance are reported, a new chain reaction of suppositions is often set off about the degree to which teachers are to be blamed or praised. But these suppositions are just that—hypotheses disconnected from much of a factual base that might shed some light on what is occurring, including the extent to which the observed results can be accurately attributed to teacher actions." This relative dearth of data can be blamed, at least in part, on what Burstein et al. (1995) point out as the inherent difficulty in measuring instructional practice.

Despite this inherent difficulty, we argue that the merits of these data outweigh the obstacles in collecting them. As an example of the importance of these data, here it is argued that we cannot know which instructional strategies lead to positive learning outcomes unless we know which instructional practices are being used and we cannot know which are being used without somehow looking directly at educational practices. In other words, achievement data may tell us a lot, but those data cannot tell us what should be done differently inside the classroom. We argue that for test data to be most informative, classroom processes need to be examined. If change in student learning outcomes is observed in the tests, we still need to know whether change is due to something going on in the classroom or something independent of that.

In this paper, we make the assumption that classroom process data, especially when collected in conjunction with student achievement data, can play a critical role in efforts to improve education. We further assume, however, that such data will not necessarily improve education and that it is therefore extremely important to have an explicit idea of exactly how data will be used to improve education and by whom. In particular, we argue that researchers, policy makers, and teachers need different kinds of data and will use data in different ways to improve the quality of teaching and learning in classrooms.

Five questions guide this paper: (1) What is the nature of classroom instruction, and what implications does this have for developing indicators of instructional quality? (2) What kind of data can be collected, and what are the advantages and disadvantages of each? (3) What kind of data ought to be collected, and how will the data be used to improve the quality of instruction? (4) What are the costs of collecting data of various kinds? (5) How can new kinds of data collection be integrated into the existing National Assessment of Educational Progress (NAEP) program?

Given these issues and questions, the goal of this paper is to consider what sorts of data can be collected on classroom processes. With this goal in mind, we examine the kinds of data that are currently collected on classroom processes and evaluate what can and cannot be learned from these data. We then look beyond current research practices and make suggestions for future data collection on classroom processes.

STUDYING CLASSROOM PROCESSES

Nature of the Classroom

Having established a broad interest in collecting data on classroom processes, we consider what kind of data might be collected. Before launching into a discussion of specific data collection techniques, we need to ponder the nature of classroom instruction. The data collected and measures constructed are only indicators. To assess the validity of these indicators, we must first think through the nature of what it is they are intended to be indicators of. Indeed, a framework for thinking about the constructs that define classroom instruction provides a necessary theoretical context in which indicators can be interpreted.

Classroom instruction, first and foremost, is a complex, dynamic, goal-directed system. One goal of the system is student learning, although there certainly are other goals as well. For purposes of this paper we will assume that achievement, as measured by the NAEP, is an important overall goal of the system we describe. The system consists of several important elements, including a teacher, students, curriculum, and materials. These elements interact with each other in complex ways. Teachers orchestrate the sequence of activities that comprise the classroom lesson. These activities represent organized behavioral interactions between students, teachers, and curriculum/materials. In addition, these lesson elements interact with key contextual factors that impinge on the classroom.

To say that the classroom is a system implies that it is more than the sum of individual features or independent dimensions. Although features might be measured to indicate indirectly the functioning of the system, it is difficult to imagine features of instruction that are always good or dimensions on which lessons should be uniformly high. For example, although in general it might be true that lessons in which students are cognitively challenged are better than lessons in which they are not, there are many instances in which repeated practice with less challenging tasks is appropriate and necessary for students' learning. This presents the researcher with a significant challenge. To define quality of instruction, one must do more than define a set of features; one must evaluate features of a specific lesson with reference to how they function in the context of a goal-directed system. Indeed, one must describe the system itself to understand the meaning of indicators.

An example will serve to illustrate the practical implications of this point. In the process-product research of the 1970s and 1980s, it was demonstrated, across many studies, that student learning of mathematics was significantly associated with rapid coverage of a large number of problems during the lesson: the more problems the teacher led students through, and the faster the pace, the more students learned as measured by achievement tests (Leighton, 1994; Leinhardt and Putnam, 1987). As often as this effect was found, however, it turned out not to hold up in cross-cultural comparisons. Japanese students achieve in mathematics at far higher levels than U.S. students, yet Japanese teachers often are found to cover only one or two problems in a single lesson, compared with 30 to 40 in an American lesson (Stigler and Perry, 1988). Clearly, the indicator of how many problems are covered has different meanings in the context of different instructional systems. U.S. teachers were using problems for repeated practice, and clearly there is something to be gained by such practice. Japanese teachers, in contrast, were using problems as the focus of students' deep thinking and reflection. Simply knowing how many problems were covered was not enough to characterize the kind of instruction students experienced.

Another truth about classroom teaching is that it is a cultural activity (Gallimore, 1996; Stigler and Hiebert, 1997). What this means is that teaching, like other cultural activities, is constructed largely out of widely shared routines that are learned implicitly and are highly resistant to change. Although in our culture we perceive variability across teachers in their approach to teaching, cross-cultural comparison reveals that such variability may be relatively insignificant compared with the large differences across cultures in the ways that teachers teach. U.S. teachers, for example, have varied ways of providing feedback to students who are working on math problems during seatwork. But these variations pale in size when we realize that virtually all U.S. teachers tell students how to solve the problem before they ask the students to solve it, whereas most times Japanese teachers do not. We tend not to notice those aspects of cultural activities that are shared, focusing instead on features that vary. But it may well be that the aspects of teaching that are widely shared in a culture are the ones that have the most impact on student learning.

One important implication of this fact about teaching is that it shifts our focus somewhat from the study of teachers to the study of teaching. Because the literature on classroom indicators has been largely an American one, it has tended to focus on aspects of teaching that vary in our culture. But we need to focus as well on identifying the shared cultural scripts that underlie most or all of what we see inside American classrooms. The improvement of teaching over time may be much greater if we focus on changing widely shared scripts than if we focus on understanding variations in the competence with which teachers use the scripts.

Research Questions

Viewing classroom instruction as a complex system and as a cultural activity leads us to identify several important research questions to guide our inquiry into instructional quality.

• What kinds of instructional systems can we identify? How can we describe these systems? This will involve, minimally, identifying the key elements of the classroom lesson and describing the ways in which these elements interact.

• What kinds of quantitative indicators can we develop to assess the functioning of different types of instructional systems? What are the processes that affect these indicators? We must quantify the descriptions developed in response to the first research question if we are going to validate them across large numbers of classrooms.

• What is the role of the student in different instructional systems? What are the processes by which students learn from classroom instruction, and what characteristics of different instructional systems affect how much students learn? These are key questions, as our interest in instruction rests on the assumption that student learning is affected by instruction.

• What is the role of the teacher in different instructional systems? How can teaching be improved? Again, we assume that teachers play a critical role in shaping the nature and quality of instruction in the classroom.

Each of these general research questions can be approached through various analytic frames. For example, classroom lessons can be described on a more macrolevel in terms of activity structures (e.g., classwork or seatwork) or from a more microanalytic level (e.g., detailed analysis of discourse patterns as they unfold throughout the lesson).

Units and Methods of Analysis

Starting with the assumption that classroom instruction is a complex cultural system, we have proposed a broad set of research questions. The complexity of instruction also has implications for the units and methods of analysis we choose.

Classrooms must be studied using units that make sense and that preserve the crucial aspects of the system. These units might be relatively large (e.g., units, grade levels), but they are probably not smaller than the classroom lesson. Classroom lessons have ecological validity from the teacher's point of view. Teachers plan their days in terms of lessons: "First we'll do math, then social studies." Lessons are goal directed and orchestrated by the teacher. The explicit goal of the lesson might be a student learning goal, or it may simply be the completion of some series of activities. Regardless of the goal, the lesson itself can only be understood in relation to the goal. Although we can study the lesson through different lenses (e.g., we can study the nature of classroom discourse or the patterning of teacher-student interactions), we will need to collect information about the context in which the processes operate.

It is also important to note at the outset that both qualitative and quantitative analyses will be required in our efforts to understand and improve classroom learning. The first research question we listed is one that must be answered through qualitative analysis. Identifying parts of lessons and figuring out how the parts interact to produce student learning require a qualitative analysis of the instructional process. Once the process has been described, however, it is useful to develop indicators that can be used to validate and refine the descriptive model of instruction.

Not only do we need both qualitative and quantitative data, we also need a way to link the two kinds of data together. As we will see, this has been a problem with more traditional approaches to the study of classroom processes.

TRADITIONAL METHODS: SURVEYS AND NARRATIVE DESCRIPTIONS

Most commonly we have relied on surveys to collect data on classrooms. Additionally, narrative descriptions have been used as a method of collecting classroom data. In this section, we review those methods. In particular, first we provide *descriptions and overviews* of the data forms. Next, we examine *what we typically learn* from data collected with each of these methods. Finally, we offer an *evaluation* of each of these methods, with some attention to both the limitations that each method has in terms of producing data on classroom processes and the potential of providing new insights about teaching and learning.

Survey Methods

Descriptions and Overviews

Surveys represent relatively straightforward ways to collect data on a host of issues related to classroom processes; however, surveys can take several different forms. For example, even if we are just surveying teachers, teachers can be surveyed about their recollections or their opinions with questionnaires (whose answers can take the form of a rating scale, forced multiple-choice responses, or open-ended answers), interviews, or diaries. In this section, we also include observational checklists, which in some ways resemble the other data forms in this section but in other ways resemble narrative observational records. In the remainder of the section, we provide a general description of the various types of survey methods.

Questionnaires and rating scales Questionnaires and rating scales are often used to tap classroom processes. Questionnaires and rating scales used for these purposes typically request information from teachers about the activities taking place in their classrooms. Others, including classroom observers and students, also may participate in completing questionnaires about classroom processes.

This data source can provide information about what is taught, how the teaching takes place, and how much time is spent on various topics and activities. As an example, Burstein et al. (1995:xiii) asked teachers to judge the percentage of class time spent instructing with various strategies (e.g., whole-class instruction, administering tests, performing administrative tasks). One of their major findings was that, "although the picture of teaching that can be drawn from survey data is quite general, it is probably valid, because . . . data clearly show that there is little variation in teachers' instructional strategies. The majority of teachers use a few instructional approaches and use them often." With these methods we can obtain data from a large number of informants who have direct access to the information we find of interest.

Diaries We use the term *diary* to represent teachers' records of their lessons, including lesson plans, outcomes, and the like. Diaries have been used, relatively successfully, to measure curriculum content. Given that we are concerned with classroom processes, one might wonder why we specified that diaries are used to measure curriculum content. The reason is that curriculum content has often served as a proxy for classroom practices, although it is not itself a direct measure of classroom practices. Barr and Dreeben (1983:107) defined content coverage (also commonly referred to as *instructional pace*) as the amount of curricular material that is covered over a period of time. They argued that although other indexes of productivity *designed for judging the effectiveness of instruction* are possible, "we have selected this one because, when treated at the level of individual children, it represents an instructional condition integrally connected with learning." Another reason for focusing on diaries to measure content when we are concerned about the relationship between teaching and learning, according to Brophy and Good (1986:360) is that "the most consistently replicated findings link achievement to the quantity and pacing of instruction."

As an example, Perry (1988) surveyed nine fourth-grade teachers' mathematics lesson plan books over the course of one year and recorded which problems were assigned. She then coded each problem as belonging to one of several mathematical topics. She also measured the students' mathematics problem-solving performance, both at the beginning and the end of the school year. Problems that most children solved incorrectly at the beginning of the year were designated as representing difficult topics, and problems that most children solved correctly were designated as representing easy topics. Generally, Perry found that problem assignment was related to student learning; more specifically, she found that spending a great deal of time on a few difficult problems led to better student achievement than covering many problems, especially problems that most students could solve before receiving instruction. In this study, a diary of what instruction consisted of was used to make inferences about teaching practices that were related to learning outcomes.

Interviews Interviews, conducted face to face or by telephone, allow us to get teachers' and/or the students' views of classroom processes. We can ask what happened and we can ask for evaluations about what was reported to have happened.

Interview techniques are especially useful, compared to paper-and-pencil methods (such as questionnaires and rating scales) when the potential responses have not been determined in advance. Interviews, especially those conducted by well-trained interviewers who know what sorts of issues are of interest and which deserve lengthy commentary, are desirable when we expect complex responses because interviewers can ask respondents different questions, depending on previous answers. If the potential responses are already known, less expensive methods may be more desirable.

Checklists Checklists often have been used to document classroom processes. When using checklists, all of the behaviors of interest must be defined in advance. Additionally, observers (i.e., the ones responsible for checking off observed behaviors on a checklist) need to agree about what constitutes the observed behavior. Thus, categories must not only be defined in advance, but must also be specified as clearly as possible so that the observers check the appropriate entry.

Typically, checklists are completed by outside observers, which makes this method different from those already discussed. In this way, checklists resemble the narrative descriptions of classroom observations, which we discuss later. However, this data form resembles the other forms of survey data in that the questions to be examined generally are already known before the data are collected.

To lay out more clearly the data that can be obtained with observational checklists, we provide a brief description of two well-known investigations that have relied on this method. As a first example, Brophy and Evertson (1976) had observers note each time a specified behavior occurred, such as teacher praise for a student's good response. From their observations and analyses, they concluded that teachers whose students had the highest achievement treated their students in a businesslike and task-oriented manner. As a second example, Stigler et al. (1987) had observers in three countries check when certain classroom behaviors and certain features of classroom organization were present. Their conclusions centered around the idea that whole-class instruction means that every student received some instruction, and teachers who relied heavily on individualized instruction had some students who, basically, were never taught. Both of these examples illustrate that checklists can provide a general snapshot of classroom life.

Uses of and Outcomes from These Methods

Survey methods are used to assess many variables related to instruction and life in classrooms. One reason these methods are used so frequently is that they are easy to use. With these methods it is easy to measure curriculum content. For example, researchers can read through teacher plan books or diaries kept for the purpose of noting what topics were covered and easily judge what was and was not taught. It is also easy to measure the amount and pace of instruction. For example, researchers can ask teachers in an interview which pages in the text were covered and can use a questionnaire to ask how much time was spent in instruction. It is also easy to measure the format of instruction. For example, researchers can ask teachers to check each form that was used on each day of instruction (lecture, small-group work, etc.).

More significantly, given the concerns motivating the present paper, these methods can even be used to measure classroom processes. For example, we can ask teachers in a questionnaire whether the questions they asked their students required short answers or reflection and abstraction; we can ask whether the students responded only to the teachers' requests or whether the students provided substantive contributions without teacher prompts. In short, researchers have used these methods successfully to document a wide array of classroom features. These methods typically have been used and analyzed in the process-product approach to classroom investigation (e.g., Brophy and Good, 1986). In general, the process-product approach assesses classroom processes—or their proxies—and relates these to student outcomes.

In addition, we note that these methods are typically used to test theories. Because survey methods must generate categories and items before the data are collected, the categories and items necessarily reflect a theoretical bias. The data collected in surveys can, for example, support or call into question a relationship that a theory would predict. In this way survey data can tell us when a theory cannot be supported and thus when a new theory is called for.

Evaluation

These methods of collecting data are used frequently, in part because they can be used on a wide scale: they are easy to administer and easy to analyze relative to other methods. The ease associated with collecting survey data makes these methods the most widely used for gathering data on classrooms. The difficulty and costliness of other methods have sometimes made them prohibitive altogether or at least have limited the number of classrooms that could be included for study (we document these more fully as these other methods are discussed).

Burstein et al. (1995:35) say that "there is still much that survey data can tell us about instructional strategy. Survey data can describe the major dimensions of classroom processes and how they vary across course levels and types of schools. National survey data, collected periodically, can document trends in teachers' use of generic instructional strategies. Such information is important for determining whether or not teaching is changing in ways consistent with the expectations of curriculum reformers and policymakers." For these reasons we imagine that the NAEP could collect and productively use these sorts of data.

Of course, with any method there are drawbacks. We see three major drawbacks to the methods just described: (1) These methods leave open many threats to validity; (2) Most significant among these threats is a lack of shared language; and (3) These methods rarely contribute to generation of new ideas and thereby do not prominently contribute to national discussion. We discuss each method in turn.

Problems of Validity Probably the most serious problem with survey methods is that responses often are not accurate, thereby making them not valid. In many instances, typical paper-and-pencil survey instruments are not to be trusted because teachers are fallible human beings and may easily forget what they have done or unwittingly skew their responses based on their individual biases. We do not mean to say that teachers are not to be trusted. What we mean is that it is sometimes difficult to produce accurate responses.

In particular, it is difficult to be precise about certain behaviors. This problem was made clear by some careful work (Mayer, 1999) on the reliability of these methods. Mayer (1999:43) writes: "We cannot rely on the individual survey questions to assess the amount of time . . . teachers use specific practices . . . because the teachers do not report their practices in a consistent manner.

Thus, the portrait of specific practices conveyed by the survey is unreliable and therefore invalid." It is much more reasonable to ask teachers what they believe than exactly what they do or how they have impacted their students with what they have done. For example, imagine how hard it would be to be precise about whether you had conveyed the concept of equivalent fractions primarily with questions, explanations, or examples. Imagine the further difficulty of knowing which of these three methods of instructional practice had the greatest positive influence on students' understanding of equivalent fractions.

Mayer (1999:43) investigated this directly by comparing teachers' responses on surveys to classroom observations of these teachers. He found that "low reliability existed for most of the practice items [i.e., items intended to measure teachers' practices] examined in this study." In short, surveys probably could never give us reliable and detailed data about classroom practice. And without reliability we cannot claim to have validly measured their behaviors.

A cousin to this problem is that those who respond to surveys are often tempted to answer questions as they imagine the researchers would like them to be answered, rather than with accuracy and honesty (e.g., Burstein et al., 1995; Cohen, 1990), thus making these methods susceptible to problems of social desirability. For example, with the recent implementation of reform-based standards, teachers are increasingly aware that their practice should reflect these standards. However, their practice may lag behind their knowledge of these standards, and so they honestly respond about what they know about the standards, even though their knowledge may not be reflected in their practice, thus making their responses on surveys inaccurate (i.e., not valid).

Although reliability is clearly a problematic aspect of relying on survey methods for documenting classroom processes, the reliability of constructs measured by surveys increases when multiple, rather than single, items are used to measure constructs (e.g., Light et al., 1990; Mayer, 1998; Shavelson et al., 1986). As Mayer (1999:43) writes: "Individual indicators of limited reliability can be grouped into a highly reliable indicator." The point here is that if we can get at a potentially important behavior with multiple approaches (e.g., use observational checklists to determine which instructional strategies were used and follow them up with interviews to learn more about how often they are used and under what conditions) or multiple items on the same measure, we are more likely to avoid problems with reliability and validity than if we rely on a single item or a single measure. Thus, we would recommend that if the NAEP were to include survey measures of teacher behavior, multiple measures should be used.

Lack of Shared Language Related to the problem of not obtaining a valid picture of classroom practices with typical paper-and-pencil survey instruments is that these instruments require an evaluation of whether teachers understand the items in the way they were intended. However, for this we need a common language that we really do not have. As Burstein et al. (1995:35) put it: "Surveys typically cannot capture the subtle differences in how teachers define and use different techniques." For example, what one teacher means when she agrees with the item "we had a discussion" may be very different from what another teacher means when he agrees with the same item. Even something as specific as "We folded paper to demonstrate equivalent fractions" is open to multiple, potentially inconsistent interpretations (Was the paper a square or a rectangular shape to begin with? How many folds were used?), thus rendering responses invalid, even to specific descriptions.

This notion is corroborated by Palincsar and her colleagues (1998), who argue that teachers' professional development should be constructed as a "community of practice." They argue that this model deals head on with two pervasive problems in the culture of American schoolteachers: "(a) the lack of consensus regarding the goals and means of education . . . and (b) the private, personal, and individualistic nature of teaching . . . which deprives teachers of collegial and intellectual support (Little, 1992)." In other words, Palincsar et al. believe that if examples are collected and used for discussion, a common language can be developed for teaching. Besides the inherent problems associated with not having a common language when teachers respond to survey items, we note that having a common language is the first critical step toward improvement and change. In this case, a common language would enable teachers to share ideas; teachers cannot be expected to implement and evaluate new practices until this takes place.

Failure to Contribute to New Ideas Third, and perhaps most importantly, these sorts of data rarely if ever contribute to the discussion of improving practice and outcomes. Why not? Because to improve practice concrete new ideas about classroom practice are needed. Without these, we cannot expect the dialogue about classroom practice to move forward productively. And, of course, all of the methods we have discussed thus far have the questions, issues, and items defined before any data are collected, thus limiting or excluding altogether the possibility of producing new, heretofore unimagined ideas about classroom practice. In this way, survey data are much better suited to supporting or questioning existing theory than developing new theory. However, this must be qualified: when theories are not supported by data, researchers are placed in a position to refine, revise, or generate new theory. In this way, survey data have the potential to contribute to theory.

Currently, most data on classroom practice can only tell us if what we want to see in teachers' practice is there or not because people (researchers, policy makers, administrators, etc.) have predefined what *should* happen. Thus, these data can tell us what is not working but cannot help generate new ideas for improvement. To generate new ideas for improvement, we would need to obtain data that permit the development of a shared language to refer to concrete examples of different practices. Several of the difficulties with survey methods outlined here are avoided by other methods, which we describe next.

Narrative Descriptions

Overview

Narrative descriptions of classrooms produce very different types of data, and have unique advantages and problems relative to survey data. Typically what is gained with narrative descriptions is an in-depth look at a small number of classrooms. In general, researchers who use this method send a small band of observers into classrooms. The observers then take notes—in other words, a narrative account—detailing what they see in the classrooms. The narrative notes typically are summarized and/or coded for the occurrence or absence of specified or interesting events that emerge from reading the narrative descriptions. If the observers take notes with enough detail, this method has the potential to yield multiple analyses on a variety of classroom practices.

We take work that we have conducted as an illustrative example of this method (e.g., Stigler and Perry, 1988). In this investigation we sent observers into 10 Japanese schools, 10 Chinese schools, and 20 U.S. schools. The observers or observer-trainers from the three countries met intensively before data collection began to iron out exactly what sorts of details were to be included in the narrative notes and exactly how often notes needed to be recorded (in this case, at least every minute). Then, when schools were in session, the observers took four days of narrative notes in each of two first- and two fifth-grade classrooms in each of the 40 schools in our sample. After the data were collected, they were summarized and translated into English and then coded for a variety of classroom practices that we suspected were either important across all sites and/or unique to one of the three sites. The summaries and coded notes yielded results and preliminary findings, which have since been explored more systematically (see, e.g., Stigler and Fernandez, 1995).

Uses of and Outcomes of This Method

Narrative descriptions give us a great deal of information. One of the typical uses of this method is to provide data for developing hypotheses and theories about teaching and learning. As mentioned, the narrative notes whose results were presented, in part, in Stigler and Perry's (1988) report provided opportunities for developing hypotheses, which were then tested more systematically in a controlled experiment (Fernandez, 1994). In other words, narrative descriptions are often the first step in the "descriptive-correlational-experimental cycle" suggested by Rosenshine and Furst (1973).

Evaluation

Problems of Money   One of the major problems with narrative descriptions of classroom observations is that they are expensive. This is true for at least two reasons: observers need to be trained very carefully and analysis is time consuming and labor intensive.

Recall the description of how observers were trained in the Stigler and Perry (1988) investigation: observers had to be brought together from three countries. They had to work together looking at videotapes of classrooms and discussing what they saw until they could agree on what should be written down in the narrative accounts. From there, the observers who attended this international training session had to go and train the remaining observers. You can only imagine how expensive the training of the observers was for this study. (But you can also imagine how worthless the data would have been without incurring this expense!)

And then there is the analysis of narrative records. Relative to survey methods, where the questions for investigation are fairly well specified before data are collected, the questions for investigation often emerge from careful reading of the data when using methods relying on narrative observation. This makes the cost of analysis—including developing coding systems, training coders to be reliable, and so forth—very expensive.

The high cost of narrative observations means that relatively few classrooms can be included in most studies. Using only a small number of classrooms, even with very rich data on these classrooms, limits the prospect of assessing state or national practices.

Problems of Reliability   We also recognize that the potential for interobserver problems is fairly high with this method. In particular, observers who take notes in the classrooms must be careful to write down, in comparable (and preferably excruciatingly precise) detail, at least everything that will later be of interest. Of course, this is not likely to happen except in researchers' and funding agencies' fantasies. Thus, researchers are left to depend on notes taken by observers who may not write down the teacher's question or may miss student responses or may neglect to note that instruction was interrupted by an announcement from the office. When this happens, the results are always limited by what was initially recorded, and conclusions must always include a cautionary note.

Even in an ideal situation, if an observational study were conducted in this fashion and found to be productive, it is hard to imagine how it could be implemented on a larger, even national scale. In particular, having a reliable group of trained observers available to collect data on a national sample seems nearly impossible.

Many of the problems associated with live observation can be overcome by capturing actual classroom processes more precisely. In particular, video has emerged as a practical way to improve the quality of classroom data.

VIDEO RECORDS OF CLASSROOM INSTRUCTION

Video has been used for many years for the study of classroom processes. However, until recently, it was primarily used for small-scale qualitative studies, often focusing on a single teacher. Video was a natural tool for this kind of study because of its richness and because of the fact that it could be played over and over again, enabling an analyst to engage in more detailed and careful analysis than would be possible in a live observation. But the use of video does not necessarily imply a qualitative analysis. In fact, video is not a method of analysis but a means of recording ongoing activity. It consists of relatively raw records of experience. On top of video records we can build both a qualitative and a quantitative analysis, provided we collect video from a large enough sample of lessons. In fact, it turns out that video is well suited to the integration of qualitative and quantitative analyses.

The most ambitious use of video to date for research on classroom processes has been in the Third International Mathematics and Science Study (TIMSS) video study (Stigler and Hiebert, 1997). TIMSS marks the first time that videotapes have ever been collected from a national sample of teachers. In the study, national samples of eighth-grade mathematics teachers in three countries—Germany, Japan, and the United States—were videotaped teaching a complete mathematics lesson in their classrooms. The primary goal of the study was to provide national-level descriptions of classroom mathematics lessons in the three countries. A secondary goal was to ascertain the impact that policy documents such as the National Council of Teachers of Mathematics Professional Standards for Teaching Mathematics have had on classroom instruction in the United States.

Although the sample sizes were not large as far as national surveys go, ranging from 50 in Japan to 100 in Germany and 81 in the United States, they were quite large for a video study. The logistical challenges of managing such large quantities of video information are considerable. Fortunately, technological advances in the computerization of video information makes the task far easier today than it would have been just five years ago. In the next sections, we discuss some of the advantages and disadvantages of video and share some strategies we have found to be especially useful for the collection and analysis of classroom video. We especially stress strategies that help ensure the objectivity of video analysis.

Advantages of Video

Video provides a number of advantages over the more traditional methods of studying classroom processes. Unlike live observations, video greatly expands our ability to analyze complex human interactions such as those found in classrooms. With live observations, we are limited to recording whatever an observer can record. Checklists can be useful, but it is possible for a live observer to make only a limited number of reliable judgments at the speed required for classroom research. There simply is too much going on. Video, on the other hand, can be paused, rewound, and watched again. Two observers can watch the same video independently and go back to replay and discuss those parts that they saw differently. Videos can be coded multiple times, in passes that require only limited judgments by an observer on any single pass. This makes it easier to train observers, for it is not necessary to load them up with responsibilities. Fundamentally, video gives us the luxury to take our time with the analysis.

The most important advantages of video derive from its concrete, vivid, and "preanalyzed" nature (i.e., the categories are derived from the data rather than vice versa, leaving the data open to a vast array of analyses). There are at least four major opportunities that arise because of this:

1. Video records of classroom lessons provide us the opportunity to discover ideas and alternatives not previously anticipated. Checklists and other live coding schemes imply that we know ahead of time what is likely to be seen in a classroom. Otherwise, how could we predict how to categorize it? Video allows us to go in fresh, to take advantage of serendipity whenever possible.

2. The concrete nature of video means that it is not as theory-bound as other methods of data collection. This makes the same video data usable to a far wider range of researchers than would be the case with questionnaires or live-coder observation systems. Video data, therefore, are amenable to analysis from multiple perspectives and are a natural focal point for interdisciplinary collaboration. Psychologists, anthropologists, sociologists, and others interested in understanding classroom processes can all make some use of a single video dataset.

3. Not only is video interesting to researchers from different perspectives, it has a longer shelf life than other kinds of data. Researchers of today would have little interest in reanalyzing most of the process-product data generated by classroom researchers in the 1970s and 1980s mainly because the theoretical context that motivated the collection of those data was so different from that of today. But imagine if we had videos of teaching during earlier periods of our history. These would be inherently interesting and easily appropriated by the theories of today.

4. Finally, video provides concrete referents for the words and concepts we use to describe instructional processes. In part because of the isolation of teachers, we lack a shared language for describing teaching. Certain terms (e.g., problem solving) are used frequently but rarely defined. Video images make it possible for multiple observers from multiple backgrounds to agree on the meanings of such commonly used words. Not only does this advance our scientific under-

standing of classroom processes, but also it facilitates the communication of research results to various constituencies.

Integration of Qualitative and Quantitative Methods of Analysis

Perhaps the greatest advantage of video is that it allows us to integrate qualitative and quantitative methods of analysis in a straightforward and direct way. Ethnographic researchers often work, at an analytic level, to integrate qualitative and quantitative data. But these data usually come from quite different sources—for example, participant observations and questionnaires. With video it is possible to integrate different kinds of data as applied to the same raw material, thus strengthening our understanding of each.

This point can be illustrated by describing the methods of analysis used in the TIMSS video study. In TIMSS we were able to spend a great deal of time engaged in qualitative analysis of the video images collected. As mentioned earlier, a critical objective of cross-cultural comparisons of teaching is to describe the different systems of instruction that have evolved in different cultures. There is no way to build these descriptions without the qualitative analysis that arises from simply viewing, discussing, and interpreting the video lessons. On the other hand, the descriptions constructed cannot be validated unless we can relate the descriptions to indicators that can be coded objectively from the larger corpus of videos. In our analyses, qualitative descriptions became hypotheses for objective validation. Coding procedures were defined, interrater reliability was established, and then the procedures were applied to the full set of videos.

The cycle did not necessarily stop at this point, however. Once codes had been applied, counted, and analyzed, and the results tabulated, we could go back to the videos to clarify and elaborate the meaning of the quantitative findings. For example, in coding the types of questions teachers asked students in Japanese and American classrooms, we found that Japanese teachers asked students to describe and explain more often than American teachers did. But even though questions in both countries were grouped into the "describe/explain" category, the questions seemed to differ from each other in quality. Going back to the video enabled us to see that Japanese teachers asked their students for complete descriptions of how they solved a problem, whereas U.S. teachers asked students to justify specific steps in a solution. Thus, quantitative analyses are used to validate and generalize the insights gained from qualitative study of the videos, while qualitative images provide meat and meaning for the findings obtained in quantitative results.

Software for Video Analysis

The analysis of video is notoriously laborious and time consuming, especially the kind of analysis described above, which requires investigators to reexamine the video continually as they proceed through the analytical cycle. This fact explains why video has rarely been used on a large scale. However, such use is now more frequent, due in large part to the advent of new technologies that enable video to be encoded and stored inexpensively in digital form on a computer. Once video is digital, many tasks that were nearly impossible to accomplish using videotape can now be accomplished easily.

Digital video, in contrast to analog video, can be stored in various formats and storage mediums. Archived on CD-ROM, it is virtually indestructible and will last for 100 years or more. Stored on hard disk drives it can be served over-local area networks and the Internet, making it possible for multiple analysts to access the video from wherever they are, whenever they wish. Digital video, unlike analog video, can be played again and again without ever degrading in quality. Digital video files can be copied an unlimited number of times without any loss of quality. Most significantly, digital video can be randomly accessed, making it possible to retrieve any particular piece of video instantly.

New commercially available software exploits the power of digital video for research. One example of such software is vPrism, marketed by Digital Lava, Inc., of Los Angeles. This software is based on software developed for the TIMSS video study. The software manages large quantities of video in a multi-media database, linking the video with transcriptions, annotations, and user-definable event codes. The user interface enables the user to view video on the desktop; define a code, mark codes in the data, transcribe, and write text annotations; construct and apply time and event sampling frames, retrieving sampled video clips for coding and analysis; search and instantly retrieve video clips associated with a particular text string or event category; and export events, together with such attributes as their duration for statistical analysis. One of the most powerful aspects of this new breed of software is that it can work with video files stored anywhere on the Internet. This makes it possible for different groups of researchers, located around the world, to collaborate in the analysis of a particular set of video data. It also provides new opportunities for sharing the findings of video studies.

Problems with Video

Despite the advantages of video, and the potential of new technologies to simplify the task of organizing and analyzing large video datasets, there are issues and problems that must be kept in mind when working with video data. First, it is important to realize that video is not a veridical picture of reality, although many people wrongly assume it is. In fact, it is highly filtered and potentially quite misleading. What you see and what you do not see on video are largely determined by where the camera operator chooses to point the camera and on how wide or close he or she defines the shot. Much of what is going on in the situation being videotaped is not visible on the screen, and sometimes what is not visible is crucial to a valid interpretation of the situation. This fact becomes quite clear as soon as one starts to analyze the contents of videotape. It is frustrating to wish the camera were pointing someplace different.

The concrete nature of video images is also problematic, even if the camera is pointed in the ideal direction. Concrete images can be quite persuasive to the human information-processing system, even if they turn out to be completely unrepresentative of what typically occurs. This fact is well known by cognitive psychologists: humans are easily misled by anecdotes, even when they are told to ignore them. There is nothing we can do about this except be aware of the potential for misinterpretation.

Another problem with video is the possibility of observer effects. Will students and teachers behave as usual with the camera present, or will we get a view that is biased in some way? Might a teacher, knowing that she is to be videotaped, prepare a special lesson just for the occasion that is unrepresentative of her normal practices?

This problem is not unique to video studies. Teachers' questionnaire responses, as well as their behavior, may be biased toward cultural norms. On the other hand, it may actually be easier to gauge the degree of bias in video studies than in questionnaire studies. Teachers who try to alter their behavior for a videotaping will likely show some evidence that this is the case. Students may look puzzled or may not be able to follow routines that are clearly new for them.

It also should be noted that changing the way a teacher teaches is not accomplished easily, as much of the literature on teacher development suggests. It is highly unlikely that teaching could be improved significantly simply by placing a camera in the classroom. On the other hand, teachers will obviously try to do an especially good job and may do some extra preparation for a lesson that is to be videotaped. We may, therefore, see a somewhat idealized version of what the teacher normally does in the classroom.

Finally, it is important to consider the issue of confidentiality in the context of video studies. Methods exist for ensuring the confidentiality of participants in questionnaire and live observational studies, but with video the challenge is far greater. How does one disguise the identity of someone who is clearly recognizable in a video? Disguising images is quite laborious. The best solution is to secure signed waivers from participants, before videos are collected, that cover the range of use-situations anticipated by the researcher. It is also possible to restrict the use of video datasets and require researchers who wish to access the data to sign nondisclosure agreements. This is not an ideal solution, however, as it means that video images cannot be used as a means of communicating study results to the public. In the TIMSS video study we produced a restricted-use dataset but also collected a few public-use tapes that could be used specifically for communicating study results to a wider audience. In future studies we plan to increase the number of videos collected for this purpose.

Practical Advice for Using Video on a Large Scale

Collect supplementary information. Although videos are notable for how much information they contain, one of the first things we notice in working with video is how much information they do not contain. Indeed, it is important to realize that video is only a partial representation of what goes on in a classroom. Often we see students working at their desks, but it is difficult to see what they are working on. Thus, the first advice we would give is to supplement a video by collecting other materials and artifacts that are relevant to the lesson. For example, student work, textbook pages, worksheets, close-up video clips of manipulatives or other materials, teachers' tests, and so on, can all be collected relatively easily. Our general rule is to collect anything that would be helpful to someone trying to understand what they see on the videotape. Teacher questionnaires and interviews also fall into this category. Often it is not possible to understand what is happening on a video without knowing what goal the teacher is trying to accomplish. Asking teachers, for example, what they intend for students to learn from a lesson is often critical for understanding a videotaped lesson.

Standardize camera techniques. It is important to note that the camera is not strictly theory free. Depending on where the videographer focuses the camera, one can get a very different view of what is happening in a classroom lesson. For this reason it is important, first, to think through what it is important to capture and, second, to standardize the procedures of camera use so that different videographers will be consistent in the decisions they make about where to point the camera. Depending on the purpose of the study, it might be necessary to use more than one camera. In any case, standard rules must be developed, and videographers must be trained to apply the rules in consistent fashion.

Clearly communicate the study's goals to the participants. When collecting video there always exists the possibility of observer bias. It is possible, perhaps even likely, that teachers will behave differently when the camera is present than when it is not. We believe that the best way to minimize observer effects is to communicate clearly to teachers what the researchers' goals are. If what you want to see is what normally happens, as opposed to, say, what a teacher could do with 20 extra hours of preparation, it is important to tell the teacher that you want to see what she would have done anyway if you had not shown up with a camera. If teachers understand the researchers' goals, our typical experience is that they will try to be cooperative.

Use intermediate representations to enhance access to video information. Video information is so complex that it taxes the information-processing capacity of the analyst. For this reason we have found it necessary to construct "intermediate representations"—representations of the content of the video that can be used by the analysts to guide their inquiry into the video.

In the TIMSS video study we used two forms of intermediate representations: a transcript and a lesson table. The transcript simply consists of a written transcription of the talk that goes on during the classroom lesson. If the talk is in a foreign language, we also use an English translation of the transcript. We have found that sophisticated analysis of instruction requires use of a transcript. Trying to understand how lesson content unfolds in the context of verbal interchange between teacher and students is difficult without a concrete transcription of the talk.

Similarly, the lesson table provides a more content-oriented representation of the lesson as it unfolds over time. In the lesson tables constructed for the TIMSS video study, we wrote down the organization of the classroom (e.g., classwork or seatwork), the activity (e.g., teacher lecturing, class discussion), and the detailed mathematical content of the lessons as they changed through time (see, e.g., Stigler and Hiebert, 1999). There are many possible ways to make such a table; the point is that some form of table is a great help to analysts as they work to understand what is happening in the video.

Work in multiple passes. This suggestion, like the previous one, derives from the inherent complexity of video information. A single analyst cannot study all aspects of a classroom lesson during a single pass through a video, and fortunately, does not have to. Because a lesson is captured on video, it is possible and highly desirable to have analysts code the video in multiple passes. On one pass a coder can focus solely on organizational aspects of the lesson; on another, on the content of the lesson. More detailed descriptions of a lesson, such as the kinds of questions teachers ask, can be constructed on yet another pass through the tape. As we will see below, software for video analysis makes it fairly simple to integrate the results of multiple passes into a single database where layers of analysis are organized by time codes.

Use time and event sampling to increase efficiency. One mistake video users often make is to assume that they must analyze all of the video they collect. In actuality it is possible to be highly strategic, analyzing only the amount of video required to answer the question that is being asked of the data. For example, if one wants to estimate the percentage of time various instructional technologies are used in the classrooms of a nation, it is usually possible to time sample from the video. Once events have been marked in a video—for example, teacher lecture—it is also possible to event sample. The number of time slices or events that need to be examined in each lesson would, of course, depend on the frequency with which the event of interest appears in the lessons. But because the data are on video, it is always possible to go back later and increase the sample from each tape according to a preliminary analysis of findings. This is something that cannot be done in a study that uses live coders in the classroom.

Set aside some tapes to be used for code development. Analysis of videotapes is largely a post hoc process. For this reason it is important to guard against the danger of being misled by chance occurrences in a sample of video. Data miners working to discover post hoc patterns in large quantitative datasets often use part of the dataset for developing hypotheses and another part for testing the hypotheses. This same strategy makes sense in the context of video surveys. In TIMSS a sample of nine lessons was videotaped in each country as part of a field test, prior to collecting the main study sample. These nine tapes were used for discovery and generation of hypotheses. Only after hypotheses had been generated and coding procedures developed on the nine field test tapes were procedures then applied to the full sample of tapes.

Cost and Feasibility

Many people assume that video is far more expensive than the more traditional methods, thus making it not feasible for use on a large scale. In fact, however, the picture is not so clear in this regard. In general, more traditional methods cost more on the "front end," meaning that it takes more planning, design, and training to get them into the field. Video, in contrast, is more costly on the "back end." The costs for collecting video data have dropped markedly over the past 10 years. Camcorders are cheap, as is videotape. And training for camera operators is far less exacting than the training of live observers who must achieve high levels of interrater reliability before they are sent into the field.

The real cost of video is in the analysis phase. Depending on how much analysis is done, the cost can be huge. Just the transcription of video, which we believe is generally required for analysis of the data, can cost several hundred dollars for a lesson. The cost of video analysis makes video especially suitable for some applications, but not others. For example, if what we want is an aggregate-level picture of what is happening in a group of classrooms (e.g., a nation, state, or district), it may well be worth the cost of analysis. If, however, we need a picture of teaching that is reliable at the individual teacher level, it probably will be too expensive.

In general, video data and the more traditional kinds of data can both play an important role in a portfolio of classroom process data. Video data should be used for theory generation, for validating the less expensive methods, and for the discovery of alternative instructional systems. Survey methods should be used for testing hypotheses generated through video analysis and for any study that requires very large samples of classrooms.

Conclusion

In weighing the advantages and disadvantages of different kinds of data, we must know how the data will be used to improve education. It is within the context of a use-model that we can evaluate the value of collecting any particular kind of data. In the following sections we examine use of classroom process data from the point of view of two kinds of consumers of the data: researchers/policy makers and classroom teachers. It is within these contexts that we address more specifically the kind of data to collect, how to sample, and so forth.

DATA FOR RESEARCHERS AND POLICY MAKERS

Policy makers and researchers are two very different types of professionals. They have different takes on the educational process and at times will use data differently. Still, we find considerable overlap between these two groups and similarity with respect to at least two critical features. First, both policy makers and researchers are trying to understand the educational system and, in their own ways, to effect change in this system. Second, both of these groups of professionals are working from outside the classroom. In other words, although policy makers primarily are trying to effect change and researchers primarily are trying to understand change, both are attempting to relate to the process of educational change from outside the educational arena of the classroom. Given that policy makers and researchers share these critical features, which means that the ways in which they can use data are distinctively different from the way in which teachers use data, policy makers and researchers are considered together in this section.

Researchers studying teaching and learning in classrooms are interested in such questions as: What kinds of instructional practices lead to improvements in student learning? They are interested in developing theories that link instruction and learning.

Policy makers have a slightly broader focus. Although they too are interested in links between instruction and learning (albeit not as intensively as most researchers), they are interested in issues of how policy affects changes in classroom practice much more so than researchers. In addition, policy makers are relatively more invested in communicating the results of their analysis to the public than are researchers.

In this section we take one model (Cohen and Hill, 1998) as an example to help us think about the different ways that researchers and policy makers use data. We also discuss how data could be fed back and used to inform such a model.

Cohen and Hill (1998)

Cohen and Hill (1998) conducted an investigation of teachers' adaptation to the California Framework (California State Department of Education, 1985). In their work they proposed a model for thinking about effecting change for students. Their investigation informs current debate because it addresses the relation between policy and practice.

They found that previous assumptions about links between policy and classroom practice were wrong: even with the prominence of the California Framework, very few teachers changed their practice. As Cohen and Hill (1998:41) stated, "Neither teachers' practice nor students' achievement was changed by most of the professional development that most California teachers had."

The point here is that although policy (here the California Framework) is designed to effect change, the desired change often does not take place. To understand why this happens, Cohen and Hill developed a model. Their model has student learning, as measured by student achievement, as the ultimate dependent measure of instructional *policy*. In this model, teachers' practice is both a direct influence on student performance and an outcome measure of policy. Furthermore, teachers' opportunities to learn, and their actual learning, influence their practice and thus, indirectly through their practice, have the potential to impact student achievement. A schematic representation of this model is shown in Figure 11-1.

Cohen and Hill are not alone in their conception of the relationship of policy to student outcomes. For example, Mandel (1996:3-29) wrote, "When dismal or promising results about student performance are reported, a new chain reaction of suppositions is often set off about the degree to which teachers are to be blamed or praised. But these suppositions are just that—hypotheses disconnected from much of a factual base that might shed some light on what is occurring, including the extent to which the observed results can be accurately attributed to teacher actions." In other words, both Mandel and Cohen and Hill argue that policy rarely, if ever, has a direct effect on student outcomes, even though that is often the intent. Instead, policy has its impact through teachers' actions, and thus outcomes in student performance need to be linked to teachers' actions.

Role of Data

We see at least three different ways that data could be used to inform the model laid out by Cohen and Hill. In particular, data are needed to generate models, test models, and communicate to the public.

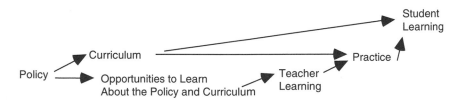

FIGURE 11-1 A schematic representation of Cohen and Hill's (1998) model of the relationship between policy and student learning.

Data Needed to Generate Models

Data can be essential for generating models—both models of the effects of policy and models of teaching and learning. Our goal here is to describe the sorts of data that allow us either to make new inferences about how policy has an impact on classrooms or to make new connections between teaching and learning. In both cases, data can be crucial for formulating useful and accurate models.

Generating Models of Policy Implementation   Without models of how policy impacts classrooms, we cannot evaluate whether policy is effective. For example, even when policy is implemented, there may be problems. And without a model of how that policy ought to affect outcomes, we cannot really say why the policy did not work.

To clarify this point, we take a look at a study conducted by Cohen (1990). He reported that even when a policy makes sense and the teachers try very hard to implement it, the effect of the policy is not always felt. Cohen came to this conclusion when he found that not only did teachers adopt new practices, they also continued to use old—and in this case counterproductive—practices. Cohen voiced the concern that the adoption of new policy is not enough: pruning away ineffective, problematic practices and materials must be done if a new policy is to have its desired effect. (See also Cohen, 1995, and Siegler, 1996, for in-depth discussions of the importance of pruning away old strategies.)

One reason that Cohen and Hill suspected that the policy was not very effective was that teachers spent very little time learning how to implement policy as represented in the California State Department of Education (1985) Mathematics Framework. But Cohen and Hill also found a clear relation between the amount of time teachers spent learning about new mathematics curricula and student learning outcomes. In this case, although the policy appeared to work well, insufficient effort was expended to get the teachers to implement it.

More to the point of our concern about how data help generate models of policy and policy implementation is that collecting data on the use of a policy (i.e., implementing practices in classrooms) and not just on the ultimate outcomes (i.e., student achievement) provides insight into how to specify policy. Both are important. We note that a stated policy might easily be undermined if contradictory practices are being implemented alongside the practices recommended by the policy. Based on Cohen's work, a new model of policy implementation—one that includes adding and deleting teaching practices—should be put forth. Of course, we would not have come to this conclusion without collecting data on classroom practices. In other words, without looking at classroom practices, any picture would be incomplete of whether or how policy pertaining to classroom practice is being implemented. And in any model that links student outcomes to classroom practice, we would need to have good data on classroom practice if we are to affect (or understand) student outcomes.

What sorts of data might best contribute to the development of new models? We suspect that the most useful data in many cases would be those that take into account both the frequency and the variation in the behaviors of interest. In this case a sampling of video records would be the most productive.

Let's work through an example to make this point more clear. For example, if we believe that small-group work is important, we need to know how much time students spend in small groups, how these groups are set up (both in terms of the work to be accomplished and the composition of the groups), and, most importantly, what takes place when children work in small groups. Of course, it is difficult to imagine tracking this without a videotaped record of lessons, with the camera focused on small groups when they were operating.

Let's continue. If we find that the policy is implemented, in this case, that small-group work takes place frequently, but the effects are not as intended, we can revise the policy so that the desired outcome is more likely. For example, we may find that small groups are set up and maintained so that the students know each other well and that the students are heterogeneously grouped so that they can draw on multiple perspectives and levels of understanding. Note that these sorts of data can be obtained from survey methods. Going back to the hypothetical example, we also find that teachers almost never call the students back into a whole class and make them responsible for the work that went on in the small groups. Furthermore, when we look at what students accomplished in their small groups, we find that they spent very little time on the intended focus of the lesson. Moreover, we find that the students do not learn very much. From this scenario (which one of us witnessed over and over again), we could recommend that a policy on the use of small groups should include making students responsible for presenting their work to the whole class, thereby revealing students' misconceptions and incomplete work.

In this example, we assumed that the effects (i.e., student outcomes) were measured successfully. Of course, this should not be taken for granted. In this example of generating models that are useful for policy makers, reliable outcome measures need to be used, too. Thus, for this example to work well, we would recommend that the video records be combined with survey methods that include student achievement measures, such as the NAEP, to support the inferences that could be used by policy makers. Although it may seem obvious, it is nonetheless important to remember that when we want to know the relation between classroom practices and student performance, we need good measures of student performance. In sum, policy models can be enhanced and revised if data are collected and analyzed on implementation of the policy.

Generating Models of Teaching and Learning New ideas are often generated by data. But where do we get these data? What sorts of data would be best for generating new theories about teaching and learning? We reiterate a point made earlier: specific examples of classroom lessons are needed. If we had these examples, a dialogue could be built about which of these lessons were good and why. In this scenario we would not have to worry as much as we do with other data sources that our language about these lessons is not understood by others: if we all watch the same lesson, for example, using folded paper to show equivalent fractions, we will know exactly how the paper is folded and how it is marked. In sum, video data can provide a shared set of examples for building language and theories for analyzing classroom practices.

Data Needed to Test and Validate Theoretical Models

The data most useful to policy makers are probably those that say whether or not teachers have implemented the stated policy and, if so, what the impact of the implementation has been on student achievement. This can then be related to student achievement data: if students perform well, the policy should remain; if students perform poorly, the policy should be revised. Thus, the first concern for policy makers is to know whether policy is being implemented. If the stated policy is indeed being implemented, it is also important to know *how* it was implemented.

Here is an example of this issue: the National Council of Teachers of Mathematics recommends that students participate in mathematical discussions. Among the many reasons for making this suggestion is that research has told us that students learn better when they participate actively than when they are passively taking in what the teacher tells them. To see whether insisting on discussions is indeed a good policy to be recommended to all teachers, we would want to know how frequently—and how well—teachers engaged their students in mathematical discussions, especially in relation to the amount of time teachers expect their students to be more passive (e.g., when the teacher stands at the front of the room and explains to the students what she wants them to know). When we know the absolute and relative amounts of time spent in mathematical discussions versus just listening to the teacher, we can relate these to student outcomes.

How do we get these data? We can imagine several scenarios, but for this sort of question we suggest that none involve teacher self-reports because teachers cannot possibly teach and note when they are using different instructional techniques and also report how much time they spent in these episodes. Thus, we recommend videotaped observations because they permit a careful and relatively accurate measure of what teachers do and do not do in their classrooms.

We also acknowledge that different types of data may be necessary to test theoretical models of teaching and learning than the types of data used to develop the models. For example, we can use videotaped records of classroom instruction to develop ideas about what might facilitate learning and then test these ideas using experimental methods. As an example, Flevares and Perry (2000) discovered that teachers vary their presentations of nonverbal information to accompany the verbal content and activities in a lesson. From this discovery, they hypothesized that the naturally occurring nonverbal information may be crucial to learning the lesson content. At this point, Flevares and Perry (1999) are systematically presenting the same lesson content in verbal form but varying the nonverbal forms and then measuring learning outcomes. Eventually, they expect to understand which nonverbal forms aid learning of different concepts.

We also wish to make the point that even when we have what we believe is a good policy, video data can clarify the policy. This point is important because policy, such as that reflected in standards, is typically vague. When policy is vague, it leaves plenty of room for interpreting and misinterpreting. As Cohen (1990:313) puts it, "The [California] framework's mathematical exhortations were general; it offered few specifics about how teachers might respond, and left room for many different [implied: some bad] responses." Thus, we suggest that clear examples, especially those derived from videotaped observations, not only allow the development of a shared language about what practices actually reflect policy—and which do not—but can hone and clarify the policy. In sum, a wide array of data forms may be necessary to test models of the effects of policy and to test theories of teaching and learning.

Data Needed as Basis for Communicating to the Public

Finally, we raise the point that data are also needed to communicate what has been learned to the public. What sorts of data are these? Of course, the answer depends on the type of data that best illustrate what we have learned. Here is a simple example: if we have learned that teachers who spend a great deal of time learning about a new curriculum do a better job of teaching it than teachers who spend little time learning about the new curriculum, we simply need to present the average number of hours spent in training of the teachers whose students learned the material well compared to the teachers whose students did not.

Let's turn to a more complex example. If we learn that stating the goal of a lesson in a clear fashion at the beginning of a lesson facilitates students' understanding of the lesson's content, we may need demonstrations of different teachers stating the goal of their lessons. Data of this sort would allow the public to get a sense of how powerful these opening goal statements can be, especially when these are compared to other teachers' opening statements, which do not include goal statements. The general point we wish to make is that the data we share with the public need to be accessible and the data need to communicate or demonstrate clearly what can be learned.

Recommendations

Classroom process data relevant to the needs of researchers and policy makers are scant. In general we need more data of all kinds that can feed information from the classroom back into the research and policy process. Specifically, however, we stress the need to expand our data collection efforts beyond traditional surveys. We recommend three new initiatives.

First, we desperately need to collect more data on how policies are implemented and their effectiveness inside classrooms. We need to know whether policies are implemented or not, and we need to understand the conditions under which they succeed or fail. Student outcome data must be linked into this effort, but outcome data alone will not be enough to understand how policies work. In particular, we propose that video surveys be used, in conjunction with more traditional surveys, to study classroom processes. Through questionnaires we can find out, for example, about teachers' opportunities to learn about new policies or new curricula. Through video surveys we can see what the new policy or curriculum looks like as it is implemented in classrooms. Clearly, both kinds of information are needed if we want to understand the mechanisms by which policy affects teaching and learning.

Second, apart from policy, we should conduct video studies to aid in the development of theories of teaching and to validate survey instruments. Video data are especially useful for theory generation. Recall the example we presented earlier in which we discussed "describe/explain" questions. Japanese teachers asked their students to describe complete problem solutions, whereas U.S. teachers asked students to present and justify single steps in a solution. Given that Japanese students outperform their U.S. peers, we could use this information to advance our theories of learning. In particular, we could hypothesize that it is not enough to retell one portion of a problem's solution and have others tell about other portions. Instead, for deep learning to take place, students may need to put their explanations in the context of whole-problem solutions. This hypothesis, generated from video data, could be tested experimentally. Video records also allow for validation of other instruments (see, e.g., Mayer, 1998).

Aside from general surveys, we can think of two kinds of data collection efforts that would be especially valuable. One would be the establishment of a national sample of "indicator" districts or schools that could serve as a testbed for developing theories of teaching and new survey instruments. We would propose to collect all sorts of data in these schools, including, but not limited to, achievement data, survey data (from teachers, students, parents, and administrators), and videotaped observations of lessons. In these settings, quantitative data could be linked with rich contextual data to yield important insights. Moreover, with the availability of multiple indicators and videotaped records, new theoretical ideas could be explored.

Another important use of video would be to study special classrooms: either those in which students have been shown to learn a great deal or those in which new or experimental teaching techniques are being used. Such data would not only advance our understanding of what works in classrooms but also provide guidance to teachers about what the process of changing teaching can look like. Examples of teachers who are in the process of changing allow other teachers to see what it is like to have mixed (i.e., new and old) practices (e.g., Cohen, 1990) and can provide teachers with direct knowledge of what may be problematic in adopting something new. In addition, examples of teachers who have accomplished a successful change can provide a model, replete with explicit tactics for instructional success. Our point is simply that special cases may well be more useful than random samples in advancing our knowledge of teaching and how to improve it.

Our third recommendation is to conduct international studies in order to increase our exposure to novel variations in teaching practices. New ideas are essential if we are to improve teaching. Systems, and individuals, have a difficult time learning without a steady diet of variability (Siegler, 1996). Innovations, alternative images, different ways of doing things, and new information are all needed to create new experiences from which the system can learn (Stigler and Hiebert, 1999). Looking across cultures can be an especially useful source of new ideas about what is possible in classrooms, but only if we use research methods that can spot what is new. Questionnaires are not well suited to this goal because on them teachers can only answer the questions the researchers were clever enough to ask. Video data, especially those that are collected outside our own country, can serve this function of generating new ideas and new hypotheses about teaching.

DATA FOR CLASSROOM PRACTITIONERS

We have described the role that data can play in helping researchers and policy makers understand the chain of influence that relates policy to classroom practice to student learning. But what about classroom teachers? What role can data play, if any, in teachers' efforts to improve their own practice?

The traditional view is that teachers can use the findings from research, and the recommendations of policy makers, to improve their teaching. So, for example, teachers are assumed to read documents such as the *NCTM Professional Standards for Teaching Mathematics* and be able to use the recommendations therein as a guide for improvement. Recent data and a lot of experience suggest, however, that teaching is not easily changed by having teachers read such documents (e.g., Stigler and Hiebert, 1997). The reason, we believe, is that general research findings, because they are general, are not situated in the complexities of classroom life. As we pointed out earlier, there are few features of instruction that are always desirable or always undesirable; it depends on the lesson context.

We propose an alternative to the traditional view. Because teaching is so complex, general research findings will have limited applicability to the improvement of practice. Such findings can serve as a guide, but they will not be sufficient. Teachers need a different kind of knowledge as well, knowledge we might refer to as localized theories grounded in practice. Teachers themselves will be the ones to develop this kind of knowledge.

What Teachers Need to Know to Improve Practice

Much has been written about what teachers need to know to perform their craft (e.g., Shulman, 1986). We will not review that literature here except to point out that there is a marked difference between the kind of knowledge teachers use, as indicated by post hoc analysis, and the kind of knowledge teachers have available in their quest to become better teachers. Most attempts to improve teaching through workshops, courses, and so forth, provide knowledge that is of limited relevance in the classroom. On the one hand, teachers are exposed to theories, generated by researchers, that are decontextualized and difficult to link to classroom practice. On the other hand, teachers are given models or examples of what they "should do" in their classrooms and asked to copy them. But in these cases the examples are not grounded in theory and thus are not easily adaptable in local classroom contexts.

Our view is that teachers, to improve their practice, need a kind of knowledge that has been in short supply to this point: theories linked with examples. This is what we mean by localized theories of teaching. To be useful, such knowledge needs to be organized around curricular goals and needs to be packaged in units that are shareable across teachers and classrooms. Currently we have no means of generating this kind of knowledge, no means of accumulating and storing this knowledge, and no mechanism for sharing this knowledge across teachers. A major goal of data collection about teaching, therefore, should be to produce data that can contribute to producing theories of teaching linked with examples, and that can help in the accumulation and sharing of this knowledge.

Role of Data for Improving Teaching

We believe that teachers must play a central role in the generation of localized theories of teaching and learning in classrooms. Teachers are the ones with the best access to relevant information about classrooms, and they are in the best position to evaluate the validity of localized theories. In addition, there are many more teachers in the country than there are educational researchers. Unless teachers are involved in a central way in this process, progress will be exceedingly slow. Of course, it will take more than data to engage teachers in this process, but data can play a central role.

Generating localized theories of teaching will require prolonged reflection and discussion of examples of classroom practice. Video can play a central role in these discussions because it allows what is normally a complex and transitory phenomenon to be slowed down and replayed for study. The theoretical descriptions of teaching that can result from analysis of classroom videos will naturally be linked to actual examples of classroom practice. Thus, what teachers learn from joint analysis of such examples will be easier to situate in terms of their own classrooms. The collaboration is important, too, for it means that teachers will be developing a shared language for describing the events and activities they see on video. This shared language is critical as it becomes the foundation on which localized theories of teaching can be stored, accessed, and communicated about with other teachers.

In the process we envision by which teachers could use classroom videos, it is interesting to ponder what kinds of examples ought to be collected. Some might think that the most important videos to analyze would be those that teachers collect in their own classrooms (see, e.g., Lampert and Ball, 1998). Although there certainly is a place for such examples in the teacher development process, they are by no means the only or even the most important examples. Because teaching is a cultural activity, and because variation in teaching methods might therefore be limited in a single culture, it is probably most important that teachers gain exposure to genuine alternatives, examples that depart significantly from what they are accustomed to seeing. Even risking possible misinterpretation, videos of lessons from other cultures, and videos of lessons in which serious efforts to reform are evident, would be a high priority for teachers because these present clear alternatives to typical and/or culture-bound lessons.

For teachers, contextual data about the lessons taped are even more critical than for researchers and policy makers. Teachers need to know what happened yesterday and what the students knew and understood before the lesson started. Test data and interview data from students both before and after a lesson would be highly relevant to teachers' analyses. Interviews with the teacher on the video would also be important, especially questions that elicit from the teacher explanations of what she or he was intending to accomplish with each part of the lesson. For teachers, the key is not sampling: lessons need not be representative, and the number of lessons need not be large. What is important is that the cases be selected to expand and inform teachers' developing understandings of teaching and learning in classrooms.

Finally, there is one more function that can be served by access to video examples. As noted by Cohen and Hill (1998), analysis of the possibilities exemplified by other teachers can provide a powerful incentive for teachers to improve their own teaching. We are reminded of the beginning Japanese teacher described by Lewis and Tsuchida (1997) who broke down in tears after watching one of her senior colleagues teach a science lesson. She explained that she thought the other teacher was so skilled that she felt badly for her own students, who, through the luck of the draw, ended up in her class. The result was a strong feeling of wanting to improve, coupled with concrete images of what improved teaching might look like.

Recommendations

Teachers can videotape themselves at the local level, but the federal government can play an important role in collecting, and then giving teachers access to, variant examples of teaching in different cultures, different subject areas, and so forth. The federal government also can document and collect examples from teachers who are unique, either through some special talent or through participation in systematic programs of reform.

The National Center for Education Statistics also should consider accumulating examples into a national database of video cases that could be accessed by teachers over the Internet. If rules were established to control quality, it would be possible to build and maintain a database to which classroom teachers could add their own examples. Nothing would do as much as such a database to facilitate the development and sharing of curriculum-based localized theories of teaching.

VIDEO AND THE EXISTING NAEP

Having discussed new methods of studying classroom processes and having thought through how data on classroom processes might be used by different audiences to improve teaching, we return to the question of the NAEP. In particular, we wish to address the issue of how new methods, particularly video, might be used in conjunction with the existing NAEP.

The primary focus of NAEP has been on student achievement. For more than a quarter of a century, NAEP has documented national trends in what students know and are able to do in various academic subject areas. Yet there has also been a growing interest in documenting changes in the context of achievement at a national level. Student and teacher questionnaires are now included in the NAEP as a means of measuring everything from student demographics to teacher preparation, instructional practices, school policies, and out-of-school activities.

We believe that video surveys can be integrated into the NAEP framework and that they can contribute greatly to the study of instructional practices over time. Of course, it is not feasible to videotape in every classroom included in NAEP, but collecting video records of lessons in a substantial subsample of NAEP classrooms is both practical and useful. Using techniques similar to those in the TIMSS video study, videotaping in national samples of classrooms can provide the first reliable means of tracking changes in instructional practices over time. Meanwhile, before data can be accumulated on instructional trends, video surveys can provide a means of studying the classroom mediators of such variables as race and social class. For example, NAEP already provides a means of tracking racial gaps in achievement over time. But are such gaps correlated with gaps in teaching quality and instructional practices? Video records would clearly be the best means of asking such a question, especially over time.

One way to implement such an effort would be to send videographers around the country, much as was done in TIMSS. But another possibility is even more intriguing: just as the Nielsen ratings measure television viewing by placing continuous monitoring devices in a sample of homes, NAEP could place video cameras in a sample of classrooms and conduct continuous monitoring of class-room processes. This idea is not as farfetched as it sounds. Cameras are cheap, and the technology for connecting them to the Internet also is cheap. It would not be necessary to record all of the camera images. Instead, sampling plans could be devised to get valid and reliable pictures of what goes on inside classrooms. If NAEP assessments could be administered more frequently in this subsample of classrooms—for example, three times a year—we would have the best data ever available for studying the relation of instruction and learning inside real class-rooms. This idea is feasible and should be considered seriously.

Another use of video surveys in NAEP should be to aid in the development and validation of better traditional measures of classroom practices such as ques-tionnaires. A well-designed sample of video data could serve both immediate research purposes and instrument development purposes, provided the two are integrated in their conception and design. It may be that some aspects of class-room practice are well measured by questionnaires, but validity studies to docu-ment this possibility are scant. Over time, using video in the development of questionnaires will increase the power of both methods of studying classroom practice. One way to approach this goal is to fund the development of a thesaurus of teaching practices. The problem of developing a shared language for indexing complex materials is a common one in library and information science. Library scientists have resolved the problem by relying on thesauruses, the meanings of which are painstakingly developed over time. Using similar techniques, we propose a project in which researchers, subject-matter specialists, teachers, and the public contribute to constructing a thesaurus of teaching practices linked with video examples. We believe that such a thesaurus could provide a foundation for developing new measures of instructional processes.

Yet another use of videos collected as part of NAEP would be in the commu-nication of study results to the public. Although testing of student achievement is a complex and difficult task, the public nevertheless has some intuitive sense of what achievement tests measure. Moreover, achievement measures themselves have been validated over many years. The study of instructional practices is different on both counts. There is little agreement as to what the basic constructs are, and, as noted earlier, we lack a public vocabulary for describing teaching practices. Not only do teachers need to develop such a vocabulary if question-naires are ever to be a useful means of studying classroom practice, but the public must do so as well if it wants to understand the information collected about classroom practices.

In terms of cost, we reiterate the fact that the cost of video data primarily resides in the analysis phase, not in the collection. For this reason we encourage the collection of larger quantities of video data, even if funds are insufficient to support in-depth analyses. Our reasoning is that an archive of nationally repre-sentative videos will become more and more valuable over time. Imagine if we had video data of instructional practices over the past 100 years. It would not be the analyses of 100 years ago that would interest us but the opportunity for analysis now. Education is a field in which many "facts" are never really established as such, most especially those that pertain to the way things "used to be." Solid data from classrooms can play a key role in mediating and dampening the polarization that characterizes most educational debate in this country.

CONCLUSION

Data on classroom processes are critical if we are to improve education, either through policy channels, research, or teacher professional development. All attempts to improve education must, if they are to work, pass through the final common pathway that is the classroom. If we fail to collect information on what is happening in classrooms, we risk missing the key processes that could effect change. But simply collecting data is not enough. We must, before we collect any data at all, develop an understanding of how the data will be used, and by whom, to improve education. We have ruminated on how classroom process data might be used by policy makers, researchers, and classroom practitioners, but this is only the beginning. The way data are used is a subject of study in and of itself. We need more empirical studies of this process. We also need to realize that there are multiple models of data use, and so we must be flexible in collecting the data we need for different purposes.

REFERENCES

Barr, R., and R. Dreeben
 1983   *How Schools Work.* Chicago: University of Chicago Press.
Brophy, J., and C. Evertson
 1976   *Learning from Teaching: A Developmental Perspective.* Boston: Allyn and Bacon.
Brophy, J., and T.L. Good
 1986   Teacher behavior and student achievement. In *Handbook of Research on Teaching*, M.C. Wittrock, ed. New York: MacMillan.
Burstein, L., L.M. McDonnell, J. Van Winkle, T. Ormseth, J. Mirocha, and G. Guitton
 1995   *Validating National Curriculum Indicators.* Santa Monica: RAND Corp.
California State Department of Education
 1985   *Mathematics Framework for California Public Schools: Kindergarten Through Grade 12.* Sacramento: California State Department of Education.
Cohen, D.K.
 1990   A revolution in one classroom: The case of Mrs. Oublier. *Educational Evaluation and Policy Analysis* 12:311-329.
 1995   What is the system in systemic reform? *Educational Researcher* 24(9):11-17, 31.
Cohen, D.K., and H.C. Hill
 1998   Instructional Policy and Classroom Performance: The Mathematics Reform in California. Paper presented at the NCTM Research Presession, April, Washington, D.C.
Fernandez, C.
 1994   Students' Comprehension Processes During Mathematics Instruction. Unpublished doctoral dissertation, University of Chicago.

Flevares, L.M., and M. Perry
  1999 Seeing what place value means: Building students' understanding through nonverbal representations. Poster presented at the biennial meeting of the Society for Research in Child Development, April, Albuquerque.
  2000 How many do you see? The use of nonspoken representations in first-grade mathematics lessons. Manuscript under review for publication.
Gallimore, R.
  1996 Classrooms are just another cultural activity. Pp. 229-250 in *Research on Classroom Ecologies: Implications for Inclusion of Children with Learning Disabilities*, D.L. Speece and B.K. Keogh, eds. Mahwah, N.J.: Lawrence Erlbaum Associates.
Lampert, M.L., and D.L. Ball
  1998 *Teaching, Multimedia, and Mathematics: Investigations of Real Practice.* New York: Teachers College Press.
Leighton, M.S.
  1994 Measuring Instruction: The Status of Recent Work. Unpublished manuscript, Policy Studies Associates, Inc., Washington, D C
Leinhardt, G., and R.T. Putnam
  1987 The skill of learning from classroom lessons. *American Educational Research Journal* 24:372-387.
Lewis, C., and I. Tsuchida
  1997 Planned educational change in Japan: The shift to student-centered elementary science. *Journal of Education Policy* 12(5):313-331.
Light, R.J., J.D. Singer, and J.B. Willett
  1990 *By Design: Planning Research on Higher Education.* Cambridge, MA: Harvard University Press.
Little, J.W.
  1992 Opening the black box of professional community. Pp. 157-178 in *The Changing Contexts of Teaching*, A. Lieberman, ed. Chicago: University of Chicago Press.
Mandel, D.R.
  1996 Teacher education, training, and staff development: Implications for national surveys. Pp. 3-29 to 3-42 in *From Data to Information: New Directions for the National Center for Education Statistics*, G. Hoachlander, J.E. Griffith, and J.H. Ralph, eds. Washington, D.C.: U.S. Department of Education.
Mayer, D.P.
  1999 Measuring instructional practice: Can policy makers trust survey data? *Educational Evaluation and Policy Analysis* 21:29-45.
Palincsar, A.S., S.J. Magnusson, N. Marano, D. Ford, and N. Brown
  1998 Designing a community of practice: Principles and practices of the GIsML community. *Teaching and Teacher Education* 14(1):5-19.
Perry, M.
  1988 Problem assignment and learning outcomes in nine fourth-grade mathematics classes. *Elementary School Journal* 88:413-426.
Rosenshine, B., and N. Furst
  1973 The use of direct observation to study teaching. In *Second Handbook of Research on Teaching*, R.M.W. Travers, ed. Chicago: Rand McNally.
Shavelson, R.J., N.M. Webb, and L. Burstein
  1986 Measurement of teaching. Pp. 50-91 in *Handbook of Research on Teaching, Third Edition*, M.C. Wittrock, ed. New York: MacMillan.
Shulman, L.S.
  1986 Paradigms and research programs in the study of teaching: A contemporary perspective. Pp. 3-36 in *Handbook of Research on Teaching, Third Edition*, M.C. Wittrock, ed. New York: MacMillan.

Siegler, R.S.
1996   *Emerging Minds.* New York: Oxford University Press.
Stigler, J.W.
1996   Large-scale video surveys for the study of classroom processes. Pp. 7.1 to 7.29 in *From Data to Information: New Directions for the National Center for Education Statistics,* G. Hoachlander, J.E. Griffith, and J.H. Ralph, eds. Washington, D.C.: U.S. Department of Education.
Stigler, J.W., and C. Fernandez
1995   Learning mathematics from classroom instruction: Cross-cultural and experimental perspectives. Pp. 103-130 in *Basic and Applied Perspectives on Learning, Cognition, and Development,* C.A. Nelson, ed. Mahwah, N.J.: Lawerence Erlbaum Associates.
Stigler, J.W., and J. Hiebert
1997   Understanding and improving classroom mathematics instruction: An overview of the TIMSS video study. *Phi Delta Kappan* 79(Sept.):1, 14-21.
1999   *The Teaching Gap: What Teachers Can Learn from the World's Best Educators.* New York: Free Press.
Stigler, J.W., S.Y. Lee, and H.W. Stevenson
1987   Mathematics classrooms in Japan, Taiwan, and the United States. *Child Development* 58:1272-1285.
Stigler, J.W., and M. Perry
1988   Mathematics learning in Japanese, Chinese, and American classrooms. Pp. 27-54 in *Children's Mathematics, New Directions for Child Development,* G.B. Saxe and M. Gearhart, eds. San Francisco: Jossey-Bass.